CARELESS HANDS
THE FORGOTTEN TRUTH OF
GARY SPRAKE

CARELESS HANDS
THE FORGOTTEN TRUTH OF
GARY SPRAKE

STUART SPRAKE & TIM JOHNSON

Best Wishes
Gary Sprake

TEMPUS

First published 2006

Tempus Publishing Limited
The Mill, Brimscombe Port,
Stroud, Gloucestershire, GL5 2QG
www.tempus-publishing.com

British Library Cataloguing in Publication Data.
A catalogue record for this book is available from the British Library.

ISBN 0 7524 3690 2

Typesetting and origination by Tempus Publishing Limited
Printed in Great Britain

CONTENTS

ACKNOWLEDGEMENTS

Many friends, colleagues and family have offered their support and encouragement in bringing this project to fruition and for this I will be forever grateful. Many have contributed informally and have freely given their time when discussing various ideas, and my sincere apologies if I have omitted anyone. Thanks to my colleagues, who know who they are, in D33 – I think they may have had a suspicion there was a book being written! Suzanne Arnold, John Bowen, Julie Davies, Alun Dodd and Rhian Ellis have been particularly supportive over the years, especially John and Alun who have contributed enormously with ideas, proofreading and providing the occasional refreshment. Alun has diligently read the drafts and offered advice and an analysis of each chapter. Thanks also to Richard Stott for granting me permission to use his research, to Ceri Stennett for arranging access to the inner sanctum of the Millennium Stadium so I could speak to the national press and Leighton Norris at the Football Association of Wales. Thanks to Ivan Barnsley and Jon Abbott for the statistics. Thanks also to Gary's ex-colleagues Jack Charlton, Leighton James, John Toshack, Brian Flynn, Mike O'Grady and Mick Bates for sharing their memories. And thanks to those former teammates who have propagated the negative image of Gary over the years for providing us with the inspiration to set the record straight. I owe an enormous debt, which is irredeemable and inexpressible, to Rosalind, her brother Vivian and mother Gwenllian, for without doubt they have always been an inspiration and provided unstinting support. Without them nothing would have been possible. Diolch yn Fawr, anghofiau byth. Thanks to Lucy, Emma and Josh for their tolerance on the numerous occasions when they couldn't access the family computer to get on with their own projects. A big thank you to my co-author Tim for his profound knowledge of all things Leeds United and for his encouragement when I was sometimes in danger of missing a deadline. The greatest thank you of all is to the man himself, Gary Sprake, for without him there would not have been a story to tell. Gary has had countless offers over the years to have his story told, but I am delighted he gave us the opportunity to put across his side of the story. Cheers Uncle Gary!

Stuart Sprake

ACKNOWLEDGEMENTS

I would especially like to thank Sian for all her help, advice and support over the last two years and Mum and Dad for always being there and backing me in everything I do. Thanks also to the Johnsons Down Under. To Alun a big thank you for inspiring the whole project and for bringing the authors together. His friendship, original ideas and continuous support for all aspects of this book has been much appreciated. Thanks to everyone at St Davids for putting up with my obsession over this period and also to Martin Brown and Aled Greville for their fan's-eye view of Gary's career. A debt of gratitude goes to the many people who helped us in our research, including Peter Shilton, Keith M. Edwards, Rob Phillips and Frances Donovan at BBC Wales. A big thank you to Stu for both his friendship and willingness to share his 'labour of love'. The biggest thanks of all are to Gary for trusting us to put right a long overdue wrong.

Tim Johnson

Firstly, I would like to register my thanks to the late Jack Pickard, the Leeds United scout for the Swansea area, for offering me a two-week trial at the tender age of fifteen, which gave me the opportunity to play for one of the best teams in Europe. Thanks also to the Leeds United manager, the late Don Revie, for having confidence in me and giving me the opportunity to play for thirteen seasons in such a great side and with some of the greatest footballers of all time. My appreciation goes to the Leeds United, Birmingham City and Wales fans, many of whom still keep in touch, for their loyalty and enthusiasm. Thanks to my partner Jackie and daughter Julia for their love and support and having to listen to my many footballing stories over the years. Most importantly, I would like to thank my nephew Stuart and Tim for their dedication and hard work while writing this book and putting the record straight. Thanks also to Holly Bennion at Tempus for her help and expert advice. To all the people I have mentioned and others too numerous to mention, I am truly grateful for their help and support in making my career in football such a memorable one.

Gary Sprake

'You can take my word for it, and there isn't a Leeds United player who will disagree with me, when I affirm that Gary Sprake is the greatest goalkeeper in the world. Bar none.'

Billy Bremner, *You Get Nowt for Being Second*, 1971

FOREWORD

Gary Sprake's football career has attracted much controversy and his reputation has been much maligned since his premature retirement in 1975. This seems unfair given that he was one of the world's finest goalkeepers between 1961 and 1975 and was admired at the time by teammates and opponents alike. Gary played during what some commentators have called the halcyon days of British football, a time when the game was blessed with an abundance of home-grown talent. The goalkeeping position was particularly strong – this view is endorsed by the fact that most teams in the top division had either a full or Under-23 international goalkeeper between the sticks. The list reads like a who's who of goalkeeping, with names such as Banks, Shilton, Bonetti, Stepney, West, Clemence, Jennings, Brown, Corrigan, Lawrence, Glazier, Montgomery and Stephenson also plying their trade in the green jersey.

When Gary and I played against each other in the late 1960s and early 1970s, Leeds and Liverpool were the top two teams in the country and we were the pace setters in the First Division. I believe that, with the exception of Ray Clemence at Liverpool, the Leeds United manager Don Revie could have attracted any of the 'keepers mentioned above to Elland Road. It is testimony to Gary's ability that Revie never attempted to sign any other name (and many did become available to him at one time or another); the reason he didn't was simple – Gary Sprake was a first-class goalkeeper. In addition to that, he was a really nice guy, the type of player you wanted alongside you in the dressing room, someone with an upbeat personality who was good for team morale. In the Wales set-up as a seasoned pro, Gary was respected by younger members of the team since he had won most things on offer, both at domestic and European level.

Unfortunately, Gary is best remembered for one 'rick' – the own goal at Anfield – when in fact he was an inspirational player through-out his career. At Leeds he played behind a team full of stars, all of whom were household names, but I saw Gary at his best on the international scene when, it can perhaps be said, he didn't have the quality of defenders that he experienced at club level. I would put Gary alongside Jack Kelsey and Neville Southall – Welsh goalies that were truly world-class – and I am pleased that this book will finally tell the truth about his career.

John Toshack

PREFACE

It is a hot, steamy evening in September 1968 and Leeds United are holding on to a slender 1-0 first-leg lead in the final of the Inter-Cities Fairs Cup in the world famous Nep Stadium against the crack Hungarian champions Ferencvaros. Leeds had overcome the Hungarians five weeks earlier thanks to a close-range effort from their hard-working centre forward Mick Jones. A mere 250 die-hard Leeds supporters have made the long journey behind the Iron Curtain, more in hope than expectation, as their heroes face a daunting task. The atmosphere is unbearably hostile and tense as 76,000 screaming fans cheer on their heroes, who have never lost a European tie on their home ground. The Leeds goalkeeper makes a series of outstanding saves from world-class players such as Albert, Szoke and Novak. In fact, every commentator and most Leeds players give this goalkeeper the majority of credit, ennobling him with the title 'The Hero of Budapest'. The goalkeeper that night was Gary Sprake, the very same 'keeper whose reputation has so often and for far too long been unfairly maligned.

Sprake is a name that for decades has generated enormous debate, seen by some as no better than a cabaret act or music hall joke. As Francis Hodgson states in his 1999 book *Only the Goalkeeper to Beat*, 'Kids far too young to have seen him play routinely shout Sprake! Sprake! at the more lamentable goalkeeping efforts of their kickabouts. His name has become a byword for hapless and laughable goalkeeping.' Yet others, like the revered football writer David Lacey in *The Guardian* and Hodgson himself, offer a more objective and balanced view; a viewpoint shared by other contemporaries and opponents, who argue that Gary was in fact one of the greatest goalkeepers of his generation, as illustrated during that famous autumn evening in 1968. All too easily, commentators and former colleagues who have their own agendas have forgotten the hero tag. The negative image has all too frequently and unfairly been used by a vindictive anti-Leeds and anti-Sprake media. Comments about that famous evening tell a different story:

'If there was one hero among a team of heroes that night it was probably Gary Sprake.' – Billy Bremner, 1971.

'In Budapest Gary was sensational, making a number of world-class saves and he won us the cup that night.' – Mick Jones, *The Life and Times of Mick Jones*, 2002.

'Against Ferencvaros the outfield players hardly touched the ball but Gary hardly got a mention after.' – Mick Bates, 2003.

'He [Gary Sprake] was sensational and his performance won us the cup.' – Paul Madeley, *Leeds United's Rolls Royce*, 2003.

'We took a rare old battering but Gary Sprake was absolutely magnificent that night. He kept a clean sheet in one of the most outstanding displays I ever saw from him. He was superb.' – Norman Hunter, *Biting Talk*, 2004.

In fact this night was only one of many memorable career highlights, others including the 1965 FA Cup final, the treble-winning 1968/69 season, 500-plus first-team appearances and 37 Wales caps. Gary's reputation should be celebrated, not pilloried nor so easily clichéd.

The media and some former colleagues fall too easily into a stereotypical trap of using Gary as an explanation for the team's underachievement. As recently as February 2004, *Shoot* magazine's Eddie Kelly highlighted this lazy style of journalism when, in an article comparing the great Revie side with the current Leeds team, Gary was awarded only six out of ten for his abilities. It was followed by the typical and ill-thought-out comment, in summary of a twelve-year career, that he was 'The weakest link. Famously threw the ball into his own net against Liverpool in 1967.' Goalkeepers by definition make mistakes and half-a-dozen over ten years hardly makes Sprake the liability that he is too often portrayed as. Francis Hodgson pertinently points out the goalkeeper is the obvious focus (of any team) and Gary Sprake became a natural fall guy and a soft target. He continues, 'Sprake became the wider public version of what the goalkeeper has always been, he became the one player in the side to carry the abuse. In his case, it came from the whole country... to ridicule Sprake was an effective way to ridicule Leeds United.' The myth has for far too long been allowed to go unchallenged. The real truth has conveniently been forgotten in the mists of time as the negative image has been invented and embellished to suit many different agendas. Indeed, David Seaman made as many mistakes and more in the last two seasons of his career yet his reputation seems to be sacrosanct among the majority of the media. In fact, some Premiership 'keepers today make as many mistakes in a single month, let alone a career. In October 2005 former Leeds goalkeeper and newly ensconced England number one Paul Robinson made two errors in consecutive weeks for his club Spurs, costing them victories against Manchester United and arch rivals Arsenal and followed these a couple of matches later with a last-minute mistake against West Ham. Robinson himself had just replaced David James as England 'keeper as a result of James' own alleged record of erratic goalkeeping. Yet very little is made of such errors in today's game and certainly neither of these modern-day goalkeepers has suffered anything like the ridicule that has befallen Gary Sprake. In reality, Gary was a great goalkeeper in an exceptional team full of gifted internationals who still remain household names.

In their excellent recent reassessment of the Revie era, *The Unforgiven*, Rob Bagchi and Paul Rogerson deal head-on with this mythical stereotype of the error-prone goalkeeper: 'Selective memories and partial observers also forget that, save for Sprake's contributions, Leeds might never have come so close to glory as they often did. Sprake alone had held Man Utd at bay in the 1965 FA Cup semi-final.' If it wasn't for Gary, Leeds would have suffered an even more disappointing defeat in that year's cup final against Liverpool. As Jack Charlton stated in his autobiography *Charlton*, 'Gary Sprake kept us in the game by making some superb saves'. Bagchi and Rogerson concede that Gary made several high-profile mistakes but take to task Revie's comments (made after the bribery scandal) that Leeds would have won more if Sprake had been replaced earlier. They argue that his agility and ability were never in question as he appeared in over 500 games for the club, picking up five winners' medals along the way. Gary remains ninth in the all-time appearances list for the club. In fact, recent biographies by Leeds legends including Peter Lorimer have been quick to point out that much of Leeds' underachievement in that period was due to Revie's own paranoia in not allowing the team out of their defensive, dossier-obsessed style of play. It is perhaps ironic that Billy Bremner's glowing words of 1971 seem to have been so easily lost in the haze of time, especially by some of Gary's erstwhile teammates.

Gary Sprake retired from football in 1975 as a result of a serious back injury at the age of thirty, with potentially five or more years left in his career. Even at this prematurely early age for retirement he had packed in more memorable and controversial events than most other professional footballers. However, Gary has not been able to rest in retirement with the luxury of a reputation and career enhanced by his actual performances on the field. When people recall his name they immediately associate it with two phenomena: the mistakes, and the controversy surrounding Don Revie with the *Daily Mirror*'s allegations of match-fixing. Any fair-minded observer can see that a career that started in amazing circumstances when Gary was a raw sixteen-year-old and ended abruptly in serious illness in a hospital bed in Birmingham in 1975 was far more eventful and interesting than this narrow view takes into account.

Anybody who spends any time in Gary Sprake's company will find not only a true gentleman but an honest one. As he will recall in this biography, he could sometimes be temperamental, resulting in some confrontational incidents both on and off the field. He is the first to admit that the mistakes were important and that they have caused no end of harm to his reputation. However, his major memories of his career are the friendship of his Leeds colleagues, the socialising, the European games and the experience of travelling and playing for Wales at international level.

Gary is not bitter at the lack of acknowledgement for his efforts among the football press or the ostracism and criticism from many of his former teammates. However, he often wonders, as he posts off the many requests for signed photographs he still gets, whether people really believe the negatives about him. He wants to tell the fans his own version of his story and this is Gary's chance to tell what has, for far too long, been the 'forgotten truth'.

ONE

A FLYING START

Gary Sprake made just about the most dramatic League debut in the history of the British game when, as a sixteen-year-old, he was rushed by taxi and then plane to play for Leeds in a vital game at Southampton on 17 March 1962 in the old Second Division. The drama had begun to develop the evening before when first-choice goalkeeper and Scottish international Tommy Younger was taken ill with a high temperature and sore throat. The following morning, as his temperature reached 100 degrees, the Leeds doctor had no option but to rule him out of the game, which immediately caused panic as second-choice Alan Humphreys was already on the treatment table with a damaged arm. Third-choice Terry Carling, who had some Football League experience, lived out in Otley, which meant that he wouldn't be able to get to the airport in time. Immediately, the Leeds manager Don Revie got on the telephone to the general manager Cyril Williamson back in Yorkshire, and the frantic rush to get a replacement 'keeper began. Just after ten o'clock that morning Williamson phoned the club's travel agent to formulate a plan to get a replacement to Eastleigh Airport near the Southampton ground. In the meantime, Gary, who was in bed in his Leeds digs near the ground, was summoned as Revie ordered his officials to 'Get cracking and organise an aircraft to fly him down to Southampton.' The young 'keeper was packed off with boots under his arm into a taxi for the thirty-mile dash to Manchester's Ringway Airport to board a specially chartered plane, which had cost the club the then not-insignificant amount of £80 to hire.

The shell-shocked Leeds youth team goalkeeper left for the 260-mile journey to Southampton in a two-seater with only himself and the pilot aboard. Shortly before one o'clock, with only two hours and ten minutes remaining until the scheduled kick-off, the plane careered down the runway. Gary remembers that he didn't have very much to say to pilot Bruce Martin, being violently sick within five minutes of takeoff before eventually falling asleep. They reached Southampton with just over twenty minutes to go before the scheduled kick-off, where another mad dash began, from the airport to The Dell. A car was provided by the Southampton club, along with a police escort, to accompany them to the ground, and they arrived barely fifteen minutes before the match had been due to start. Although Leeds had obtained special permission from the League to delay the kick-off this was only to be by a quarter of an hour. For the sixteen-year-old Gary Sprake, however, this was a blessing in disguise as he had no time for first-night nerves. Almost four decades later Gary recalls the day as if it were yesterday.

I was having my usual Saturday morning lie-in when the telephone rang downstairs and the landlady, Mrs Hillyard, came rushing upstairs to tell me Mr Williamson wanted to speak to me. He told me of the predicament the first team were in and that I was to make my way to the South Coast. We left Manchester at around 12.45 p.m. and for the next two hours or so I was terribly sick. When the plane landed Mr Revie was waiting on the runway and he had to all but carry me to the car – I was so weak through vomiting I could hardly stand. The game just passed me by. I remember Freddie Goodwin scoring an own goal and after the game Revie told me that I had done really well and thanked me for my efforts. I then caught a train to London where I changed for the long journey north. Around 6.30 p.m. I had my first meal in over twenty-four hours, a large mixed grill.

Don Revie had faced a difficult decision on whether to risk Gary, as his first senior game had only been five days earlier in a West Riding Senior Cup tie against Halifax Town at The Shay, but to an extent his hands were tied as long-serving full-back Grenville Hair was the only alternative custodian for the game.

During the Southampton game, Freddie Goodwin, the Leeds centre half and captain, put through into his own net for the opening goal. Although Leeds equalised a minute later the Saints added a further three goals, none of which was attributed to the young 'keeper. He did, however, have one memento from the game – stud marks on his chest after a collision in the seventy-fifth minute with Saints centre forward Reeves, which left him unconscious for over two minutes. It was a remarkable beginning to what would become an equally remarkable, and often controversial, career. Leeds may have lost 4-1 but Gary had proved himself to be both brave and confident, demonstrating even at that early stage the qualities that were to take him to the pinnacle of his profession: the sound positional sense, the faultless taking of crosses and the ability to make difficult saves look easy.

While his debut may have caught the national imagination, it was life as normal when he turned up for duty back at Elland Road the following Monday. He was back down to earth with a bump, his first job cleaning out the dressing room bath with a scrubbing brush. Phil Brown of the *Yorkshire Evening Post* made a shrewd observation in that Monday's edition, arguing that Gary wouldn't be doing too many more chores. 'Sprake was not at fault for any of the goals conceded, having no chance with any of the efforts that beat him,' wrote Brown, 'In a year or two he will go far.' The following week, however, it was back to the reality of junior football as he lined up in goal to face Wolves at Elland Road, with the youth team on a good run of only two defeats in twenty-two games.

Don Woodward of the *Daily Express* summarised the incredible debut thus: 'Gary the Goal, sixteen years old and six feet of Welsh confidence, yesterday relaxed after the most dramatic of soccer weekend trips.' The nature of his debut itself had been sensational and was in stark contrast to the experiences of his former teammates back home in Swansea. While Gary was turning green, interspersed with a whiter shade of pale, as he made the nerve-racking flight from Leeds to Southampton, many of his friends were preparing for local league football or their Saturday afternoon jobs. However, for the young Welshman there would be no return to this traditional lifestyle as he set out on the journey that was to bring him so much fame in a team wherein success and notoriety came in equal measure. If Don Revie's reputation at Leeds United is synonymous with controversy then central to these issues is the name Gary Sprake.

However, his dramatic debut nearly didn't happen at all, as he had left his first Leeds trial convinced he had blown any chance he had of a career as a professional footballer. In only his second game of the trial period Gary turned out for the Leeds Juniors in the Northern Intermediate League, losing 6-1 to Rotherham United:

I was extremely nervous, which was understandable, but even so I didn't think I played very well at all. After the game I went back to the digs and confided to Billy Bremner and Norman Hunter that I was very homesick and missed my family back home in Swansea too much. We were a typical close-knit working-class family and were very supportive of one another. I told the lads

I had decided to catch the first train home the following day. In the meantime my parents had no inkling of my decision and they were both surprised and delighted to see me that Sunday afternoon. There were many reasons why I had come to this decision: partly the result of the game, the Yorkshire accent was strange to me – but most importantly I was only fifteen and had never been outside Wales before and felt hopelessly unsettled.

The very next day there was a knock on the front door and, once again, his mother Gwladys and stepfather Walter Wood had the shock of their lives, being confronted on the doorstep by the Leeds manager Don Revie.

He told my parents that I had loads of ability and potential and in his opinion would make a very good goalkeeper. He said he would take me back to Leeds with him straight away, something my parents and myself immediately agreed to as we were so impressed with his actions and his persuasive nature. I later found out that he had successfully used the same personal touch to sign other players such as Peter Lorimer, Billy Bremner and Eddie Gray.

These exciting experiences as a trainee footballer seemed a long way from his childhood upbringing in the small Swansea village of Winch Wen, where his footballing talent was first unearthed by Jack Pickard, Leeds United's South Wales scout who was also responsible for unearthing the greatest Welsh footballer of all time, John Charles. Both Charles and Gary were snatched from under the nose of Swansea Town as teenagers by this acclaimed talent scout. Pickard himself had moved from his native Leeds to Swansea before the First World War and had been appointed as the Yorkshire club's South Wales scout in 1935 by then-manager Billy Hampson. While Charles was taken onto the Swans' ground staff, Gary was overlooked in favour of another local lad, Colin Park, both of whom had been vying for the Swansea Schoolboys goalie's jersey as fifteen-year-olds. The young Sprake was selected only twice as it was Park who played in the majority of these games and subsequently signed on the dotted line for his home-town club. As in the case of John Charles, the Swans made a terrible error of judgement as Park was selected just once for the first team while Gary went on to success at domestic, European and international level. Once again, Jack Pickard had proved himself invaluable to the Leeds club with his in-depth knowledge of the game. As Gary recalls today:

There were outstanding young footballers in the majority if not all of the local school and youth teams in the Swansea area at that time. Scouts were attached to almost all the First and Second Division clubs, each trying to spot the next John Charles. It was Mr Pickard who famously ensnared the original and his reputation was second to none, so much so that other scouts would try to find what games he would be watching each weekend, hoping to put one over him. As well as Big John, Jack was responsible for finding Terry Yorath in Cardiff and I remember two other Swansea lads joining me up in Leeds, Dennis Hawkins and Geoff Scrine, although unfortunately they never made it. Even though I made it I will never forget the kindness of Jack Pickard. He followed my career with great interest, both with Leeds and Wales, attending most of the matches during my early career. He was very proud of the fact that he discovered me. We spoke a lot over the years and he was the perfect gentleman, always keeping in contact with my family as well. I will be forever grateful for the opportunity he gave me to play for such a great side as Leeds and consequently my country. Thanks Jack!

As a youngster growing up in Winch Wen Gary was immersed in a culture steeped in football history. It was association football that captured the hearts and minds of the city's sporting population more so than rugby union. Swansea was and still is regarded as a hotbed of footballing talent, with many local players going on to Football League and international stardom. Perhaps the biggest conveyor belt of ability has been the east side of the city as, besides Gary and Jack Kelsey, the area still provides a rich seam of talent, with Andy Melville and John Hartson both having worn the famous red shirt of their country with distinction. Gary's first memories of Saturday afternoon football were watching the local team with his friends from Cwm Primary School at the Halfway Park in Winch Wen. He had a particular interest in these games for in goal was brother Dennis and at centre half first cousin Desmond, while stepfather Walter was on the committee. During this time, opportunities for Gary to play in organised games himself were rare as Llansamlet School, like most schools in the South Wales valleys at that time, was still rugby-dominated. Most of his sporting experience came from playing rugby at centre for the school team, with only the occasional game of football at the headmaster's discretion. If the football-loving pupils were lucky they were allowed to play a competitive fixture every couple of months, although even then the headmaster would happily cancel games on a whim. Onw such occasion Gary and his friend Terry Connell were summoned to the headmaster's study one

Wednesday morning to be told they had to make the five-mile journey to Townhill to inform the opposing school that Llansamlet would be unable to field a side for that afternoon's fixture. The headmaster gave them half a crown for the bus fare, but the boys had a better idea: why not borrow two bikes from the shed, cycle to Townhill and pocket the cash? A great idea, almost foolproof except for one thing: the rightful owners of the bikes wanted to go home before the likely lads returned. When they did return they were faced with irate teachers and a head-master who believed that football was a game for miscreants and took great joy in the fact that he had apparently been proved right. Even worse, the police had been called. After duly receiving the usual school punishment at the time, the cane, there was to be one final humiliation, namely the return of the half crown.

Gary left school at fifteen with no formal academic qualifications, mainly because he missed the eleven-plus through illness, to pursue a career as a fitter and turner with Tom Smith & Clark in Port Tennant, Swansea, alongside neighbour and footballing friend Ronnie Squires. As for his footballing career, along with most of his schoolmates he went on to play for local team Cwm Youth. Other friends played for local rivals Bonymaen Colts in the under-sixteen league. It was while with Cwm Youth that Gary came to the attention of Jack Pickard who, being impressed with what he saw, offered him a fourteen-day trial at Elland Road. Firstly, however, he had to demonstrate that he could handle the more physically rigorous demands of senior football. The game was between the works' team and local opponents Swansea Boys' Club in the West Wales Senior Cup and Gary conceded his first hat-trick, scored by the opposition striker Bob Coates. Although he played in goal during this trial game most of his games for Cwm Youth had been at inside right. He had only originally been picked in goal because of his height and his handling skills from his rugby. Pickard must have seen enough potential in those brief goalkeeping perform-ances to have been left with a strong impression. On the very same day as his hastily arranged game Gary had also been selected in goal for the Cwm side against Swansea Town in the West Wales Youth Cup, a huge grudge match for the small village team against their mighty neighbours. When Gary failed to turn up, any chances of a cup upset against their professional opponents were lost as Cwm crashed out of the tournament with outside right Byron Hughes having to take the goalie's jersey. Meanwhile, in the trial game, he had done enough in this one appearance in senior football to convince Pickard he had the ability to warrant the price of a return train ticket to Yorkshire. Given Leeds' recent history of profligacy the fare would now appear money extremely well spent.

His mates quickly forgave him for his absence when an explanation was given, for no-one outside of the Sprake household had previously known of the hastily arranged game and the reason behind it. His parents were against the idea of their son moving so far away but the eventual acceptance of a trial was a team effort by the whole of the Sprake family rather than any individual. Gary's mother and stepfather had to be convinced by the rest of the siblings that their little boy had to leave home to seize what could prove to be a once-in-a-lifetime opportunity to make good. The personal visit of Leeds manager Don Revie during the middle of the trial period did much to reinforce their convictions that Leeds was the right choice for the young 'keeper. *The Herald* of Wales reported that the Swans had lost a 'talented youngster' to their Second Division rivals:

> The strapping Gary Sprake today signed professional terms for Leeds United, one year earlier than expected. Manager Don Revie has been so impressed with him; he has put Sprake on the books months before the usual age. Strangely Sprake was dropped from the Schoolboy side after just one appearance, the emphatic win over Newport Boys. Sprake's home is, coincidently, next door but one to where Jack Kelsey once lived. It would be more coincidental if Sprake succeeded Kelsey in the national side.

The same paper added somewhat prophetically that 'his prospects seem good'.

Although, along with most of his mates, he would regularly walk the four miles to stand on the North Bank at Swansea to cheer on his heroes whenever the local youth fixtures didn't clash, Gary never really had any driving ambition himself to become a professional footballer. His favourite player at that time, if he really had one, was the Swans' goalkeeper Johnny King, who played over 300 games in a long and distinguished career. Perhaps the greatest inspiration for him in his early days should have been another who had escaped the clutches of the Swans, the Arsenal and Wales legend Jack Kelsey. As mentioned in the *Herald* article quoted above, Jack and Gary had been brought up in the same row of ten houses in Jersey Road, Winch Wen, which were owned and leased to the workers of the zinc smelting works, the Swansea Vale. Yet this small valley's street produced three players who went on to sign professionally with First Division clubs; besides Gary and Jack there was also Brian Jones, who was signed by Arsenal after starring for Wales Schoolboys against England at Wembley, but later returned home to South Wales because of homesickness. Next door but one to the Sprake family lived the Kelsey clan and Gary should have been in awe when the famous player came home for his summer holidays. Jack would take time out for a kick around with Gary and his mates in return for them washing the big man's car – even though they would have done it for him anyway as this form of transport was a rarity in this traditionally working-class community. They would set up makeshift goals on the waste ground opposite their homes and Jack would spend hours practising, playing and coaching with the star-struck youngsters. This was typically generous of this great professional and Welsh sporting legend. Such childhood experiences would have been a great inspiration to any youngster, especially an aspiring goalkeeper, but not so much Gary. He only played the game because he had a natural ability and was good at it. He never really had any ambition to play local league football, let alone follow his illustrious neighbour into the national side. Even in later years as a seasoned professional with Leeds and Wales he remained down to earth, preferring to spend his leisure time going out with his mates outside of the game. If you asked him who his opponents were he would only know because it was rammed down his throat by his dossier-obsessed manager or by the coaching team. If you asked him the name of any other player in any other team outside of the First Division he wouldn't have a clue. Football to him was only a job, even though he was pretty good at it.

I was more interested in playing with the oval ball during my secondary school years, even though I enjoyed playing football. Rugby was the team game I played, but I just enjoyed having a kick around with my mates on the waste ground in front of my house. At the time we played for fun and not one of us even considered the possibility of becoming a professional. There wasn't really anybody to influence us. In those days you could only buy a red or blue top, unlike today's shirt sponsorship and the multitude of shirts available to kids. Even though I lacked ambition in my early years I realised after my senior debut that I had the potential to go a lot further and I subsequently became more confident in my own abilities. In fact, for the next ten years I believed myself to be an excellent 'keeper, one of the best around. My only problem was I appeared to be laid back, but this was a misconception, I was fiercely determined and wanted to win as many medals, titles and caps as the next person.

A lack of initial ambition was not the only reason why Gary's spectacular rise to prominence was surprising, for as a child he suffered serious illness. He was first diagnosed as having St Vitus's dance, a manifestation of rheumatic fever, in his primary school years. This illness affects the nervous system, leaving the recipient unable to keep still – hence the term 'dance'. Gary's symptoms included involuntary, jerky and spasmodic movements, which meant he was constantly in motion and forever twitching. On one occasion his mother Gwladys popped down to Llansamlet to do some shopping and on her return, as she went upstairs, she was mortified to find Gary chopping up her wardrobe with an axe, perhaps thinking he was doing her a favour by collecting firewood. Another similar incident was recalled by Tina Kelsey, Jack's sister, surrounding the events of Queen Elizabeth II's Coronation in 1953. As a treat Jack had bought his parents a television set so they could watch the event. All the neighbours were summoned to the Kelsey house as they now owned the only television set in the area. Unfortunately Gary had one of his 'attacks', ripped the aerial from the top of the set and the neighbours – along with a furious Mr and Mrs Kelsey – missed the crowning of the royal. In total during this period he lost over a year's schooling, including missing the eleven-plus exam, which meant like many of his peers he was confined to a second-rate education. However, unlike the rest of his schoolmates, who would spend most of their working careers within the local factories, life as a professional footballer would give him an opportunity to sample a very different lifestyle with its many advantages and potential pitfalls.

In his early teens Gary recovered from his illness and remained healthy for a number of years due to the care provided by his mother. If the weather became inclement after Gary had left for school, she would walk the mile or so to the school with his raincoat so he wouldn't get wet later in the day. Byron Hughes recalls that the villagers of Winch Wen didn't need weather reports: 'You knew it was going to rain when you saw Mrs Sprake walking down the road, coat under arm.' At the age of thirteen, however, Gary once again suffered from rheumatic fever and was off school for eighteen months. Peter Lorimer suggests that, towards the end of his Leeds career, Gary's nerve had gone and he would have facial twitches before important games. Was it loss of nerve, or perhaps the effects of a latent earlier illness? What is clear, however, is that it is a miracle how Gary overcame such a debilitating illness that affects legs, arms and muscles. For him to have played any kind of sport was amazing but to have played at the highest level reflects the courage and dedication of a quite extraordinary person, especially as he never let anyone except the management and medical staff at Elland Road into his 'secret'. Gary overcame these serious illnesses and argues that they never hindered his career.

I had regular yearly medicals during my time at Elland Road and not once did they discover any heart abnormalities. As for my supposed nerves, yes I suffered terribly before each game and would become violently sick, but once I got onto the pitch everything was fine.

Gary has been lucky throughout his life to have had the benefit of a close-knit and supportive family. This family environment was to continue at Leeds when he became an integral member of the 'family' created by Don Revie, where every member looked out for each other. Critics of Leeds United – and there were many outside the city – believed that this went beyond a family atmosphere and created a siege mentality (a phenomenon that Gary has personally encountered more than once since his infamous and controversial falling-out with Revie in the mid-1970s).

While playing at the very top with Leeds he had the support of his first wife Kathy and their daughter Julia and, after retirement from the game, the support has come from his partner Jackie. Throughout every stage of his life it has been the Sprake family that continued to play an important role.

Gary Sprake was born into a typical working-class family on 3 April 1945, the youngest child of Albert and Gwladys. His eldest brother was Alfie, followed by Jean, Glyn, Dennis and Sylvia. Tragically, another brother, Ken, had died as an infant before he had even reached the age of one. Albert himself died at the prematurely young age of forty-four from a massive heart attack when Gary was only ten months old. Unbeknown to him at the time, Gary would see many of his family suffer from this disease over the years. His mother later remarried a local man, Walter Wood, and Gary gained another two half-brothers, Jeffery and Colin. Both Walter and Gwladys died of heart attacks in their early sixties. Glyn suffered his first heart attack at the age of thirty-eight and a fatal one five years later, while Alfie, Sylvia and Gary himself have all successfully undergone bypass surgery. Dennis also passed away at the relatively young age of fifty-eight, from cancer.

On the spring day that Gary was born, during those death throes of the Second World War, it was a typical day in Winch Wen – damp, dark and overcast with low-lying cloud. If he had been born in the middle of August the same conditions would have prevailed, for the village overlooked the Lower Swansea Valley and its factories, including the infamous Swansea Vale Smelting Works. The works, known locally as 'white man's grave', billowed out sulphuric acid and the locals often found themselves fighting for breath as they went about their daily business. Young boys and girls would be breathless as they played in the street and no-one within a three-mile radius of the works could grow either grass or vegetables. The works itself was an evil necessity as it was the major local employer, with both Gary's sister Sylvia and brother Glyn being employed there, along with his father and many uncles and cousins. The working conditions were very tough but the wages were relatively good as there was plenty of opportunity for overtime and this allowed Glyn to purchase one of the few televisions in the area. According to lifelong family friend and neighbour Mike Sullivan, Gary was particularly close to his brother during his teenage years and would spend every evening the mile or so away from his parents' home with Glyn in Neath Road, Llansamlet. Was it brotherly love or the fact Gary liked to watch the only television in the Sprake family? Alfie and Jean had both moved away in search of employment that didn't involve the daily grind of working in temperatures of over a hundred degrees and Dennis worked in his father-in-law's coal business. When Gary moved away every member of the family got together to help his mother and father with the expense of new clothes. Even at this young age he was always smartly dressed and the money raised went on new trousers, a blazer and sports jacket. Without his brothers and sisters he would perhaps never have made it to Leeds and in the early years before he had a car he would travel by train from Leeds to Alfie's house in Preston to spend time with his brother and entertain the young kids in the kickabouts on the grass verges outside Alfie's house.

Gary has fond memories of the closeness of the Sprake family, but one of his greatest regrets is that he didn't get to know his father.

My dad died when I was ten months old, but I'll always remember my mother, brothers and sisters telling me he was a loving father and husband who would work long hours to give us that little extra. I'm sure he would have been very proud of what I achieved, God bless him. When my mother remarried, however, I couldn't have wished for a better stepfather than Walter Wood. He was a lovely, gentle man with whom I got on extremely well. He also worked very hard to provide us with food and clothes and I remember him handing over his wage packet every week. In fact, all the men in the locality used to hand over their wages to the mother. I think it's a Welsh trait, but I don't know if they were handing over money or responsibility, leaving all the bills to the woman of the house. My mother then gave Walter his pocket money, which he spent on fags, a few pints down the Colliers Arms or a little bet on the horses. That was the way of life in those days.

Gary never forgot the help and support of his family in these crucial formative years. During his Leeds career every member of the Sprake household had tickets for any game they wanted and it was Gary who footed the bill, as players were only allowed two complimentary tickets each. With seven brothers and sisters, together with partners and children, the bill was enormous, especially as even the top footballers who were relatively well paid compared with their contemporaries were far from the millionaire players of today's Premiership.

Even though the tickets used to cost me a small fortune, it was worth it. I didn't mind because I loved them all dearly. I know they were very proud of me and what I achieved. It was a thank you from me for their support. I used to enjoy meeting family and friends before and after a game. It's sad these days that the top stars are surrounded by bodyguards and games are planned with such military precision. I used to enjoy the banter with my family and the crowd, even if I was sometimes called a Welsh bastard or a useless so-and-so.

Indeed, as a young boy the co-author can remember many Sprake family trips to the big League or cup games and Gary would always introduce his young nephew to his colleagues in the dressing room after the games and he would be awestruck in meeting these 'international stars and household names'. Up until his late teens the co-author would bask in the reflective glory of having one of the world's finest goalies as an uncle. Whenever there was a football match to be played on Llansamlet's Recreation ground the young nephew would always be made captain with first pick of the players for his team. Francis Hodgson in his book argued that the chant 'Sprake, Sprake' was a pejorative term used on football fields and playgrounds throughout the land when young kids made goalkeeping errors. For the co-author, however, the name 'Sprake' had many advantages and opened many doors: playing for the primary school team at eight years of age, receiving preferential treatment from grammar school teachers and coincidentally even finding that his first job interviewer was Leeds born and bred and a lifelong supporter. Needless to say the job was in the bag.

Money, however, was not an issue where family was concerned, as Gary demonstrated by buying the house that his parents had rented off his father's employers so that his mother would have security. Before his mother's death, when he was twenty-five, he would travel home as often as possible and spend time with family and friends. And there was nothing the local kids would love more than to try to put a penalty past one of the finest goalkeepers in the land. When his mother became ill Gary would travel down from Leeds every Saturday after the whistle for the arduous pre-motorway era ten-hour drive, spend the Sunday with her and then drive back to Leeds for training on the Monday.

It was the least I could do; my mother was a very special woman. She unfortunately passed away a month before my daughter Julia was born, which was very sad as I wish Mam could have held her. I think I inherited many of my mother's characteristics: she was a very fiery person who would defend her family through thick and thin, sometimes when we were clearly in the wrong. When we played against Liverpool in the 1965 cup final my mother travelled with the rest of the family from Swansea on the train. I remember my brother Glyn telling me that after a few stops on the tube a crowd of Liverpool supporters got on. They started saying things in front of my mother about the Welsh so-and-so in the Leeds goal, not realising who she was. The next thing this 6ft-something Scouser was being hit over the head by an umbrella-wielding 4ft-something Welsh lady. She kept up the attack until he and his mates apologised.

On his frequent visits home, he never acted the high-profile footballer, being first and foremost son, brother and friend, and he never went out of his way to seek attention or the high life. He would stay with his mother or brother Glyn rather than in a swish hotel in Swansea and he would always seek out old mates like Terry Connell. He would spend hours in the local pubs like the Colliers Arms, Winch Wen, play darts and cards in the Llansamlet Workingmen's Club with old neighbours and school friends or go out with Terry for a few pints to reminisce and catch up with local news. They would go not to town-centre hotels, where Gary would have been instantly recognised, but quiet country pubs in the villages surrounding Swansea where they would consume large quantities of locally produced ale. In those days, unlike today, there was a culture of drink-driving. There weren't so many cars on the road and the police devoted their time to catching burglars and robbers, which meant people would have a few pints and drive home. On a couple of occasions, however, they would end up in the 'in' places, like the Three Lamps on the High Street, and needless to say the smartly dressed, good-looking guy with a middle-class income and fast sports car would attract the attention of the local young ladies. It wasn't just in Swansea that Gary would find himself a big hit with women. Several of his former Leeds colleagues, including Mick O'Grady and Mick Bates, recently recalled that Gary had a good deal of success with the opposite sex. Although, as Jack Charlton remembers, this wasn't always without a degree of controversy:

> A few of the lads went out to a nightclub, 'The Ace of Clubs', and we were having a drink at the bar. This girl with her boyfriend kept looking across at Sprakey who didn't even notice her. The boyfriend came over to Gary. Me, Billy and the rest of the lads assumed he wanted his autograph. The next thing we knew was that this guy had poured his pint all over Gary. Sprakey was a well-dressed lad and was wearing a mohair suit; in fact I sold it to him. Myself, Billy and a few of the lads stopped Gary getting involved and the bouncers threw the guy out. Gary disappeared and we thought he had gone to the toilets to clean himself up. The next thing this guy came flying back through the doors. As the guy had been ejected Gary knocked him straight back in again. Although he was usually quiet and shy you never messed with Gary and it wasn't the only time he got into a scrape in town.

During his career, even when married, there were many more escapades involving drinking and various women from the time he was a young apprentice to the time he finished with the game and beyond.

Gary suggests that these incidents seemed to start at an early age and followed, or sometimes dogged, him throughout his life. One of the first things he remembers about his early days at Leeds was both the camaraderie that Revie engendered and the meticulous attention to detail. These were the reasons why the 'boss' organised pre-season trips to Holland, to foster team spirit and gain a captive audience for what was to become dossier-obsession on the following season's opponents. After playing a friendly in Amsterdam in early August, Revie allowed his young and not-so-young charges the following day off for relaxation and sightseeing around the Dutch capital. The players did the usual trips in the morning and then found themselves at a loose end for the afternoon and evening. A quiet period back at the hotel perhaps to recharge the batteries? One of the senior pros had another idea;

what about a drinking competition, young versus old? Strong Dutch beer was consumed in copious amounts (even though Gary will still argue today that there wasn't a drink culture) until they were down to the 'finalists'. Representing the seniors was the awesome presence of big Jack Charlton, while the dubious honour of representing the youngsters rested on the under developed shoulders of the seventeen-year-old goalkeeper. A few pints later, amazingly, the young Welshman emerged victorious and to celebrate the winners decided to throw as many bikes as they could find into the river. The police were called – even in liberal Amsterdam such behaviour was frowned upon – and the culprits were arrested. The Leeds manager was called upon not only to act as the peacemaker but also to pay the £50 fine needed to obtain Gary's release from jail as he had been the one deemed most guilty and incarcerated. Looking out for Gary was something Revie did extremely well. On this occasion and unbeknown to him, he would be called upon several more times over the next ten years.

After receiving a severe dressing down from the management it was back to Leeds for Gary and to the digs that were now home. His first digs were a five-minute walk from Elland Road in Cemetery Road, Beeston, which was run by Mr and Mrs Leighton. It was a large house and Gary's housemates were Billy Bremner, Norman Hunter and Hugh Ryden, who all slept in the attic. In the two years that he lived there, there were many pranks played that would not have been unfamiliar to sixteen-year-olds the length and breadth of the country. The early 1960s were not renowned for good-quality sanitation and the old Victorian house was no exception. If the lads wanted to relieve themselves during the night an old zinc bucket was at hand. Norman, although an exceptional footballing talent, could not, with the best will in the world, be called a 'thinking man's' player. And it was usually he, at the end of each prank, that was the victim of the judge (Billy) and the jury (Gary and Hugh)'s judgement, which inevitably ended up with the same punishment involving the said bucket and a toothbrush. However, apart from the lack of toileting facilities, the three apprentices experienced a relatively comfortable lifestyle as they were paid a weekly wage of £2 per week at sixteen, rising to £5 at seventeen. Their food and board was paid for by the club and this enabled Gary to send his mother half his wages every week, which he did religiously up until the time he got married at the age of twenty-three. He also saved enough money to pay £1,500 for the family home back in Swansea.

Unlike the players of today, there was no nutritional advice or sports-related science for these professional athletes. If you read any football magazine of the 1960s and 1970s, inevitably most players' favourite meal by consensus of opinion would be steak and chips. Gary recalls asking Norman his favourite dish and he replied he quite liked the blue and white one next to the teapot on Mrs Leighton's dresser! Good wholesome food was the order of the day and the landlady was a very good cook with everything freshly prepared using ingredients from the local corner shop. Mrs Leighton believed herself to be a good cook and was never surprised to see the young would-be football-ers fighting over her homemade bread at tea-time. What she didn't realise, however, was that they were trying to get the cleanest slices, for Mr Leighton always used to butter the bread directly after putting coal on the fire. Another favourite pastime of the young apprentices, throwing suits out of windows, was not invented by Sam Hammam and the Crazy Gang at Wimbledon, as Gary will testify. From an early age he was always regarded as the smartest dresser at the club and his roommates would often throw his clothes, which were hung on a piece of string stretched across the attic the four of them shared, out onto the street below. After darkness he would creep downstairs to retrieve them, only to find an angry Mr Leighton waiting in the hallway. After being caught breaking the ten o'clock curfew he would be summoned to see Revie the following day and either a rollicking or a couple of quid fine would ensue. On weekends the lads could stay out until midnight, although sixteen-year-olds didn't have a lot to do in downtown Leeds. Once Gary realised that there were other things in life besides football he moved out to another house in Oakwood Lane, Oakwood, where he stayed from 1963 until he married local lass Kathy O'Boyle in 1968. Fed up with sharing his clothes and toi-letries, he moved in with Mr and Mrs Thackerey and it was here that he experienced for the first time the pampered life of a professional footballer. The landlady was a smashing woman, a good cook who did all his washing while Leeds United picked up the tab at the end of every week. As a young professional at eighteen his wages rose to £20 per week and by the time he left for a newly mortgaged home of his own at twenty-three he was earning the considerable sum of £70.

One observer who watched Gary make his mark in the game, literally, and became a long-term admirer of the Welshman was Liverpool manager Bill Shankly who commented in one of his weekly newspaper columns:

Whenever I see his name it takes me back to the day when, as an eighteen-year-old he appeared in a reserve match at Liverpool. I didn't see the game but Sprake left his mark at Anfield. He had scratched a line from the goal-line to the eighteen-yard box. Left his mark did I say? It was more like a trench! I was blazing mad. I rang Leeds straight away to complain about Sprake and I told them I would sue Leeds and Sprake for damaging the pitch. I suppose it proved that Gary had his own ideas about how to do his job. He has proved also that he is a great goalkeeper, but what I said then still applies. If he wants to make marks on the pitch he should organise a goalkeepers' union and get them to persuade FIFA to draw a white line.

Gary was to continue to develop these goalkeeping idiosyncrasies, giving him somewhat of an iconic cult status. One of the most famous images of the Leeds and Wales 'keeper is the endless amount of chewing gum that he got through during games. Today's custodians adorn high-tech gloves which can seem almost as big as the goal they are protecting. In Gary's day such equipment was a rarity and this certainly made life more difficult for 'keepers. However, being innovative, Gary devised a method to overcome these problems. He would chew endless packets of Wrigley's throughout the game. Not, as most commentators and fans thought, to help his concentration but because he used it to make his palms sticky. Gary would chew the gum and then spit it into his hands and rub them together in an attempt to give him an advantage in catching the old, heavy and wet leather ball. As Peter Shilton recalls:

> When I played against Leeds for the first time I walked into the area and it was littered with paper. When we turned around for the second half the same thing happened. After the game I realised they were chewing gum wrappers. As I shook hands with Gary at the end of the game my hand stuck to his. The crowd must have thought we were really good friends as it looked as if we were walking off holding hands.

Don Revie was, at that time, nurturing a family atmosphere and his young players were placed with carefully selected families while top-quality professional coaches such as Les Cocker, Bob English, Syd Owen, Maurice Lindley and Cyril Partridge were enlisted. They were given the mandate to turn promising youngsters into one of the greatest teams of their generation. Revie had a vision and was granted a certain degree of autonomy by his chairman, unlike today, when boards of directors and chief executives are answerable to multi-national conglomerates or billionaires or, as Leeds were famously to find out in 2004, the Stock Exchange. The club owners of the 1960s were the local butcher or factory owner. The very popular chairman at Leeds from 1961 to 1967 was Harry Reynolds, a self-made millionaire who had made his money out of a steel stockholding business. Gary has fond memories of his former employer:

If it wasn't for Harry Reynolds Leeds would never have achieved the success they did. He put as much effort and time into the club as he did his steel business. He may not have involved himself in wage negotiations, leaving that side of things to Don Revie, but it was his money that went into team strengthening and contracts. He would leave the football matters to Revie, although after every game he would come into the dressing room and hand out fags to Billy and Big Jack, the two smokers in the side. I suspect that Jack would have got his hands on them anyway. There weren't many better people than Jack for scrounging!

A football club was not a plaything, but part of their small business empire where profits needed to be made. Revie's backroom team were top-quality coaches, but not one had the expertise or specialist knowledge to coach the goalkeepers. Today, every club in the League employs a specialist coach, but this wasn't in the financial interests of clubs back then. Instead, the goalkeepers' coaching was left to the senior custodians and the young Welshman learned a lot of his trade through tips passed on by Tommy Younger and Brian Williamson.

It was strange to be given advice by someone whose place you were trying to take. We used to stay behind after the other lads had finished and, along with Les Cocker, would work for around an hour every day. We would take crosses, work on angles, have penalty-saving competitions and do goalkeeping exercises. Even though we were competing for the first-team spot we were told time and time again it was for the good of the 'family', the collective that was Leeds United.

When Gary became senior goalkeeper himself, albeit at the very young age of seventeen, he would pass on those very same tips. He helped to groom David Harvey, who was to supplant him, somewhat controversially, seven years later. It was obvious that Harvey had mimicked

Gary's style, without perhaps reaching the same heights. In fact, Harvey recalled in the *Leeds United Book of Football* (Second Edition) how he played 'second fiddle' for over 300 games. As well as supervising the 'keepers, Les Cocker's main objective was to condition the players' fitness levels through running and gym work, although Gary argues that the real tactical nous came from Syd Owen.

He was the coach that was most aware tactically and did a great deal of the defensive coaching. Syd also travelled to away games to compile the dreaded, mind-numbing dossiers on the opposing players that we were to face the following week. He would pass them on to Revie to read out, they would last about an hour, by which time the lads would be bored silly – I know I was – although nobody would dare tell any of the coaches this and certainly not the boss himself!

Don Revie had very little input on the training ground; he would plan the day-to-day activities for Cocker and Owen to carry out. Occasionally he would involve himself with corner kicks and free-kicks, always trying to be innovative, a perfect example being the brilliant and forward-thinking masterstroke of placing Jack Charlton on the goal-line in front of the opposing goalkeeper. Unbeknown to the rest of the squad, Revie wanted to test it out on the training pitch, so the usual weekly practice match was the perfect opportunity. At the very first corner Big Jack stood in front of Gary, backing into him and standing on his toes as the corner was delivered.

I pushed him away and told him to stop messing around, but the next corner he did exactly the same, so I just punched him on the back of the head and we ended up on the ground wrestling. A few punches were thrown before Jack started laughing, telling me it had all been pre-arranged. I don't think the boss expected my reaction, but it proved to him how unnerving it was for goalies and it became a very productive tactic.

Big Jack recalls how he used to wind Gary up but knew how far to push it:

You didn't mess with Sprakey; he looked soft, but was very fit, very hard. In training he would save shots from less than five yards away, diving at players' feet and these exercises would go on for hours and hours. Gary also had a quick temper and could be volatile in both training and games.

Being a fiery Welshman there were many more alleged training ground confrontations, especially when other teammates tried to take liberties. In his autobiography, *Marching on Together*, Eddie Gray recalled that he felt both the wrath and the infamous right hook when trying to make a fool of the goalkeeper with his dragbacks instead of just putting the ball in the net during a training session. Gray also wrote of the time that Gary allegedly lost his temper with fellow 'keeper David Harvey, grabbing him around the neck and physically lifting him onto the clothes hooks in the dressing room. Gary, however, denies that either incident took place, believing Gray's comments to be yet another attempt to besmirch his character and reputation. The Welsh 'keeper has somewhat unfortunately gained a reputation outside the club of being a poor trainer, a reputation that has become much repeated over time. However Cyril Partridge (*Leeds Leeds Leeds!* magazine, 2004) takes issue with this, arguing that 'Sprakey was a very enthusiastic lad and a good trainer. He'd come into training and tell everyone that no-one was going to score on that particular day, and they never did!'

So with meticulous planning both on and off the field, the scene was set. It was time to unleash the untried yet highly talented youngster onto the demanding stage that was professional football.

TWO

THE GREEN, GREEN GRASS OF HOME

It was perhaps fateful that the match perceived by many observers and Leeds fans as heralding the club's glory years was against Gary Sprake's home-town club at the Vetch Field, Swansea in the seventh game of the 1962/63 season. The debuts of Norman Hunter, Paul Reaney and Rod Johnson and Gary's second first-team appearance came in a 2–0 victory that became a watershed in the history of Leeds United. Probably every football fan's dream is to watch their team develop successful young home-grown talent and then to give them licence to go out and represent their club with passion and ability. Every team is dearly loved by its supporters but none finds a place in the fans' hearts as does a good young team. The television pundit Alan Hansen's famous comment that 'you win nothing with kids' can be questioned if you look at many of the young and successful British teams produced over the years: not only 'Fergie's Fledglings', who went on to disprove Hansen's theory that same season, but famous teams such as 'Buckley's Boys', the 'Busby Babes' and 'Drake's Ducklings'. Today Arsene Wenger at Arsenal is following suit, not with the home-grown and nurtured talent that was the trademark of the astute Don Revie, but with his purchase of the likes of Jose Antonio Reyes, Cesc Fabregas and Robin Van Persie, gifted youngsters to supplement his Premiership-winning team. The football-loving faithful of Elland Road will forever hold dear in their hearts the rookies that Don Revie introduced during the early 1960s who went on to become household names.

Along with that of Gary, Don Revie's reputation has been much maligned with the passing of time, with pejorative labels such as 'Don Readies' being handed out by an all-too-critical media. Yet his uncanny knack of unearthing raw talent and turning them into internationals can only be matched by Sir Alex Ferguson at arch-rivals Manchester

United decades later. Ferguson, however, presides over the world's richest club, while Revie had to attract those youngsters to a below-average club playing in the second tier of the English pyramid. The game wasn't awash with the millions of pounds it is today, which finance academies and centres of excellence. Youngsters couldn't be attracted by the prospect of multi-million-pound contracts and jobs and houses were not available as incentives for parents to move near to the club courting their children. Yet Revie put in place a network of scouts around the United Kingdom to ensnare a proliferation of the Home Nations' finest schoolboys. Spotted in Wales were Gary and Terry Yorath; from Scotland came Bremner, Lorimer and Gray while Hunter, Cooper, Madeley, Reaney and Harvey (although a future Scottish international) were from England. Almost a full team of internationals were nurtured from aspiring youngsters and to that list can be added those who represented Leeds with dignity over a number of years without achieving full international recognition. These included Mick Bates – who would probably have got into any other top-flight side if he had not demonstrated such tremendous loyalty – Albert Johanneson, Rod Belfitt and Rod Johnson. What is yet more amazing is that, like Gary himself, not all of these youngsters were schoolboy internationals as many were spotted on local parks instead, playing in front of the dozen or so scouts attracted by the high-profile schoolboy games.

There have been few events in the chequered history of Leeds United that so set supporters' hearts aglow as that day, 8 September 1962, in south-west Wales, as Revie set the football world alight by unleashing not one or two, but four teenagers onto the demanding stage that was the old Second Division. The talent of this quartet, and the undoubted qualities of others such as Lorimer, Gray, Cooper and Madeley in the reserve and youth teams, gave hope for the playing future of Leeds United. This was a club whose previous reputation and fortunes seemed to be perennially ranked among the also-rans of the lower leagues. Many youngsters have been one-game wonders, or had to go back into the reserves to further their experience, but the youngsters that Revie fielded that day were the cornerstone of Leeds United's first team for the next ten years or more. They were eventually to obtain legendary status among the Leeds faithful, who even now are able to religiously reel off the names of that famous 1960s and 1970s line-up that became automatic choices on the team sheet after the Swansea game.

As a result of a spate of early season injuries and poor League form Revie addressed his problems with the introduction of youth. A back injury prevented John Charles from appearing in front of an adoring home-town Swansea public and he was replaced by the debutant centre forward Rod Johnson, a Leeds-born England Youth international. Dropped from the previous game was the acting captain Grenville Hair, so Paul Reaney, the London-born but Leeds-raised full-back, made his debut. Also dropped was club captain and centre half Freddie Goodwin, to be replaced by Gateshead-born Norman Hunter. Making up the teenage quartet in only his second appearance was Gary, standing in for the out-of-form veteran international Tommy Younger. In some quarters Revie has since been depicted as indecisive, dossier-obsessed and loyal to the point of blindness but at the Vetch Field that day his boldness reaped dividends. The introduction of four seventeen-year-olds in place of seasoned professionals was truly a masterstroke. After a string of poor results Revie gambled on this drastic measure, even though ideally he would have wanted to bring along these youngsters slowly in the Central League. Earlier in the week Leeds had faced Liverpool in a reserve fixture at Anfield with what the *Yorkshire Evening Post* called 'one of the youngest and most successful Leeds sides ever' at that level. Revie and his coach Syd Owen had slowly been nursing them along and even though they were beating all before them the 'boss' believed they were still far from ready for the intensive rigours of regular first-team football. In fact, the reserve team that lined up that day didn't have one seasoned professional to look after them, the team sheet looking like this: Gary Sprake (17), Paul Reaney (17), Barrie Wright (16), Mike Addy (19), Paul Madeley (17), Paul Hunter (18), Ronnie Blackburn (20), Rod Johnson (17), Peter Lorimer (15), John Hawksby (20) and Terry Cooper (18). A few days later, after the Liverpool game, four of the youngsters – Sprake, Reaney, Hunter and Johnson – were summoned to the manager's office to be told that they had been selected to play against Swansea Town the following Saturday.

In a little over a year since he signed as a professional, the Leeds management had learned two things about Gary Sprake. Firstly, that he had a short fuse and secondly, if they could help him overcome that, that he had a talent that would take him to the pinnacle of his profession. Syd Owen was to experience at first hand the red mist that would occasionally descend over the young Welsh goalkeeper. Owen was a stickler for discipline and had an unpleasant habit of tending to bully the young apprentices – a point commented on by both Terry Yorath and Norman Hunter in their autobiographies. In a training session just after he arrived at Elland Road, Owen attempted to motivate Gary with the comment that he would 'never make a goalkeeper as long as he had a hole in his arse'. Rather than take the advice, Gary reacted in what was to become a trademark fashion by giving the coach a right hook to the side of the face. Amazingly Revie chose to ignore this indiscretion, perhaps thinking he could harness this part of the youngster's character for the good of the team, the 'fighting spirit' he was attempting to nurture in his side. Norman Hunter, in his autobiography *Biting Talk*, argued that Owen took a different view of Gary, never having much time for him. Gary's explanation of this incident provides a fuller understanding of Hunter's comments.

The boss was a disciplinarian and wanted to keep everyone in line. If you crossed him you would be fined, although for some reason he ignored this major indiscretion with Syd. Owen himself held a grudge against me from then on and this might help to explain Norman's comments that he had little time for me. After the incident I don't think we spoke more than a few sentences during the rest of my Leeds career.

There was much optimism about the forthcoming 1962/63 campaign and the summer acquisitions of the legendary John Charles from Serie A and Jim Storrie from Scotland, allied to the experience of Bobby Collins, Willie Bell and Tommy Younger, promised much. However, even though they were only six games into the season, alarm bells began to ring around Elland Road. Prior to the Swansea game Leeds had won two, drawn one and lost three; scoring eight goals while conceding nine. An indifferent start to the season meant that supporters were preparing themselves for, at best, another season of mid-table mediocrity. Their next opponents had hardly set the division alight either, although they were three places above Leeds in tenth. It was time, therefore, to give youth its head, even though somewhat earlier than anticipated. Revie argued in the *Yorkshire Evening Post* that events had overtaken him; even though he wanted the youngsters to mature in the Central League, he also wanted to belatedly kick-start the new campaign.

Gary had experienced a never-to-be forgotten debut at Southampton the previous season, but his second game was just as daunting, returning to his home town as a Leeds player for the first time since his move to Yorkshire two years previously. In the crowd that day were his brothers, sisters, cousins, nephews, former school friends and former Swansea League teammates, all wanting to see the local boy make good. If playing in front of all his friends and family was problematic, getting them all tickets proved even harder. The Leeds 'keeper had to find around twenty or so to keep everyone happy, especially as they all wanted to see the action but not actually pay for the privilege. Gary's teammates, with the exception of John Charles, had to hand over their ticket allocation to meet demand. The young goalie was no stranger to the Vetch for, on his many visits home, both in mid-season and during the summer, the Swans had willingly allowed him to train with their first team. In those days clubs couldn't afford to send scouts to watch their next opponents but the Welsh club had a very good idea of what they would be facing, with the promising youngster having been hugely impressive during the many training sessions he had spent with them over the previous two years. As a result of these sessions Gary had made many new friends, including Barrie Jones and Herbie Williams, who also went on to represent Wales at international level.

Unlike the youthful reserve team sent out at Anfield a few days before, this new team was full of leaders. The Scottish veteran Bobby Collins had proved to be an inspirational signing; tenacious, gifted and a true leader, looked up to by the youngsters and seasoned professionals alike. The one-man 'awkward squad' Jack Charlton was the defensive linchpin who, after the Swansea game, blossomed into one of the all-time greats at both club and international level. In an interview given to the *Yorkshire Evening Post*, Jack recalled the Swansea game being the first time he was granted autonomy by Revie. Jack wanted to defend his way, zonal rather than man-to-man marking, and with the absence of so many senior defensive players he was allowed to get on with it. The other leader on the pitch that day was Billy Bremner, still only twenty years of age but showing maturity, organisational skills and leadership that belied those tender years. In fact he was already by that time something of a veteran, having clocked up close to 100 appearances. This experience told as he cajoled those youngsters around him to greater things, never allowing them to let their nerves get the better of them.

At seventeen years of age and in only his second senior game, watched by dozens of family and friends, it would have been understandable if Gary had been overcome by nerves. However, unlike his debut, he had time to prepare normally for this game. Leeds started the match very tentatively and were second best in all the early exchanges as a result of the wholesale changes that had been made. The local boy soon settled, however, thanks to two comfortable saves, one from Barrie Jones, the other from Colin Webster. Far from being overawed, the youngsters played a high-tempo game, chasing every ball and closing down the Swans in the final third – tactics that Revie had adopted with great success earlier and ones that were copied by David O'Leary in his tenure as Leeds manager. The high-tempo, aggressive football was to become a trademark of the Leeds United style and every fan of the club came to expect players who pulled on the famous white jersey to display this commitment at all times. Unfortunately, during Leeds' terrible last two years as a Premiership club, the fans became distinctly unimpressed with the inability of Terry Venables, Peter Reid and Eddie Gray to motivate their teams to play in the style set so proudly by Revie's legendary side.

All the debutants acquitted themselves well, demonstrating skills that would hold them in good stead for the next ten years or more. Reaney used his pace to good effect, both in defence and overlapping in attack, while Hunter injected pace and ball-winning skills into the backline. Even though the home side enjoyed the early pressure it was Leeds who edged in front through Johnson, on his debut, with a mazy run past several defenders before a clinical finish from an acute angle. This prompted an immediate response and Gary was forced into action on several occasions, allowing him the opportunity to demonstrate his enormous potential. He displayed his full repertoire of skills: the faultless handling of high crosses, which was to become a trademark; saves from both close and long-range shots and excellent positional sense. What was most pleasing for the young Leeds 'keeper was the recognition given by the home fans. Round after round of applause rained down from the terraces he had stood on no more than two years previously. His performance that day was described by Phil Brown in the *Yorkshire Evening Post* as 'story book', helping inspire all around him. Jack Charlton coped with all that was thrown at him, Collins and Bremner worked tirelessly throughout, setting up attacks and protecting those around them and they were justifiably rewarded when Leeds scored their second goal.

Leeds had performed tremendously, eventually overpowering and outplaying their more experienced opponents. The four youngsters had promising games, including the young Welshman, who excelled. Yet this game set a precedent; when fans are asked to recall matches they remember the score and scorers but never look beyond the result to the goalkeepers' contributions. Another clean sheet, another victory, and as so often demonstrated in the following years, a faultless performance from the man between the sticks. With Gary Leeds were certainly receiving value for money as he was still only earning £2 per week. Following his debut six months previously, the young goalkeeper had alternated between youth and reserve teams. Now, however, he was to be first choice, barring injury, for the next 500 games – a remarkable and record-breaking achievement that would span over a decade and that still makes him the goalkeeper with the most appearances ever for the club.

Throughout my career I was extremely nervous before games, but on the occasion of the first game at the Vetch my only feeling was of being excited at the prospect of playing before family and friends. Swansea had a very good side in those days and produced some excellent players like Barry Hole, Brian Purcell, Roy Evans and Mike Johnson as well as an abundance of internationals. I was very proud the boss had given me the opportunity to play. I thought I had played well and after the game my family and friends confirmed this, along with the boss who gave me the weekend off. I celebrated by having a couple of drinks with my family, even though I was underage.

After the success of the four teenagers during the Swansea game, Don Revie faced a dilemma: should he keep the same team or revert to the old guard? Revie confessed to Phil Brown of the *Yorkshire Evening Post* that his view that he should bring on the youngsters slowly had not changed since before the Swans game. However, the four had made such an impression that Revie did keep faith with three of them. Perhaps it was asking too much to pick Johnson in place of the legendary John Charles, even though he had had an excellent debut. As it turned out Revie hadn't finished with his policy of giving youth its head as three weeks after the Swansea game Peter Lorimer beat Gary's own record to become the youngest Leeds player at fifteen years and 289 days.

Gary's home debut, along with that of Reaney and Hunter, came with the following week's visit of the much fancied (and ultimately promoted) Chelsea, managed by the relatively inexperienced Tommy Docherty. Chelsea had already kept six clean sheets in the seven games they had played and had battered Sunderland into submission at Stamford Bridge the previous Saturday. Chelsea had shown their intent on achieving a quick return to the top flight after their relegation the previous season. As well as accomplished footballers, Chelsea had a physical presence that would undoubtedly pose a threat to the inexperienced Leeds side. Their smallest player was the 5ft 9in Terry Venables, although at the Vetch Leeds had included the much more diminutive Collins and Bremner. Over the next ten years or so Leeds and Chelsea would become bitter rivals with some games resembling open warfare, most notoriously the 1970 FA Cup final replay.

Games against Chelsea were always hard and physical and relationships were fired by the press. They always billed the games as the north/south divide. Added to that, we were hated by both the London media and fans of southern clubs. I particularly liked playing against Chelsea because I was never afraid of a physical confrontation. I had some very interesting battles against Peter Osgood and there was always a bit of needle between us. He would always have a go at winding me up and I don't think there was one game where we didn't clash. He was a very skilful, if sometimes arrogant player. He would have been even more effective if he didn't react, but Big Jack, Norman and I would wind him up. He would spend the rest of the game seeking revenge rather than playing football. He was different to Ron 'Chopper' Harris; he was the same type of player as Norman. What you saw was what you got. A hard, but fair defender.

Revie and his backroom staff had to meticulously plan for Leeds' toughest game to date. Yet two minutes into the game those plans were in disarray as right half Eric Smith was on his way to hospital with a broken leg after a collision with Welsh international Graham Moore. At first it appeared Moore had come off second best and once play restarted insult was added to injury with the referee awarding Chelsea the free-kick. Billy Bremner dropped back from midfield and a backs-to-the-wall performance was envisaged by the Elland Road faithful. Yet the players demonstrated a will to win in a gritty performance that was to become Leeds' trademark. Rather than being overrun they produced a magical display, particularly from the gifted outside left Albert Johanneson, who scored two excellent goals.

I remember Albert as a very skilful player. He had great ball control with electrifying pace and could also score goals. Albert was shy and nervous both on and off the pitch but was a great favourite with the Elland Road faithful. When we played away, however, he unfortunately suffered racial abuse from a small minority. The worst I witnessed was a game at Goodison Park. They were making monkey noises and some idiots threw bananas at Albert. As you can imagine he was extremely upset and being a timid person it affected him deeply. Even though players used to wind each other up during games, opposing players never once made racist remarks towards him. I think it was a terrible shame the way some fans treated him as Albert was a very nice man who sadly died through drink-related problems.

Chelsea had threatened with their short passing game and on twenty minutes Gary was called upon for the first time, plucking the ball expertly out of the air from a Chelsea corner. Fears that this would be a tough home debut for the young goalkeeper proved unfounded as an uncompromising rearguard action led by Jack Charlton restricted Chelsea to one long-range effort by Moore, which was comfortably saved, and a vicious cross-shot by the same player that was confidently dealt with. The youngsters in whom Revie now entrusted the club's future had once again demonstrated determination, passion and professionalism belying their tender years. For the young Welshman in goal, things were looking very promising – two games and two clean sheets in faultless displays of safe handling and accomplished saves. Especially pleasing was the understanding he was developing with centre half Charlton.

My first impression of Jack was that he was a really nice, friendly and down-to-earth person. Many people think he was blunt, arrogant and miserly. On a personal level I was close to Jack. As a young apprentice my girlfriend Kathy and I used to babysit for Jack and his wife Pat. Believe it or not he used to pay me a couple of quid, although I spent some of it on his son John. Jack, Billy Bremner and me also used to go out for a few pints together in one of our locals where we would play darts, cards and dominoes with the regulars. Sometimes we would have a few pints on a Thursday night, even though the club had a forty-eight-hour curfew before games. No one ever grassed us up to Revie though. On a professional level we had a great understanding, always talking to one another, deciding when I should come for crosses or leave them for Jack. We did have many arguments on the field, mainly because Jack would never admit to being in the wrong or that he had made a mistake. He would give me a terrible dressing down if he thought I had made a mistake. He would just let rip in front of everyone; he never thought beforehand, but it was over as soon he had made his point. That was one thing about Jack: he never held a grudge, although with his memory he probably genuinely forgot! Some people say we couldn't play together, but Jack played over 700 games, while I played over 500, so it couldn't have been a bad partnership could it?

What was pleasing for Revie, and particularly for club chairman Harry Reynolds, was the fact that for now it appeared the chequebook could be put away. Having spent the then quite considerable sum of £135,000 over the preceding twelve months on new players, both the chairman and manager were delighted with the dividend these youngsters were now paying, with Revie praising them for playing with wisdom that belied their years. Money, it seemed, was not everything (something the club management of the early 2000s could have taken heed of. Somehow the Elland Road faithful in the 1960s could not have imagined the gruff Yorkshireman Reynolds feeding the goldfish in his office!). After a profitable fortnight, Leeds were on the road for two away games against opponents that it was thought would not provide as severe a test as Chelsea: the lesser-known lights of Bury and Luton. Bury had installed as player-manager Bob Stokoe, who would become a thorn in the side of Revie over the next ten years or so. Stokoe was building a big, hard and physical side and this proved the undoing of Leeds in 1962, just as Stokoe's Sunderland would in the FA Cup final eleven years later. Phil Brown reported that their direct and uncompromising style of play proved too strong for the teenagers. Bury could not be hassled or jostled off the ball with Stokoe a commanding presence at centre half. Leeds found themselves 2-0 down at half-time before pulling a goal back through Storrie. However, the home team, who had been sitting on their lead, then moved up a gear, adding a third before the final whistle. It seemed the honeymoon period was over. According to Phil Brown, the only players to emerge with any distinction were Bremner, who worked heroically against physically stronger attackers yet distributed the ball beautifully, and Sprake who, having conceded a weak header for the first, thereafter produced a number of very good saves. As Brown points out, even the great John Charles was struggling and found it very difficult to readjust to the physical demands of British football after his successful time in Serie A. His readjustment period had not been helped by a series of niggling injuries.

After the severe confidence test of conceding three at Bury, Gary's next challenge was the away trip to lowly Luton Town who, almost a quarter of the way through the campaign, were showing relegation form. Leeds went into battle without their star man, Charles, who was 'rested' for the clash, proving that at an early stage in his managerial

reign Revie was never going to shirk painful decisions. In fact, this
was the youngest ever Leeds side to take the field, with an average
age of only twenty-two. With another eighteen-year-old debutant,
Mike Addy, the side included six teenagers. Leeds raced into a two-
goal lead through Storrie and the outstanding Collins, who was again
irrepressible, but after the half-hour the highly influential Bremner
was injured and spent the rest of the game hobbling on the wing.
Against what was effectively ten men, Luton pressed forward but found
Gary in outstanding form and, as Luton threatened to take control, he
made three blinding saves to keep Leeds in the game. As early as the
Southampton debut the previous season he had shown that he had
both the ability and speed of thought to become a great goalkeeper.
Even though he was to be portrayed as laid back throughout his career,
he took his performances very seriously, reflecting, perhaps sometimes
too much, on each and every game from his debut onwards. Gary
himself admits that during his early career at Leeds he did sometimes
struggle with his anticipation but these skills improved with experience, as did his judgement. This was evident in the faultless display
against Luton, beaten only by a dubiously awarded penalty just before
half-time and a wicked deflection after he had had a shot covered
two minutes from the end. Leeds had surrendered a two-goal lead
because of the injury to Bremner, who spent two-thirds of the game
as a passenger on the wing.

After the impressive results of the Swansea and Chelsea games the
next four games saw the 'goals against' column rise by nine. The visit
to the Baseball Ground for the clash against mid-table Derby County
was therefore vitally important as Leeds' fans seemed to perceive that
the club's brief upturn in fortunes had been yet another false dawn. In a
dour game against opponents who had only achieved one win in their
previous thirteen matches Leeds set out their defensive stall – a trait
that was to become second nature to the team over the next decade.
Leeds threw a defensive blanket around the young Welsh 'keeper and
when in the second half they breached the defence Gary responded
by producing four fine saves. The reporter Ken Tossell of the *Daily
Mirror* argued that 'the two best shots of the game, a thirty-yard rocket
by Young and a snap-shot drive by McCann were brilliantly saved by
Sprake'. Gary's performance had once again gone a long way towards
Leeds coming away with a confidence-returning 0–0 draw.

Unfortunately, while gaining this vital point Leeds suffered a series
of injuries. Missing for the League Cup clash with Blackburn were

regulars Charlton, Bremner, Collins and Johanneson, while Charles, although recovered from a badly gashed forehead after the Derby clash, was away on international duty with Wales. This gives an indication of how the new competition was actually regarded at this time, as it was not to be very often that Wales would take precedence over Leeds in competitive games involving Gary. In their League fixture preceding the tie, Blackburn, with their sprinkling of full internationals, had overcome the mighty Manchester United. Leeds therefore went into the game as no-hopers, especially given the makeshift team Revie was to field. Gary, however, went into the game with his position assured because the veteran Tommy Younger had announced his retirement leading up to the fixture. Not only had the young 'keeper attracted the nation's attention with a string of masterful performances, but Younger had also seen enough to convince him that it would take something special to oust the seventeen-year-old Welshman.

Tommy was a big man and a very good 'keeper. He took me under his wing when I first arrived at Leeds and taught me a great deal. He coached me in all aspects of goalkeeping: narrowing angles, positional sense and taking crosses. He spent hours with me on the training pitch and in the gym. He used to knock crosses in to me, then he would throw a medicine ball in the air, then he would put me under physical pressure by knocking me about when I was catching this big heavy ball. No wonder I was a hard player, although with hindsight no wonder I ended up with arthritis! I will always be grateful to Tommy for his help.

During the game itself the new Leeds number one had looked as if he was on police duty, directing the traffic with his newly acquired white gloves. The only traffic, however, was the one-way variety emanating from the Blackburn Rovers attack and heading towards him time and time again. Gary alone stood between Rovers and an embarrassing scoreline in a Leeds performance that lacked experience and confidence. His judgement once again belied the tender years and his agility impressed all. Local reporter Phil Brown stated that it was a gruelling test for the four youngsters: Hunter, who coped well; Reaney, who had a difficult game against his experienced opposite number and left his goalkeeper exposed on several occasions; Johnson, who lacked service from an overrun midfield; and Gary: 'Sprake responded by being the hero (and what a busy hero he was) of the match. He made a succession of saves; high, low, long range and point blank. The second half showed the high natural abilities in this fair-haired Welsh boy even when confronted by a rampaging First Division forward line on its own ground.'

Although beaten by two first-half strikes, Gary seemed to be holding Rovers almost single-handedly before the exhausted away defence was overrun completely, conceding a further two in the last five minutes.

They had a side full of internationals but surprisingly I wasn't that nervous. We were not expected to win so we just took it as an opportunity to develop. It was good for me because I was given numerous opportunities to make saves, such was the pressure we were under.

Although Revie's team had been thoroughly outplayed in a resounding 4-0 defeat Gary had demonstrated that he could compete with some of the best the First Division had to offer. Indeed, the morning after the Blackburn game the boss called him into his office and more than doubled his wages to the astronomical (for a seventeen-year-old) sum of £5 per week.

While one Swansea-born player seemed to be securing his Leeds career another's was sensationally coming to an end. John Charles, who Revie had brought back from Serie A in an attempt to reach the top flight, had been transferred back to Italy. His performances had never reached the heights that everybody had come to expect from the great man and the chairman couldn't refuse a deal that showed a profit of a couple of thousand pounds. Come kick-off the following Saturday Reynolds may have had second thoughts as the gate had dropped by over 10,000 from the previous game. On the playing front, however, it seemed that a great weight had been lifted off Charles' old teammates, as Gary recalls:

Revie never consciously changed the way we played before the game, but we appeared to play with more variety. When John was in the team all the attacking moves went through him; probably we had become too predictable, but in that Norwich game Jim Storrie played in the central position rather than out wide. John was a fantastic player but his absence seemed to make the other players work much harder – perhaps they had become over-reliant on him and now everyone had something to prove. It's strange but when you have such a good target man everything seems to go through him. It's the same when I watched Wales play under Mark Hughes; it all went through Big John Hartson, even though players like Giggs, Bellamy and Davies have tremendous pace. These tactics can become predictable.

In fact, Leeds started at a frantic pace and the forwards, who suddenly realised they were the stars, not the supporting cast, gave the home side the lead with two goals in the first ten minutes through Storrie and Bell. Reporter Rex Traill believed Norwich were a better outfit than the early scoreline suggested: 'they were by no means inferior, coming into the game more and more, with Sprake having as much to do as his opposite number. The longer the game lasted the better he performed, turning excellent saves into first-class passes with his accurate throwing of the ball.' Collins had sprayed passes around with aplomb through-out the game but not even he surpassed the quick, long throw out that the home goalkeeper made when setting up Johanneson for the killer third goal. The ball had travelled from Leeds' six-yard line to the back of the opponents' net with only two players touching the ball.

While Gary was earning rave reviews from many commentators in both the local and national press, it was his burning desire to catch the attention of the Welsh selectors. To do this, however, he had to perform well against the two Welsh sides in the Second Division, Swansea Town and Cardiff City, as the selectors never ventured outside the Principality.

I wanted to do well, obviously, in every game I played, but it meant so much more to show my fellow countrymen how capable I was. Then, hopefully, I would gain recognition at Youth and Under-23 level.

After the inspired early season performance against Swansea his next chance was the trip to Ninian Park in the run up to Christmas. Cardiff, although settled in mid-table, were the division's top scorers, having scored in all of their home games. Another coincidence was the fact that the home side's attack was led by Mel Charles, another Swansea man, who a few seasons before had broken the British transfer record when moving from the Swans to Arsenal.

It was incredible that throughout my career I played against so many players from my home town. I'd be very surprised if there were many towns in that era that produced so many fine players. Some, you could argue, were even world class. The people of Swansea have always been known as 'Jacks' after a dog by the same name who rescued countless people from the sea by swimming out to them and dragging them back to shore. The people of Swansea have also got a tremendous sense of humour and I used to engage in banter before and after the game with my fellow Jacks. During the game we all used to try our hardest to put one over each other though. During my career I think Swansea-born players would have held their own against any side in Europe. I could have selected myself in goal or my former neighbour Jack Kelsey. My team would have been Sprake/Kelsey, Herbie Williams, Mel Charles, Mel Nurse, Barry Hole, Leighton James, Terry Medwin, Ivor Allchurch, Barrie Jones, Cliff Jones and of course John Charles. I don't think many would have come out on top of that lot, even in today's Premiership! All with the exception of Herbie were seasoned internationals and I would argue that Leighton, Ivor, Cliff and John were all world class.

Gary, like many footballers, especially at Revie's Leeds, had his own superstitions and from his first game onwards was accompanied to every game with his toy soldiers, which he placed in the back of the net in his cap. Before the game he also ensured that he tied up his right boot before his left and that he trotted out second onto the pitch behind the captain. Pundits throughout the country, however, were arguing that the young goalkeeper was making his own luck with a string of dazzling displays week in, week out. The Welsh public were to be given the chance to witness this themselves at Ninian Park on 21 September. The young Welshman was desperate to demonstrate his attributes to the people of Wales and was well satisfied with his performance in helping to secure Leeds a point from a scoreless stalemate. Ironically, his best saves denied his Swansea-born opponents Ivor Allchurch and Mel Charles. As Tom Lyons from the *Daily Mirror* reported at the time:

> A beanpole topped by a mass of blond curls gave a terrific display and twice rescued Leeds. He made a brilliant one-handed save to turn an Allchurch drive round a post. This effort, that brought a standing ovation from a sporting Cardiff crowd, not least because he demonstrated unbelievable agility, but demonstrated out-of-the-ordinary bravery, having been knocked unconscious after crashing into the post while making the save. He also did well to hold a rocket-like header from Charles.

As Gary recalls:

Apart from playing for Leeds and Wales the biggest thrill I got was returning to the land of my fathers, especially when I was pitting my wits against fellow internationals. There was another reason to do well; Don Revie would promise me I could return home to Swansea for the weekend if we didn't get beaten.

The award-winning local *South Wales Echo* journalist Peter Corrigan made a shrewd observation of the match:

> Young Sprake didn't have a lot to do, although what he did was perform with an air of authority that was pleasing to watch. This young Welshman is obviously one to mark down for future reference.

The Welsh media were urging the national selectors to take notice of a seventeen-year-old that by now had become an automatic choice in a side pushing for promotion from the second tier of the English pyramid – a point reinforced by fellow journalist Bryn Richards: 'young Sprake appears to have booked the Wales jersey in the very near future.' While Gary earned the plaudits for his display in gaining Leeds a valuable point, the Englishman Jack Charlton felt the wrath of the home crowd for his display. Bryn Richards, although full of praise for fellow Welshman Sprake, was grudgingly admiring of Big Jack: 'The centre half was the kingpin, but some of his tackles were on the rugged side and they didn't please the crowd, but he kept Charles under subjection.' Tudor James of the *Sunday People* described Gary's save from Allchurch thus: 'he cricked his back in the superhuman effort' while reporting that 'Allchurch had enquired whether Sprake was psychic, believing he had been denied a certain goal.'

As 1963 approached, Leeds were handily placed for a promotion push. Going into the last game of the old year, against fellow promotion candidates Sunderland, Leeds had won eight, drawn eight and lost six. Sunderland would be a severe test, especially as they were on an unbeaten thirty-one-match run at home. It was also going to be Gary's biggest test to date, coming up against one of the most prolific scorers in the history of the British game, Brian Clough. Leeds went down 2-1 but Gary more than held his own, with the *Sunderland Argos* reporting that 'Sprake made two magnificent saves, one from a Clough header, another from a rasping shot after Clough had weaved his way past four defenders.'

Even though Gary played for over a decade this was his only appearance against the prolific scorer.

Clough was a very good player but an even better manager. Our paths never crossed but he was an exceptional man. I had just left for Birmingham when he arrived at Leeds for his ill-fated stay. My ex-teammates never rated him. I remember them telling me that the first thing he told them was that they were all cheats. He told them they hadn't earned all the trophies they had won under Revie – little wonder his stay was so short-lived.

Even at this very early stage of his burgeoning career, Gary was earning rave reports from around the country. Journalists, Leeds fans and opposing supporters were taking notice of his confident displays. The *Daily Mirror* ran a sports poll, 'Success United', in which fans had to vote for their team of the week. Gary was becoming a regular fixture, voted in alongside such greats as Bobby Charlton, fellow Welshman Roy Vernon and Charlie Hurley.

Leeds started the new year in an optimistic mood. Their defence was solid, conceding just over a goal a game with Charlton, Sprake and Hunter putting on consistently excellent displays. From March until the middle of May 1963 they remained unbeaten and an air of optimism was sweeping around Elland Road. That optimism proved unfounded as Leeds had a disastrous month of May madness, losing three games on the trot and ending up five points behind champions Stoke and four points behind promoted Chelsea. It would not be the last time they would fall at the final hurdle.

Although the season had ended in disappointment, with Leeds finishing fifth, Gary could be pleased both on a personal and professional level. In his first full season he had made thirty-three league appearances, three FA Cup and two League Cup appearances. He had conceded thirty-four goals, under a goal a game, and helped keep thirteen clean sheets. His wages had more than doubled from the previous season, from £2 a week to £5 a week, enabling him on his seventeenth birthday, towards the end of the 1962/63 season, to buy his first car, a Singer Gazelle. While Norman Hunter took great delight in his Vauxhall Viva, Gary was showing a bit more class. He was reaping the rewards of his profession, also gaining a taste for fast cars and the opposite sex – two things that would continually get him in bother over the next ten years or so.

My first full season went really well, better than I could have ever have dreamed of. There were many reasons for this. I wanted to prove to Syd Owen that I did have what it took to play professionally. I wanted to impress the Welsh selectors, but most importantly I did not want to return to the lifestyle of my mates like Ronnie Squires back home in Swansea. I never considered myself any better because I played football. But, and it was a big but, I never forgot my first job as an apprentice fitter and turner. I had to go to Tomkins' slaughterhouse in Llansamlet to repair the chain lift. I'll never forget the smell and sight of the carcasses as long as I live. What an incentive to succeed as a professional footballer. While I was more than pleased with my first full season there was another opinion that mattered more: Don Revie's. He had recently introduced a new pay policy; everyone was assessed on individual performances and paid accordingly. Some didn't like it, arguing that it was a team game and the policy could prove divisive. Big Jack had other ideas though. I remember him saying in a team meeting that he shouldn't have the same wages as any useless so-and-so – although Jack never quite used those exact words!

In fact, Revie's view at the time reinforced Gary's own self-assessment, telling local reporter Fred Willis: 'He has got a great future ahead of him and I am very proud. He works very hard and like the rest of the youngsters has given us no trouble. Provided he does not let the publicity go to his head, I think he is almost certain to play for his country.'

Not a bad assessment, recalls Gary. I worked very hard, I had a great career, I wasn't greatly affected by the publicity and I played for my country. As for giving Revie trouble, well… four out of five wasn't bad.

Gary's performances on the field had caught the nation's attention but he was still like every other teenager in the country. His favourite pop star was Elvis and every weekend he could be found dancing the night away in the Mecca in Leeds city centre. Gary was developing the life of a pop star himself, regularly attending parties, a prototype David Beckham perhaps?

We used to go to the Mecca where Jimmy Saville was the manager, he used to introduce us to the radio DJ's and pop stars. It used to cost sixpence to get in but Jimmy used to get me and some of the other players in for nothing. We joined the Tudor club, which was the VIP area within the club. Myself and Paul Reaney were there most weekends. Big Jack would sometimes come along but the girls thought he was too old. Paul and I used to have a great time though! I did develop a soft spot for my adopted land as the Yorkshire people were really friendly, but Wales was where my heart was. I used to make the journey home every five weeks and stay the whole close season. Revie told me, along with the rest of my teammates, to make the most of the break. After our disastrous run-in he was determined that next season we would achieve promotion. The boss was never one to make rash promises, so when he did we knew he meant it.

Although promotion was the major objective of the new 1963/64 season there was to be no team strengthening. Revie had decided to stick with the old guard and his crop of prodigious and precocious youngsters. Controversy was also on the agenda, both on the footballing front and in the wider world. John Charles had sensationally been stopped from making his debut for Cardiff City because the Ninian Park club still owed £16,000 of his transfer fee to Roma. In Argentina, the legendary Alfredo di Stefano had been kidnapped (a phenomenon that still occurs in poverty stricken South America), while at home the public had been stunned by the Great Train Robbery. As the big kick-off got under way there was an ongoing manhunt for the perpetrators.

Preparations for the season's opener against Rotherham were not going according to plan. Midfield star Billy Bremner, who was home-sick and missing his girlfriend back in Scotland, had asked for a trans-fer; Celtic were showing a keen interest, although Revie desperately wanted to keep the player. The impasse had not been broken as they took to the field, lining up Sprake, Reaney, Bell, Bremner, Hunter, Charlton, Collins, Weston, Johannson, Lawson and Storrie. In his pro-gramme notes Revie had called on the fans to produce an intimidating home atmosphere throughout the season and the fans responded by showing their support even during a dour 1-0 victory, the winning goal coming from Weston. Despite the clean sheet Gary remembers the more exciting news of that day.

After the game Revie told us that he was, after all, strengthening the squad, but would not reveal the player's identity. We did not have to wait long; the next day at training we were introduced to Johnny Giles from Manchester United. The boss wasn't sure he could hold on to Billy and wanted cover. As it hap-pened Billy stayed and the two of them became the best midfield partnership not only that Leeds ever had but possibly that the country has ever seen. They were a fantastic midfield pairing; both had tremendous skills and their range of passing was superb. Both could play the short pass or spray long passes all over the park. Billy was predominantly a one-footed player but Giles had two great feet. They were also hard players – Giles was one of the hardest men I played with or against, although on times he could be cynical with his over-the-top tackles. They had a great understanding, almost telepathic.

The Welsh wing wizard Leighton James endorses Gary's opinion: 'Billy was a hard player, but Giles could be both dirty and sly, he would kick you after the ball had gone.'

Over the first four months of the season Leeds suffered only one defeat, away to Manchester City. Although they could produce attractive, free-flowing football, in the majority of games results were ground out. All the youngsters were making mistakes, but Revie was tolerant. Gary recalls:

We all made mistakes, but the boss saw it as a learning curve. I made a few but no more nor less than anyone else. I was not pilloried; for the boss it wasn't an issue.

A view taken by many managers and goalkeepers since about the perils of being between the sticks. In what proved to be his final game in charge of Newcastle during the 2004/05 season, Bobby Robson witnessed his goalie commit a howler that cost his side the game. Rather than lay the blame at Shay Given's door, Robson took the view that a goalkeeper's mistake may be the culmination of the team's failings. The centre forward didn't close down quickly enough, the midfielder gave away possession too cheaply or the defender was ball-watching. Tim Howard, after being dropped by Manchester United in the same season, gave the *Guardian* a blunt assessment of a 'keeper's lot: 'Every player makes mistakes, but it is always the 'keeper that is made the scapegoat' – a view shared by Revie and Gary's teammates throughout his illustrious career at Elland Road. Until, that is, a certain newspaper article in 1977.

Following the early season defeat by Manchester City, Leeds put together a then club record of sixteen games unbeaten. Gary in this period looked forward very much to the visit of Welsh clubs like his home-town team Swansea Town to Elland Road. Despite not playing particularly well, Leeds were picking up the points, a quality that ultimately produces champions. Mid-table Swans, however, would be no pushovers, for in their side was the much-vaunted Barrie Jones. His wing play was much admired and he was being tracked by most of the top sides. An exciting winger, he was later the subject of a British record transfer.

I remember Barrie was a really quality player. I was really looking forward to another Welsh player entering the top flight, either as a teammate or opponent. He did get a move, but strangely it was to Second Division Plymouth Argyle. No one knows the intricacies of transfers, but Barrie could easily have plied his trade at the top level.

Leeds overcame the Swans thanks to goals by Johanneson and a rare effort from Willie Bell. The following three games produced victories and Leeds entered the Christmas period top of the table with only one defeat and with over half the games played. The Boxing Day fixture was at home to second-placed Sunderland, with the return fixture two days later at Roker Park. With twenty-odd games to go these games were being hailed as championship deciders. The first game at Leeds was played on a 'horror' of a pitch. It was not a spectacle as each side cancelled the other out and the game petered out in a 1-1 draw. The only incident of note for the 40,000-plus crowd was the clash between Sprake and the Sunderland forward Sharkey. After scoring his goal, Sharkey was over-exuberant in his celebrations.

Rather than just get on with it he was telling me how hard he was – but I was training with really hard men everyday. They didn't come much harder than Charlton, Collins, Bremner, Hunter and Giles. That was one of our qualities. I may have been young and inexperienced but I could look after myself. So when he said that, I just whacked him in the kidneys, something I perfected over the years. The linesman was flagging furiously, but luckily for me the referee ignored him. Perhaps he thought he was flagging for offside and overruled him.'

Unfortunately for Leeds the record-breaking run ended on 28 December as they went down 2-0 in the away game. Revie, picking horses for courses, had dropped the cult figure Johanneson because he was expecting another physical battle. This proved to be the case, with Gary facing an aerial bombardment and he dropped a cross at the feet of Herd who, after a goalmouth melee, was eventually able to slot home from close range. To add insult to injury, it was Sharkey who added the second, but this time the celebrations were muted. Without the flair of Johanneson Leeds had nothing to offer. As Gary remembers:

That was perhaps the first time I witnessed how negative the boss could be. He became obsessed with not losing, putting up the shutters. If we did go behind we sometimes had little to offer. Albert was a flair player who could, and would, win games on his own.

For the remainder of the game the Leeds goalie was back to his best, with Phil Brown reporting that Sprake 'after the first goal never lost concentration, making a magnificent full-length fingertip save from a

Sharkey cross-shot'. So the run had come to an end. As Brown stated, 'All good things come to an end, but at least it ended with credit.'

On the journey home the boss told us to regain our focus, to concentrate and to remain unbeaten for the rest of the season. He may have tolerated our mistakes at the start but now he could see our potential was being realised, that we were, in fact, capable of winning the title.

Leeds did regain their focus, remaining unbeaten for a further three months in the League until a defeat away to Preston North End. Meanwhile there was the FA Cup, with some pundits tipping Leeds as the dark horses for a place at Wembley.

Football is and always has been full of twists and ironies and for the young Welsh custodian it was ironic that their first opponents in the FA Cup would be Cardiff City. He once again had the opportunity to impress the national selectors and demonstrate his outstanding ability in front of compatriots, friends and family who had made the short journey up the A48. Unbeknown to Gary, however, there were others sitting in the Ninian Park directors' box taking more than a passing interest – the scouts from Serie A giants Lazio. Tudor Jones of the *Mirror* reported that the Rome giants were preparing an offer for Sprake after studying their scouts' reports. 'Lazio has always paid top wages to colourful goalkeepers and they are wondering if Sprake can attract crowds to the Olympic Stadium and become another Sentimenti,' reported Jones, before he added knowingly, 'I have a feeling that Don Revie will fight tooth and nail to keep Gary at Elland Road.'

Before the game I approached the boss to see if the rumours were true. He said they were but he would never sell me. That was the end of the matter as far as I was concerned. I was still a teenager who was just settling in Yorkshire. I don't think I wanted to go to another foreign country. If I were playing today, however, I could have used that interest to at least double my wages. In the days before agents we were the property of the club. Although wages were relatively good, the clubs were the ones that profited the most.

The previous season Gary had almost single-handedly ensured Leeds reached the fourth round for the first time in twelve years by defeating Stoke City. This year, however, hopes were high of going much further.

When the coach arrived outside Ninian Park Gary had cause for concern. Revie had demonstrated confidence in his young star but when the team kit was unloaded, Gary's lucky toy soldiers, cap and gloves were missing. Welsh reporter John Lloyd stated that 'Gary bought new gloves, did without a cap and made his own luck.' In a game that saw two players break their legs, the Leeds captain Freddie Goodwin and Cardiff's Alan McIntosh, the Leeds goalkeeper, according to Lloyd, broke Welsh hearts:

> A couple of Sprake's first-half saves from John Charles wonder headers would have done credit to any 'keeper in the game. If it wasn't for scintillating Sprake, Cardiff would have won by two goals.
>
> In the event it was the tireless Billy Bremner who got the only goal of the game, topping a masterful midfield performance with a torpedo-like strike that flew in at the near post.

After the game Don Revie gave his assessment of the game to Lloyd: 'I am proud of all my lads, but what a player Sprake is, and what a player Bremner is. I've just told Gary he can have the weekend off in Swansea; it's thoroughly deserved.'

Dewi Richards of the *Western Mail* reported that

> City played well but were thwarted by some brilliant goalkeeping by Sprake. He has blossomed to such an extent that he should keep the Welsh jersey for many seasons. His cutting out of high crosses could never be bettered, while he made some magnificent ground saves when all seemed lost. Compared to the superb Sprake, his opposite number Dillwyn John appeared mediocre. John Charles was more robust than usual but the plucky Sprake stood his ground throughout.

Peter Corrigan of the *South Wales Echo* described his performance as

> the main reason why City did not score. He received a tremendous battering and three times had to have treatment off both trainers. His performance was world class and some of his saves were out of this world. His air work nullified the threat of John Charles.

I remember I had to show agility and braveness, especially against John. I think that was the most physical game he played – he wanted to prove something to Revie for letting him go after a disappointing second spell at Leeds. John didn't have to prove anything to anybody but if he had I wish it had not been against me. I may have been given two days off, but I was black and blue and spent most of the weekend on the sofa. But John was a real gent and although physical he was always fair and never dirty in any way.

Leeds were cruising in the League and were consolidating their position at the top of the table, so the FA Cup was proving to be a nice diversion. And the fourth round draw meant that Revie could pit his wits against one of the country's top managers and teams: Harry Catterick and League champions Everton. For Gary however, it was touch and go whether he would be fit to pit his wits against top opposition in what was still a season of professional development. His personal life was threatening to affect those ambitions. He was in danger of becoming a victim of the increasing positive publicity he was attracting and was starting to live the life of a pop star. The week before the tie he had crashed his sports car and needed sixteen stitches in a head wound after he collided with a lamp post. Tina Kelsey recalls the weekend of the third round.

> We knew that if Leeds got a result in Cardiff that Gary would be home
> in Winch Wen. That was confirmed on Saturday evening when we heard
> the sound of screeching tyres as he hurtled through the lanes between
> Llansamlet and our row of houses. You knew he was around; he thought
> he was a racing driver, like the time he was driving too quickly down
> Carmel Road, couldn't stop at the junction, flew across the main road and
> demolished the telephone box.

Unfortunately, it wasn't the last time that a car accident was to play an important part in the life of Gary Sprake.

Gary did just pass the last-minute fitness test and lined up against opponents from a higher league for only the second time.

Don Revie was really worried about the tie, not because we were playing more illustrious opponents but because he thought we would have stage fright. A crowd of over 50,000 was expected and he thought that we were too young to handle the occasion. Willie Bell was the oldest defender and he was only twenty-three, although Billy Bremner, while still only twenty-one, had some big-match experience with Scotland. We also had Bobby Collins, a tremendous competitor and leader of men. He was also an ex-Blue and wanted to show his old club he could still do the business.

Just fewer than 50,000 turned up to watch what Eric Stanger of the *Yorkshire Evening Post* described as a 'memorable yet turbulent match that was played at a furious pace.' Stanger went on, 'Hunter was out-standing, providing stout defence that meant Sprake was only called upon once to claw away a Temple shot.'

I remember the game for its cut-and-thrust nature and the intimidating noise generated by the Leeds supporters. It was quite intimidating in the tunnel for most of us, although when I looked across there was my fellow Welsh interna-tional Roy Vernon leaning against the wall having a fag. I don't think many of the Premiership's athletes would do that today.

The game ended 1-1 with the young Leeds matching the League champions in every department. Scott had opened the scoring, but Weston notched the equaliser. Stanger observed that 'it is Leeds and not Everton who will be looking forward to the replay'.

If Gary and the Leeds youngsters had been intimidated by the crowd at Elland Road they were in for a shock four days later as they took the field in front of 66,000 screaming fans, the majority Blue-nosed Scousers. In another game played at an astonishing pace, Leeds were forced to play on the counter-attack. Revie had once again showed tactical nous, leaving out Johanneson for the more defensively minded Hawksby. This meant that Leeds were playing the League champions in their own backyard with six players under the age of twenty-one. Eric Stanger reported that Bremner, Giles and Collins were outstand-ing and only in the last twenty minutes did Everton show their greater class and experience:

> Gabriel had given Everton the lead, but Sprake came to the rescue with fine saves until twelve minutes from time Vernon mesmerised the defence before driving beautifully past Sprake.

Frank McGhee of the *Daily Mirror* offered his account of Leeds' development:

> Marshalled superbly by Collins, Leeds looked the better side for long spells. However, Vernon had a purple patch, once cutting in and forcing Sprake into the kind of save that will win the kid many, many more caps for Wales. In an exciting contest Everton took complete control of the closing stages. Leeds were only saved from complete humiliation by the

brilliance of Sprake. He made five saves that were the combination of instinct and ability.

Leeds had gone some way to enhancing their reputation but now it was back to the bread and butter of Second Division football, with promotion the most important item on the agenda. Back at this level the Leeds machine was proving relentless. After the defeat against fellow promotion candidates Preston North End Leeds put together a seven-match unbeaten run that meant that a point against Gary's home-town club Swansea would ensure promotion. In another twist, Leeds were back at the Vetch, where the new team had been shaped the previous season.

In the three-way fight for promotion between themselves, Sunderland and Preston, Revie was making few predictions. As he told Bill Mallinson of the *Yorkshire Evening Post*, 'We will play this game like any other and do our best for ninety minutes.' Revie produced a shock before kick-off, replacing Johanneson with the untried winger Terry Cooper from the reserves, who made his debut at outside left.

While Leeds were celebrating promotion to the First Division, the Sunday newspapers were focusing on something that would follow Revie's side for the next decade or so: English football was embroiled in a bribery scandal. Everton had suspended their international Tony Kaye, while David Layne and Peter Swann had been suspended by Sheffield Wednesday. A Sunday tabloid had also accused a York City player of accepting £180, which was delivered to him by registered post. Amid the mayhem, Lincoln City had also suspended four players. Such was the furore that Cliff Lloyd, the head of the PFA, demanded talks with both players and clubs.

While Revie and Leeds would controversially enter the bribery debate a few years later, the local press remained focused on the young team's achievements, Phil Brown arguing that 'this was the best of the away victories'. Leeds produced incisive attacks and even though the Swans needed a point to ensure another season in the Second Division they were up against the meanest defence in the country. Leeds raced into a three-goal lead with two from Peacock and one from Giles, then sat back to defend, for a Swans goal would have affected their goal average. As Brown reported:

> Leeds adopted two styles of play, incisive for the first half, whilst defensively protecting their lead. Sprake made a series of ground and air saves of the

highest quality in the second half. Collins was immaculate, but every player played their part including Cooper, United's best forward.

After the game, Revie was offered a new contract as a reward for his and the team's achievements.

I remember that Revie told us we had to go all-out for the championship, believing we would never have a better chance. We were two points in front of Sunderland with two games to play against Plymouth and Charlton who were both fighting relegation. The boss brought back Albert Johanneson, using his experience in place of Cooper. Albert never made a difference, in fact we were all dreadful – our worst performance of all. Our passing went astray, we hardly made any chances and myself and the rest of the defence were terrible. It was lucky we did our lap of honour before the game because we were dreadful and were lucky to escape with a draw after another rare effort from Willie Bell.

The BBC was launching a new station on the day of the game: BBC2. Unfortunately, there was a power cut and the launch had to be delayed – it seemed after the performance against Plymouth that the lights might also be fading on Leeds' title aspirations.

Before the championship decider away to Charlton, the newspapers were once again reporting on the scandal that refused to go away. Walsall were dragged into the mire after suspending a player and rumours surfaced surrounding Bradford and Halifax. On the political front the spy Grenville Wynne was swapped for a Russian spy and there was a feel-good factor sweeping the country, with unemployment levels at a record low.

Leeds' fans and officials were also feeling good. The fans were on the verge of seeing the country's finest players in the coming season and for the directors there was the princely sum of £1,500 if the title was won. Revie once more alternated between Cooper and Johanneson; this time the youngster took the field. The rest of the team had a familiar look, lining up Sprake, Reaney, Bell, Bremner, Charlton, Hunter, Giles, Weston, Peacock, Collins, Cooper. The first five minutes set the pattern for the rest of the game, with Leeds on top throughout and playing like champions. Gary had one of his quieter games and full-backs Reaney and Bell had the freedom to overlap and show their attacking capabilities. The match was easily won with two Peacock strikes. For the first time in five years Leeds were back in the top flight. In the final run-in they had only lost two out of twenty games, and only three games all season.

Gary Sprake had played in all but one of the League games, plus three FA Cup ties and three in the League Cup. Forty-seven games in total, thirty-seven goals conceded – again, as in his first full season, under a goal a game, with nineteen clean sheets. Impressive statistics, but would they impress Revie? The answer was a resounding 'yes'.

On the journey home the boss said he would not be making any predictions or prophecies. He did say that we had done everything he had asked of us, so we deserved the chance to compete at the highest level. He made one promise: there would be no close-season signings.'

The goalkeeper and his teammates now had the chance to show what they could do on the biggest stage of all: the English First Division.

THREE

START OF AN ERA

At the start of the 1964/65 season the so-called 'Age of Affluence' under the Conservative party was coming to an end but there was still a feel-good factor enveloping a major part of the county of Yorkshire. New research had confirmed that beer sales were at an all-time high with each adult in the land drinking, on average, nine glasses a week. A fair share of that was probably being sipped by the Leeds players, staff and supporters as they celebrated their ascendancy to the top tier of English football. Perhaps even Leader of the Opposition and fellow Yorkshireman Harold Wilson was raising a tipple to celebrate the return of top-level football to this particular corner of the White Rose county as he prepared for the forthcoming autumn General Election. As August approached, a wave of cautious optimism swept through the city of Leeds as the club's supporters waited in anticipation for the return of the glorious game, where for ninety minutes every Saturday they returned to their spiritual home, within which, of course, each and every one believed himself to be a football expert.

Now back in the top flight, Leeds, with a crop of highly rated youngsters, had captured the nation's attention by losing only three League games during the previous season in an uncompromising division. Unfortunately, they had also come to the attention of the Football Association as a result of their very poor disciplinary record; of all ninety-two League clubs, Leeds had the most players booked, censored, suspended or fined. The club officials offered the excuse that it had been the long and hard pursuit of the championship that had resulted in such a long list of miscreants. The FA, however, dismissed the claim, citing Ipswich Town as a model of good behaviour with the least amount of players committing misdemeanours despite their season-long battle against relegation. Don Revie vigorously defended his team and refuted the allegation that Leeds were a dirty side, telling Eric Stanger of the *Yorkshire Evening Post*, 'I tell all my players to play hard, but fair, I just hope the first couple of games in the new campaign are not hard. If you get a bad name in this game it tends to stick.' Words of wisdom that would prove to be applicable to him throughout and even after his managerial career and a warning also to his then fresh-faced goalkeeper Gary Sprake.

For lots of games in the previous season we were busy rather than brilliant. We had a tremendous capacity for hard work and we believed that work ethic would see us through, hopefully, to mid-table security in the First Division as in those days the gap between the First and Second Division was nowhere near the gap that exists between the Premiership and the Championship today. The first game of the new campaign was the visit to Villa Park and I remember me and the other youngsters being a little overawed by the occasion. Before we knew it we were a goal behind when after four minutes Tony Hateley beat Jack in the air and set up my fellow Welsh international Phil Woosnam, who drove the ball past me. After that though, we did settle and our confidence grew. The lads tackled hard and we played a higher-tempo game. Albert played one of his best ever games for Leeds and grabbed the equaliser before Big Jack got the winner. However, our real hero was Bobby Collins; he had been an inspiration to us all in our championship-winning side and he carried on that form against Villa. He may have been a small man but he was huge in stature for Leeds United. We had shocked many of the pundits by beating of the country's most established teams at their place.

On the same day, League champions Liverpool defeated Arsenal 3–2 at home. United's opening home fixture was to be the visit of the Reds from Anfield.

I remember Harry Reynolds, the chairman, in the days leading up to the game rubbing his hands in anticipation of the bumper crowds he was expecting for the season. For some reason we seldom used to have 'ground full' notices up. Whether they thought we would be candidates for relegation or they didn't expect us to play exciting football, the crowds were never as big as the club hoped and it become a real bugbear of Don Revie and the board. By this time we had a wonderful team spirit and allied that to plenty of skill and flair. After a good victory in our first game we also quickly developed more confidence in our own abilities. Added to this we did have a hard streak that ran through the side and we soon realised we could be more than a mid-table outfit.

Those in the crowd of just over 36,000 did witness an enthralling encounter, as the *Yorkshire Evening Post* reported that Bremner was like a pocket-sized dynamo, Charlton remained cool and calm under pressure and the game was played in a good spirit, although it was stopped after Liverpool supporters threw missiles at Sprake.

That was the way it used to be throughout my career. In the 2004/05 season, Roy Carroll of Manchester United was hit by a coin in a European fixture. He was fortunate he only experienced it the once. I can't remember how many times I was pelted with coins, stones, snooker balls and the occasional half a brick – and they would warn me that the other half would soon be on its way! And the coins used to come in handy; they sometimes hurt on contact, but I had the last laugh. I used to collect them in my cap; they never realised it, but the opposing fans used to pay for my beer after the game. Also, the more hostile the crowd got the more it hardened my resolve to do well. As the seasons wore on, possibly because of our success, the more violent some away fans got. Towards the end of my Leeds career it became even more intimidating, such as the time at Loftus Road when the home fans brought sharpened plastic discs and one hit me and split my eye open.

After the game had restarted, Liverpool took the lead as right-back Paul Reaney inexplicably crashed into his 'keeper, knocking the ball from his grasp, with Hunt following in to level the scores after Albert Johanneson's opener for the home team. Gary argues that during this period the team were continually learning:

Paul made mistakes from the time he made his debut to the time he hung up his boots, as did each and every one of us. For the boss, though, it was never an issue as he used to say no one intentionally sets out to mess up. In fact, I never once throughout my career heard the boss berate anyone, even when I made some major mistakes. Billy Bremner and Johnny Giles would rove around the midfield, doing hundreds of brilliant things – they could make one or two mistakes and still step off the pitch in a blaze of glory. I could give a perfect display of faultless goalkeeping for eighty-nine minutes and make a string of fine saves but if I made one slip I would come off with the jeers ringing in my ears, but the boss would put his arm around me and tell me to work twice as hard for the next game.

Reaney's mistake wasn't fatal as Leeds came back into the game and raced into the lead courtesy of a Yeats own goal and strikes from Weston, Bremner and Giles. Liverpool grabbed a consolation after Gary had pushed a Milne effort onto the bar, but the Liverpool defender knocked in the rebound.

Not in our wildest expectations did we think we would beat the champions, let alone hammer them 4-2.

The third game of the campaign saw Leeds visit Molineux to face a Wolves side that over the years had caught the nation's attention with their brand of attacking football. Eric Stanger of the *Yorkshire Evening Post* reported that Leeds started poorly, with the defence particularly hesitant, but a Jack Charlton equaliser in between Jim Storrie's first and second put them in front and the Leeds 'keeper made 'an admirable save from Broadbent that gave Leeds the two points in a 3-2 victory.'

Amazingly, Leeds had won their first three games and sat proudly at the top of the table.

After the first three games we had taken maximum points and the boss instilled in us an optimism that we could now aim to be a top-four side, even though we were facing world-class players on a weekly basis. The biggest test of my career would be the fourth game of the season. I don't know if they had computers in those days, but there must have been some sort of glitch as we were now due to face Liverpool at Anfield, only two weeks after the home fixture.

The *Yorkshire Evening Post* reported how the champions Liverpool were intent on revenge after the drubbing they received from the young upstarts in the reverse fixture. Leeds fought a rearguard action with 'Bremner, Sprake, Charlton and Hunter forming a formidable barrier'. With Bobby Collins battling away in midfield, Liverpool were held at bay for long periods and it was Collins himself who surprisingly gave Leeds the lead with a free-kick that bent past the Liverpool goalkeeper. Leeds defended resolutely but it only seemed a matter of time before wave after wave of Liverpool attacks bore fruition. Gary was finally beaten by Thompson in the sixty-seventh minute, followed by a Smith effort in the seventy-sixth, as Leeds lost for the first time. By the end of their first three months in the top flight they had played fifteen games, winning nine, drawing two and losing just four, scoring thirty-three goals and conceding twenty-seven. If the pundits were expecting Leeds' games to be dour affairs they were shocked by the goals for and against columns. Twenty points out of a possible thirty was a surprising yet excellent return for a youthful team in its first season in top-flight competition.

There have been many teams who have entered the top division and been able to grind out results or catch opponents unaware with either their exuberance or collective team spirit, such as Swansea City under John Toshack, who led the old First Division in the early 1980s. Most of these teams were unable to sustain the pace of the top flight, or else the opposition got wise to their tactics, but even though the country's elite teams had a pretty good idea of what to expect from Leeds they were unable to stop Revie's youngsters from flourishing.

Unfortunately our reputation had gone before us and the first games were littered with fouls, free-kicks and bookings. Our younger players, wherever we went, were singled out for harsh treatment, especially Billy. By the time November came we were on a winning streak and felt confident of getting something at Goodison Park, even though Everton were deemed one of the 'big' clubs. The tone of the game was set from the first minute when Big Jack was the victim of a crude and late tackle. I believe it was this game that moulded us as a team, when we decided it was now going to be us against the rest. I remember the game degenerating into a series of vicious and spiteful brawls with little heed being paid to the actual football. Players from both sides were having running battles with their opposite numbers and just after the half-hour the referee had had enough and took both the sides off to cool down. When we came back out the Everton fans kept shouting 'dirty Leeds' even though it was their team that was to blame. We were tarnished unfairly and we never seemed to live that stereotype down. Wherever we played we would always be known first and foremost as 'dirty Leeds'. Throughout my time at Leeds, however, Don Revie never once told us to go out and kick people. Yes, he told us to be hard and never shirk a challenge but he never encouraged us to be dirty. The thing was, with the possible exception of Eddie Gray, we were all hard players who thrived on physical confrontation.

When the football match did restart, Leeds carried on the fine run with Willie Bell scoring a rare goal that proved to be the match-winner.

The games against the big clubs were coming thick and fast, with the visit of Arsenal next on the agenda. Leeds, playing with supreme confidence, easily disposed of the Gunners 3-1 with goals from Charlton, Belfitt and Storrie. The *Times* correspondent offered his assessment of Leeds' performance thus: 'There was no sign of Arsenal disturbing the serenity of Sprake.' One of Gary's ambitions since turning professional had been to play at Old Trafford as, much like today, Manchester United were the best-supported side in the land, with over 53,000 packed onto the terraces for every home match. After playing all the country's big clubs, Gary was looking forward to pitting his wits against United's world-class players such as Charlton, Law and Best, under the master tutelage of the great Matt Busby. Old Trafford was shrouded in fog as the teams settled into the top-of-the-table clash, with 10,000 Leeds fans crossing the Pennines, perhaps more in hope than expectation, as Manchester United had won their last nineteen League and cup games. In fact, the game was held up for seven minutes in the second half as the thick blanket of fog meant that visibility was down to a few yards. Once the game started it was Leeds who proved themselves superior, even though Revie had been expecting a footballing lesson from one of the world's leading clubs. They took the game to their illustrious opponents and local reporter Edgar Turner recalled that 'the Leeds defence had tamed the most lethal attack in British football today'. He argued that, despite finishing 0-0, the match belonged to Leeds and in particular to the mastermind, Bobby Collins.

> Not even the rain and fog could conceal the speed, agility and defensive covering of Leeds. Leeds also missed two gilt-edged chances in the final minutes to emphasise their increasing superiority.

He added that 'Manchester United also had their chances in the first half, but Sprake made three glorious, almost unbelievable saves from Law twice and Charlton.'

Apart from my international debut, this was my finest game to date, a full house, over 10,000 of our fans and a world-class strike force to put me through my paces. After the game the boss called us together and said that this was his greatest game as a manager and he was proud of us. If Everton had been a defining moment for us physically, this was the game that made us realise we could compete with the best the country had to offer.

After a 1-0 win against West Bromwich Albion on 28 November Leeds went on an unbeaten run of eighteen games in the League, which meant that by mid-April they had reached the pinnacle of English football. During this period Leeds had won twelve and drawn six, scoring thirty-three goals and conceding only fourteen, with Gary keeping seven clean sheets. One of the most satisfying results was the 4-1 thrashing of Everton at Elland Road, which demonstrated that not only could Leeds mix it with the best, they could also turn on the style and compete in footballing terms with any team in the top division.

We always tried to play a high-tempo game as far up the pitch as possible and as much in the opposition half as we could. This may be perceived as attack-minded but really our tactics were very rigid and we tended to go onto the pitch with a cautious approach. However, the boss must have got it spot on as we were in uncharted territory; never before in the history of the club had they been in touching distance of the Football League championship.

Leeds could consolidate their position in the next home game, for the opponents were Manchester United, who had been vying for top spot along with Chelsea all season. An all-ticket crowd of almost 52,500, the highest of the season, squashed into Elland Road for a game the fans saw as potentially vital in deciding the outcome of the title. Leeds entered the match on the back of a twenty-five-game unbeaten run in all competitions, which had not only taken them to the top of the division but seen them reach Wembley in the FA Cup. In a match played in gale-force winds neither side settled well as the nerves dominated, but the match was settled as early as the fourteenth minute when Manchester winger Connelly scored with a sharp snap shot that flew wind-assisted into the net. With the strong wind at their backs in the second half, Leeds pressed forward in search of the equaliser but could not break United's stubborn resistance. In fact, Connolly's strike was the only real action of any note in the game. It appeared, with four games left, that Leeds' title chances had been blown away.

If the Premiership stars of today moan about fixture congestion they would be advised to search the archives of the 1960s and 1970s. In April we had to play eight games and with one week left of the campaign we still had to play four games, including home and away fixtures against Sheffield Wednesday on consecutive days.

After the demoralising defeat against Manchester United, Leeds had to travel to Sheffield Wednesday for a local derby. As *The Times* reported, 'Leeds did not look like title challengers, in the first half they went two goals behind and they had Sprake to thank for keeping the score down.' Wednesday scored a third after the break and it seemed Leeds' chances of the championship had slipped away. The following day, a revitalised Leeds entertained Wednesday and convincingly dispatched them 2-0 with goals from Storrie and Giles. Over the week, therefore, the lead had changed hands three times as on Saturday Chelsea sat top, by Monday they were replaced by Manchester United and a day later, with two games to go, Leeds were in pole position, although the Red Devils had a game in hand. In the penultimate game of the season in a game of Russian roulette involving three teams it seemed Leeds had the luck of the fixture list as they visited lowly Sheffield United. There have been many local derbies where the form book has been turned on its head but this was not one of them as Leeds totally dominated the game, chants of 'easy, easy, easy' ringing down from the terraces. Gary was a virtual bystander as goals from Storrie, Bremner and Peacock kept their title chances alive. It was now down to the final game of the season against bottom club Birmingham City, a must-win encounter if they were to keep the pressure on Manchester United, who faced Arsenal.

As the game began it seemed the arduous campaign and the pressure of the moment had finally caught up with the youthful legs and minds of Revie's team. The Blues scored after just four minutes and went on to score another two, despite having had a man sent off, the last coming from the penalty spot after Cooper had scythed down his opposing winger who was rushed off to hospital with a suspected dislocated shoulder (some observers suggested that this was merely the latest example of Leeds' alleged dirty tactics throughout the season). In one last show of character Leeds pulled back to draw the match 3-3 with goals from Giles, Reaney and Charlton. However, it was all in vain as Manchester United had beaten Arsenal 3-1, meaning that Leeds could only win the title on goal average if Aston Villa scored eighteen or more goals in the last game against Manchester United. It was not to be!

In their first season in the top flight the youngsters, with a sprinkling of old heads, had shown outstanding qualities and resolve. They had kept going to the very end and in finishing runners-up had a remarkable haul of sixty-one points. In the post-war two points for a win era that total would only be bettered on three occasions by teams who won the title. On top of this, Manchester United's title run-in had been truly remarkable as they had won ten of their last eleven games. Contemporary reports show that without doubt Gary Sprake played his part in ensuring Leeds finished second in the First Division, and his consistently excellent goalkeeping ensured that many points were won or saved.

Leeds United's magnificent efforts in the League were also matched by an incredible FA Cup run. After Southport were easily dispatched in the third round this set up an encounter with Everton, who had disposed of Leeds, after a replay, at the same stage the previous season. Leeds were drawn at home in what proved to be another violent encounter, with *The Times* reporting that 'the match was a bitter struggle, which could have been played without a ball.' On two occasions, however, the ball was used: when Storrie scored and then when Everton notched an equaliser. For the second year running a replay was required and the authorities were beginning to despair of the fixture's increasing reputation for brutality. Those fears proved to be unfounded this time around as the teams produced a rousing cup tie. During the first hour Leeds held Everton at bay before Charlton scored a typical headed goal from a corner. Bremner played Weston in for the second before Everton's Pickering pulled one back a minute later. The *Times* reported that

> in the dying minutes Sprake faced a raging sea of blue, although Everton should have won it just after half-time when the unmarked Temple brought Sprake to a blinding save at point-blank range. Almost at once a thirty-yard Pickering rocket brought the 'keeper in full length to make a marvellous save.

Leeds had reached the fifth round thanks to a major contribution from their goalkeeper, but Gary was not called upon to make a save as Shrewsbury Town were dispatched 2-0 in the next round to set up a meeting with Crystal Palace. *The Times* described the quarter-final as 'a cup tie, but not a football match'. A record home crowd witnessed a ruthless and ugly display with *The Times* football correspondent calling Palace 'a team of bulldozers'. 'My notes should have reflected a football match, but it read more as a crime sheet,' he lamented. On the football side Leeds recorded a 3-0 victory with Gary in the Leeds goal called upon only once, in the last few minutes, to tip a long-range shot over the bar.

The draw for the semis paired Leeds with a team that were increasingly becoming rivals, Manchester United. Each team had notched a 1-0 away win over the other in the League, and this game would be a season decider. In fact, in an exhausting season the game needed a replay to produce a positive outcome. Leeds went into the tie on the back of a twenty-three-match unbeaten run, buoyed by the fact that they were still in the hunt for the title. They had proved in the matches over three-quarters of the campaign that they could compete with the best. However, if the football purists were hoping for a classic game of football involving the land's top two sides at neutral Hillsborough they would have been bitterly disappointed by the goal-less draw. From the opening exchanges the referee, Mr Windle, lost control and the game degenerated into a shabby, spiteful and bitter encounter littered with petty, niggling and violent clashes.

The referee totally lost the plot as Big Jack and Denis Law exchanged blows on the halfway line; Billy Bremner and Paddy Crerand went in to act as peacemakers and got booked for their troubles. After that it was just a free-for-all. He was very weak and missed, or ignored, the physical intimidation of both sides.

This view was confirmed by the report in the *Yorkshire Evening Post,* which stated that '65,000 people watched a boxing and wrestling match, but could have watched the real thing far more cheaply' while *The Times* reported that 'both sides should take a good look at themselves in a cracked mirror'.

While the first game was a wretched affair, the replay was a far more memorable match with Manchester United playing at their best, launching wave after wave of penetrating attacks. Everyone played their part, especially Bremner and Collins, while big Jack Charlton's powerful heading rescued Leeds on numerous occasions. For Eric Stanger, however:

> Leeds owed much to Sprake, who made fine first-half saves to deny both Herd and Charlton. And in the second half once more Leeds had to thank Sprake. He saved brilliantly from Best and also diverted Law's shot.

Manchester United controlled the game and had given Leeds a rare gruelling time. With a quarter of an hour left, however, Leeds had their biggest scare as Gary dropped a cross from Connelly, but showed remarkable athleticism to turn Law's follow-up shot over the bar. With minutes remaining, Leeds began to press forward and Dunne in the Manchester goal had to make three great saves, the best to repel a Cooper volley. Weary legs meant the game was opening up and the Leeds defence had to deal with five consecutive corners. With two minutes remaining and Bremner playing in an advanced role that he had been familiar with at the start of his career, Leeds won a free-kick near the halfway line. Giles floated it in and Bremner flashed a header into the net. This was a goal of historic proportions, as Leeds would appear in an FA Cup final for the first time. Trouble at Leeds matches was never far away, be it with players or supporters, but this time it was some Manchester United fans who vented their disappointment at referee Windle by knocking him to the ground at the final whistle. The national press agreed with the local reports, believing that

> Man Utd should have settled things in an inspired quarter of an hour when Sprake was the hero, whose performance was the highlight of the whole dramatic clash. He held a Best header with masterful ease and later, after a quick passing movement involving three players, the ball was played to Law. It was odds on a goal, but the Manchester fans' roar of 'goal' was choked as Sprake made a remarkable point-blank save.

After a long and gruelling season Leeds were at Wembley for the first time. Even though they had done magnificently in their first season in the top flight they were regarded by many as the underdogs against a vastly more experienced Liverpool. This wasn't the only problem for Leeds:

Since the win over United in the replay we had played eight games in three weeks. Over Easter we played three games in four days. It would not have been too bad if we were in a mid-table position and could relax, but we were fighting for the championship. With a young, inexperienced and small squad we found it extremely hard. Today, there would be squad rotation, where managers can rest players or players are replaced with teammates of equal ability. In those days chairmen would not sanction big squads, so we just had to get on with it. Also, Revie was inflexible in his approach; we had to follow the same routines because of his superstitions, when really we would have liked nothing better than a few days away with perhaps a beer or two.

Even though the end of the League campaign had been something of an anticlimax, it did not stop the good folk of Leeds doing all they could to get their hands on tickets for the final. There hadn't been many sell-outs for the First Division home fixtures but everyone, it seemed, wanted a trip to the capital. So much so that tickets costing 7s 6d were exchanging hands on the black market for £25 or more. For Gary Sprake it meant another trip to the ticket office at Elland Road as there was no way his seven brothers and sisters, their partners and children were going to miss the biggest game of his career.

For the twenty-year-old goalkeeper it turned out to be an anxious wait in the days leading up to the game, not because he was unsure of his place in the team but because another important event had arisen on his calendar in the shape of his driving test. Gary had bought his first car on his seventeenth birthday, but he had overlooked one important point – had never taken his test. After the local police had ignored this fact for over a year the long arm of the law decided enough was enough after he had driven onto and got stuck in the middle of a roundabout. The test date allocated by the Department of Transport was to be Cup Final week.

On the day of the test I remember I was extremely nervous and did not want the hassle of a resit. As the examiner got into the car I asked him if he liked football. When he replied he did, I told him that I had put two of my cup final tickets in the in the glove box. He never said a word. I followed the route, and he informed me in a matter-of-fact way I had passed the test. He then opened the glove box, took the tickets and left.

The newly qualified driver did not need the car the following week as Leeds journeyed south in a luxury coach, staying at one of the capital's finest hotels. Although not pampered like today's stars, the players of Leeds United were being treated as never before. While Revie recognised and rewarded the players' achievements he was still locked in his superstitious routine in the build-up to the big game.

He hired the facilities at Hendon, even though the pitches were rock hard, because the last four winners had trained there. It was out of the way and involved a little more travelling, but there was no persuading the boss once he had made his mind up. There were tough decisions to make with team selection and someone was going to be disappointed, the unlucky ones being Don Weston and Terry Cooper.

Before the game Revie's meticulous planning did go slightly awry as the police motorbike outriders who were escorting the team bus lost it in the heavy London traffic. In farcical style they then mistakenly escorted one of the official supporters' buses to the ground. All of this meant that the team bus arrived late, throwing Revie's minutely planned timetable into disarray and not doing very much to settle the team's nerves. When Leeds United did take the field it was possibly their strongest eleven, lining up as follows: Sprake, Reaney, Bell,

Bremner, Charlton, Hunter, Giles, Storrie, Peacock, Collins, who had just won the Football Writers' Player of the Year award, and Johanneson, who became the first black player to appear in an FA Cup final. By the age of twenty Gary Sprake had made his Wales' debut in front of 90,000 at Hampden Park, played in front of full houses at most League grounds and now he was to appear in front of 100,000 at Wembley, with millions looking on worldwide. The occasion would have fazed many, but not the young custodian from the Lower Swansea Valley, who was to put in a five-star display and disprove the theory that he would bottle it during the big games.

The match itself was no spectacle with both sides showing too much respect for one another. In fact, the *Yorkshire Post* described it as

> unspectacular, a footballers' game with rigid tactics, with both teams fright-ened of each other with Leeds looking both emotionally and physically drained. It appeared that Leeds have been the victims of a long and hard season, where they had to play for every point until the very last game.

The paper went on to report that 'Sprake was an heroic figure in an overworked defence.' Phil Brown of the *Yorkshire Evening Post* reinforced this assessment of Gary's performance:

> He brilliantly tipped over a Hunt pile-driver and made a superlative save from Thompson after the winger ended a mazy run by firing in an angled shot from the left, which Sprake finger-tipped away as it made its way into the net. He also tipped over a twenty yarder from Smith. If Leeds had a hero today it was Sprake.

The Swansea-based *South Wales Evening Post* described his perform-ance thus: 'Today at Wembley heroic Gary Sprake produced a masterful display in an otherwise drab final.' *The Times,* in the run up to the game, had suggested that if ever a final was going to require extra time and possibly a replay it was this one, as the teams and managers had enormous respect for each other and would cancel one another out. Their prophecy was proved to be close to the mark. The paper's post-match report offered this analysis:

> Liverpool fully deserved victory. Whilst the Leeds forward line was put out of gear with Storrie hobbling on the left wing, both defences enjoyed long periods of ascendancy. Whilst Lawrence was seldom worked, Sprake made

three dazzling saves to take Leeds into extra time; one before the interval from Hunt and two from Thompson in the second half. Hunt dived to head past a gallant Sprake for the opener, Bremner equalised when he flashed in a volley after a knock down by Charlton, before St John's header won it for Liverpool. Leeds on the day did not have the invention to upset a more sophisticated foe.

Teammate Jack Charlton recalls:

I played and trained with Sprakey for the best part of twelve years. In that time, both on the training ground and in competitive matches I saw him do some amazing things. He was so natural, a terrific shot-stopper and very athletic. He would be up and down in training saving shot after shot. Many believe that night against Ferencvaros was his best game and he also had many other great performances to his name. For me though the Liverpool final was his best, he was absolutely incredible and kept us in the game to the very end. It was a great pity the rest of us never performed to that level, or somewhere near it, because he did not deserve to be on the losing side.

Another former teammate to praise Gary in his memoirs is Norman Hunter, who states, 'Gary Sprake was absolutely outstanding, keeping us in the game with a string of fine saves when otherwise we might have been dead and buried.' In fact, a review of the recent DVD of the final in *Leeds Leeds Leeds!* magazine (June 2005) states,

In truth it wasn't a great game, the rain played havoc with the famously heavy pitch and the apparently heavy match ball of the day, but it's worth watching for Sprake's performance alone. He's been much maligned since, but you can see why the commentator describes him as probably the best 'keeper in the country.

The cup final loss was a major disappointment for the team at the end of what could have been a monumental season.

Before the game we all felt jaded and without substitutes it did not help that Jim Storrie was injured and became a passenger on the wing for the majority of the game. The boss tried to raise our spirits but ultimately we froze on the day. Bremner and Collins were forced into deep positions because of Liverpool's tactics and once again we lacked that little bit of creativity and cutting edge. Even though we experienced bitter disappointment, which would become a familiar theme over the next few years, and had nothing tangible to show for our valiant efforts, we did demonstrate a resilience and team spirit that would make us stronger for the forthcoming season. I think, like many teams in their first season in the top flight, we had played beyond our potential. What had been realised, however, was our collective resolve. Throughout the 1950s when people talked about Leeds United it was really John Charles they were actually reminiscing over but now we were a real team. It was a team effort that was being recognised by the football world. The boss had blended us youngsters with astute signings like Storrie, Peacock and Giles. Many experts predicted we would be 'one-season wonders' but in that first season we produced a consistency that would last for ten years or more and which I feel was not surpassed by any other team in the country. For everyone outside of the city we would always be known as 'chokers' or also-rans, forever the bridesmaids. If you use today's qualification criterion we would have been one of Europe's superpowers, a consistent member of European football's elite. We would have been perennial qualifiers for the Champions League, for throughout my career with Leeds we never once finished outside the top four and were always competitive in the cup competitions as well, at home and abroad.

This view was endorsed at the time by the great Liverpool manager Bill Shankly who, when interviewed by the *Yorkshire Post*, magnanimously offered this assessment: 'Leeds are a fine side, this could help them become a great side, and the experience gained from European games can count for so much.' The next season would provide Revie's young but highly talented side with that opportunity and, as runners-up both in the League and cup, they deserved it.

For Gary it was time for a well-deserved break. In his first season in top-flight football, despite being a raw nineteen-year-old, he had been almost ever-present, missing only one League game. In the League campaign he had conceded forty-eight goals while keeping twelve clean sheets. In the amazing FA Cup run he played in all the eight ties, conceding four goals and keeping five clean sheets. In the League Cup Gary was rested for each tie – an indication that even then the competition was perceived by managers like Revie to be something of a second-rate exercise.

While the superstars of today's Premiership fly first-class to exotic locations for their breaks, things were somewhat different in 1965. In the latter stages of his career Gary and family would take a trip to the footballers' playground of Majorca, where they would regularly mix with players from other clubs. At the end of the 1964/65 season, however, it was back home to Swansea for the summer, where he would seek out old friends and former work mates like Cliff Dacey, Tudor Counsell and Terry Beynon from Tom Smith & Clark, where he had started but never finished his apprenticeship. His former colleagues still laugh today about the time when the company's owner Tom Smith refused to let Don Revie talk to Gary at the factory and warned the persistent Mr Revie that if he didn't leave he would have him arrested for trespass. A week after playing in a Wembley cup final Gary had other footballing duties to perform – he was guest of honour at Winch Wen FC's end of season presentations at the Jersey Beach Hotel, Aberavon, to present his former teammates with their medals for winning the Swansea Senior League's Gwalia Cup. Over the next month Gary would relax in the company of his friends and relatives, catching up over a pint or two in the local hostelries.

How times have changed. I used to spend the days chatting with the neighbours, walk up to Ye Olde Corner Shoppe on Winch Wen corner and settle the bill my mother had inevitably run up with the proprietors Mr and Mrs Rosser over the preceding months. In recent years the shop has become a family home and all the other local shops have been replaced by supermarket chains. I am glad they were not around then – Mam would have had a field day and I would have struggled to pay the bills she would have racked up.

FOUR

THE EUROPEAN EXPERIENCE

After a quiet summer break at home with the family reflecting on both the excitement and the disappointments of the 1964/65 season it was back to the grind of pre-season training and the arduous cross-country runs organised by the sergeant major-like Les Cocker. Gary smiles as he reflects that

Pre-season training was really hard and it was one long run after another. I have got to admit that you would rarely find me at the front of the run. I usually lagged behind as much as I could get away with.

As the 1965/66 season was about to kick off, severe weather was prevailing over Europe, with over 2,000 killed in a Turkish earthquake, while parts of Britain were plunged into chaos as storms and floods caused power cuts. In the world of football, FIFA made a decision that for Leeds United had come a year too late: they were to allow the introduction of substitutes. The club could only rue the fact that they might have had a much better chance of beating Liverpool in the cup final a few months previously if the injured Jim Storrie could have been replaced. There was to be no major overhaul of the squad for the new season, Revie believing that only a little 'fine tuning' was necessary. In fact, there was to be only one new acquisition, the much underrated Huddersfield Town left winger, Mike O'Grady. The Leeds-born player had originally been overlooked by his home-town club, an error that now cost them £30,000. Although there may not have been many major signings Revie's knack of grooming young players was in evidence as Mick Bates, Peter Lorimer and Paul Madeley, who had appeared spasmodically over the last couple of seasons, were now given their chance. Revie also included for the first time the promising Eddie Gray, but perhaps the masterstroke was the conversion of left winger Terry Cooper into a full-back.

The boss could be a very conservative character but he was still way ahead of his time as a manager. Converting Terry to a full-back was far-sighted, for he developed into one of the best full-backs in the world. People talk today of Roberto Carlos's attacking flair but TC could be compared with anyone. He certainly gave us an extra dimension with his mazy runs and pinpoint crosses.

Although the previous campaign had ended in bitter disappointment the Elland Road faithful could still look forward to the forthcoming season as, for the first time in its history, the club would be playing in Europe in the Inter-Cities Fairs Cup. This would be the first season of over a decade of continuous European competition that saw them in memorable battles (not always footballing) against the Continent's finest. Leeds were to prove themselves a surprise entity, just as they had been domestically the previous season. European clubs would soon sit up and take notice as Don Revie now pitted his tactical acumen against foreign coaches. The historic first game was against the Italian side Torino at home and the team lined up Sprake, Reaney, Madeley, Bremner, Charlton, Hunter, Peacock, Collins, Cooper, Lorimer, Giles.

Revie was always thinking of ways to gain an advantage over opponents; for this game he gave all the outfield players different numbers. I think Billy wore the number nine shirt and all the others had different numbers on their backs. When the team was announced to the 33,000 crowd there were gasps of astonishment. When we lined up for the kick-off, however, we were all back in our rightful positions.

Leeds played a high-tempo game that set the pattern for their European campaigns. They would go for all-out attack at Elland Road but throw a defensive blanket around Gary in the away ties. The home side got the reward for their attacking display when Bremner, belying his small stature, rose to power in a header just before the half-hour. Peacock doubled the lead with another header just after half-time. With Leeds pressing for the killer third goal they were caught by a typical Italian counterattack after Cooper lost the ball, it being moved forward quickly before Orlando squeezed the ball past Gary for a confidence-boosting away goal. United went into the away leg as massive underdogs but a defiant rearguard action meant they went into the break with a clean sheet. Just after the break, tragedy struck for Leeds, and for Bobby Collins in particular.

Bobby went in for the ball and the Italian, Poletti, just went over the top. I could hear the thigh break from where I was half a pitch length away. Like the Everton roughhouse of a game the year before we once more showed amazing courage in the face of uncompromising, spiteful and vicious tackling. We had a fiery baptism in the face of their crude gamesmanship and deceitful tactics. Bobby had been our inspiration in the rise to the top; what a cruel way to end his season – in fact that tackle did much to end his career; he was never the same after that as he was already well into his thirties. I would go as far to say that Bobby was Revie's best signing while I was at the club. He was a model professional, a very skilful player and a hard man who could certainly look after himself. He was only five feet four, but in five-a-side matches in training he would always be arguing with Big Jack and Norman about his over-zealous tackling. There were never any fights, just good old arguments. After that tackle he was in tremendous pain, but when Les Cocker rushed on to treat him he just said, 'you live by the sword, you die by the sword.'

Despite the sickening blow of losing the influential Collins, Leeds held onto a goal-less draw to emerge victorious, 2–1 on aggregate, in their first ever European tie.

The next round saw them drawn to play behind the Iron Curtain against SC Leipzig in the old East Germany. The tie went ahead with the pitch covered in a blanket of snow and ice, conditions that would have led to a postponement of the game in the UK. Gary was to be disappointed as once again a Leeds game was to clash with a Wales international, this time against Scotland. However, he was to put the disappointment behind him and turn in an excellent performance to help his club achieve victory, with the *Yorkshire Evening Post* stating that 'Sprake was in wonderful form on the ice'. All the action came late in the game as three goals were scored in the space of three minutes, Lorimer in the eightieth and Bremner in the eighty-first before the Germans pulled one back in the eighty-third. For the second leg it seemed like the East Germans had brought the Arctic conditions with them as it was Yorkshire that was now in the grip of snow. The match went ahead and Leeds were chasing shadows as their quick-footed opponents glided over the treacherous conditions. They spurned numerous chances, meaning that Leeds progressed to the next round. Jarred & Macdonald in *Leeds United; The Complete European Record* (2003) state that the Germans complained about Leeds' underhand method of making sure they kept their feet on the treacherous surface, with the accusation that 'some Leeds' players seemed to have had nails sticking out of their studs'.

The boss would sometimes resort to anything to gain us an advantage. Even though he denied it after the game, we did sometimes have cardboard glued over our studs so that when the referee and linesmen checked our studs they could feel the smooth cardboard, but once they had gone we would drag our boots along the track surrounding the pitches, to reveal much sharper studs. They would sometimes be used to facilitate a better grip on the surface, other times to intimidate opponents. In this game it was both.

The third round saw Leeds entertain the Spanish giants Valencia, who were going for a hat-trick of wins in this competition, and the Elland Road faithful were to witness a remarkable game. The media dubbed the game 'The Battle of Elland Road' and reported on scenes that included a mass brawl between opposing players, police officers running onto the pitch to stop players fighting, three players sent off, the referee trying to hold Jack Charlton back to stop him exacting revenge on the Spanish goalkeeper and then the eventual removal of both sides from the pitch so they might cool down and order be restored. In between there was some football played, with Valencia taking the lead after both Reaney and Hunter had hesitated to let in Munoz after seventeen minutes. Soon afterwards, perhaps as a result of his frustration, Hunter committed a needless foul that incensed the Spaniards. Thereafter their Latin tempers got the better of them and, aided by the leniency of Dutch referee Leo Horn, their game degenerated into a series of fouls, shirt-pulling and verbal intimidation. Lorimer scored the equaliser after considerable Leeds pressure with twenty minutes remaining and, as the home team pushed forward in search of a winner, they were awarded a corner with quarter of an hour to go.

As Big Jack took his familiar position in the six-yard box the goalkeeper took a swipe at him. Jack went to get his own back but was surrounded by three or four Spanish defenders, one of whom kicked him – but what really infuriated Jack was the fact that the 'keeper then spat in his face. At this point Jack completely lost it and chased the perpetrator behind the goal and I've never seen a goalkeeper run so fast. The next thing I knew nearly every outfield player had joined in, trading punches until the police and officials were able to eventually restore order. Jack and the guy who originally kicked him (Vidagany) were sent off. It was amazing and really funny to see a full England international who was a near certainty to play in the World Cup finals at the end of the season completely lose the plot – he could have been suspended and perhaps lost his

England place. But that was Jack; he always fought for what he believed was right, in this case literally, and hang the consequences.

The Times reported that 'Last night at Elland Road mania replaced football with the police entering the field of play to restore order.' before concluding the report, 'in the dying minutes Sprake dived full length to save the game'. When the teams returned both were a man short and soon afterwards the Spaniards were down to nine men after Sanchez saw red after bringing down Storrie. Although fined £50 Jack Charlton escaped suspension, which meant he was available for the second leg in the volatile and partisan Mestalla Stadium. If they were to progress to the quarter-final in their first season in Europe they would have to produce an extraordinary performance.

The weekend before the tie Leeds had been knocked out of the FA Cup by fierce rivals Chelsea, so hearts were leaden as they flew to Spain. After the brutal first leg the respective football associations had rejected calls for both teams to be kicked out of the competition and there were real fears that this game would see a spill over of the violent events at Elland Road. Leeds adopted the same strategy they employed in previous away legs; they allowed Valencia possession and were quite willing to perform a rearguard action with the occasional counterattack. Charlton was outstanding at the heart of the defence to atone for his aberration at Elland Road, while behind him Gary was an unbeatable last line of defence as he had been in every away tie to date, with The Times arguing that 'Valencia found Sprake in his best form'. Revie's tactics worked to perfection for, with fifteen minutes left, Madeley, free from his defensive duties, released O'Grady who beat the offside trap to fire home the deciding goal.

Ujpest Doza, having scored six to overcome Cologne in the previous round, were now the visitors to Elland Road. A close game was envisaged by the pundits but within forty scintillating minutes Leeds had almost put the tie out of the Hungarians' reach, racing into a four-goal lead with strikes from Cooper, Bell, Storrie and Bremner. After the break the Hungarians pushed another attacker forward and got their reward as Dunai grabbed what was, on the face of it, a mere consolation, the tie seeming out of reach of the inept Ujpest side.

Gary remembers everybody at the club thinking that

The away tie was going to be no more than a stroll in the park, so much so that the boss let us relax two days before the game, allowing us to go sightseeing and shopping for souvenirs. Within minutes of the game starting, however, we knew we were in for a much harder night than at Elland Road.

Revie again employed the tactic of using Jack Charlton as the defensive lynchpin and Big Jack did not disappoint with another commanding performance. When Ujpest did break through they found Gary in outstanding form in the Leeds goal. The Hungarians opened the scoring from striker Fazekas, with the *Yorkshire Evening Post* describing the action thus: 'In the 38th minute Sprake made an incredible save from a thunderous free-kick from Solymos, but the rebound fell to the more alert Fazekas.' After that it was one-way traffic to the Leeds goal with Billy Bremner stating in the *Yorkshire Evening Post*, 'I've never spent so much time chasing shadows, never has a side played so quickly and accurately.' Only a series of wonderful saves by Gary kept Leeds in charge, before O'Grady freed Lorimer to equalise and break Magyar hearts. Jack Charlton told the same paper 'That was the hardest match I have ever played in,' while in his post-match interview Don Revie argued 'That was the greatest performance by a Hungarian team since the national side walloped England in 1953.' Local reporter Alan Thompson argued that

> Sprake was magnificent, saving superbly in the first minute from Bene. In the second half even the partisan Hungarian crowd were cheering the defiant Sprake and the match ended as it had begun, with Sprake making another brilliant save. It begs the question, 'Why then did Leeds survive to book their place in the semi-final?'

The *Yorkshire Evening Post* conclusion: 'It was down to a tremendous team spirit and a superlative goalkeeping display from Gary Sprake, who made two out-of-this-world saves in the first twenty minutes.' In a recent interview given to the authors at his pub, the Commercial Hotel in Leeds, as well as pouring an excellent pint of cask-conditioned bitter Peter Lorimer, now a member of the Leeds United board, provided a frank assessment of Gary's performance in this game.

> Although goalkeepers are paid to make saves and it's their job I remember Gary's performance against the Hungarians went beyond what you normally expected from a goalkeeper. I remember this game vividly and I think it was probably his best game for Leeds; he was outstanding. Although we had a comfortable first-leg lead his performance was excellent in the away

leg where we were really up against it throughout the game and before I scored an equaliser it was Gary who kept us in it.

Remarkably, Leeds had progressed to the semi-final stage of European competition at the first attempt and their opponents were to be the crack Spanish outfit Real Zaragoza, whose attack was renowned throughout Spain as the 'Famous Five'. Leeds were not perturbed as they had a famous five of their own with Sprake, Charlton, Hunter, Bremner and Giles able to compete with the best the Continent had to offer. Once again Revie relied on the defence to hold out for a draw to take the Spaniards back to Elland Road to finish the job. Big Jack was a tower of strength and behind him Gary once again showed sure handling and excellent positional sense. Leeds' tactics frustrated the home side for an hour until Bremner gave away a penalty and even though Gary partly saved the kick it hit the post and fortuitously trickled across the line. The Spaniards then followed on from where other European teams left off by singling out a Leeds player for particular attention, on this occasion Johnny Giles. He was kicked and punched before his revenge on his perpetrator led to both being sent off. On reflection, Revie would have settled for the 1-0 defeat, confident as he was of overcoming Zaragoza in the return leg. In the return at Elland Road the Spaniards did not allow Leeds to settle into their normal attacking rhythm. However, Leeds gradually began to dominate the match. Charlton created havoc with his aerial strength and it was from one of his knock-downs that Johanneson put Leeds ahead after twenty minutes. As they pressed forward in search of the second goal that would put them into the final Leeds were stunned on the hour when the Spaniards equalised with a stunning half-volley from Canario. Three minutes later Charlton again got his head to the ball to put Leeds in front once more and level on aggregate. Zaragoza continued attacking in a pulsating game and right at the death Gary kept Leeds in Europe with an excellent save from Lapetra. At this time away goals were not taken into account and Leeds felt confident after a lucky toss of the coin gave them a home tie in the play-off. However, after just fourteen minutes of the play-off the dream had evaporated as Zaragoza stunned the home side and fans into silence with three goals. In typical continental style they then sat back, invited Leeds to attack and then hit them on the break, although Leeds twice hit the woodwork before Charlton got a consolation.

Although the European adventure had come to an end at the last-but-one hurdle, Gary had been given a chance to pit his wits against the cream of Europe's strikers.

I thoroughly enjoyed the experience, even though I believe the boss got the tactics wrong away from home. We invited too much pressure. Having said that, it meant I was constantly in action and could therefore show what I could do. Opposing managers and the foreign press appreciated the way we played; they respected the way we defended because that was the way they played. We had more positive press abroad than we ever got in England. The Italians, particularly the fans, liked the way we went about our business, they enjoyed the fine art of defending and the swift and incisive counterattacks. The Italian and Spanish players were very temperamental and volatile, resorting to niggling fouls, hair-pulling and sometimes viciousness. However, when I had the ball they let me take it to the edge of the area, unlike the big, robust English forwards who would clatter me at every opportunity. The Iron Curtain players were very disciplined and very technical. It was a wonderful experience and certainly developed my game.

Notwithstanding their success in reaching the semi-final of the Fairs Cup they were also very keen to be successful on the domestic front during the 1965/66 season. In what may have been a blessing in disguise, Leeds made early exits in both domestic cups as West Bromwich Albion knocked them out at the second stage of the League Cup and Chelsea put them out of the FA Cup. In the League Leeds were trying to better the runners-up spot of the previous season and a promising start saw them win the first two games. The third game saw them travel to the footballing academy of West Ham United and *The Times* described the encounter as a 'game of contrasting styles' between the cultured passing of the home team and the 'route one' football of Leeds. Making his debut for the Hammers was eighteen-year-old winger Harry Redknapp who, according to *The Times*, 'showed a tactical approach, speed of thought and a football brain.' Leeds, however, stuck to their rigid game plan, which bore fruition when Lorimer flicked on Sprake's long punt to Peacock, who rifled in the opener. West Ham drew level after Peters bundled home from close range. West Ham were to provide the bedrock of the England team that was to go on to win the World Cup at the end of the season.

Everyone knows that if it wasn't for Bobby Moore Norman Hunter would have won lots more caps for England. Norman was a good tackler, an excellent distributor of the ball and a wonderful reader of the game but Bobby was the consummate professional. He was all the things Norman was but he also had a calm and assuring temperament. You could probably count on one hand the number of mistakes he made throughout his career. He was magic! Peters was a very good midfielder, although no better than Billy and Johnny, but it was a pleasure to play against Hurst. He was a brilliant centre forward who played the game as it should be played. He wasn't the archetypal, robust English centre forward; he was the thinking man's player. He never once fouled me, and I can't remember him scoring against me either!

After only two defeats in the first thirteen matches Leeds were once again vying for top spot with Spurs, Liverpool and the surprise package Burnley, who were to be the next visitors to Elland Road. *The Times* reported on the feel-good factor that was surrounding Elland Road: the board had plans to make the ground the 'Wembley of the North', the team were in all four competitions and crowds were up on the previous season. A hero's welcome greeted Bobby Collins as he took his place in the directors' box for the Burnley game after being released from hospital following the brutal tackle in Turin. Storrie opened the scoring for Leeds before, thirty seconds later, Gary committed the cardinal sin: he took his eye off the ball, which went through his legs for the equaliser, although *The Times* reported that 'he atoned for the mistake with a splendid save from Elder'.

After the end of a pulsating match the referee rushed towards the tunnel and he starting clapping as both teams went off. It was very different to other games that we had played in when the referee had taken both the teams off for violent play.

Apart from these very rare aberrations, the contemporary reports suggest that Gary was one of the most consistent performers in Leeds' first two seasons in the First Division and the debut season in Europe. The undeniable truth, contrary to the created myth, is that at a very early stage Gary Sprake was a world-class goalkeeper whose saves helped amass many points for his team and did much to help, rather than hinder, their quest for honours. This can be confirmed by *The Times'* report of the next home game against Arsenal:

An exhilarating match with Leeds playing with flair, fast and furiously.
Both sides produced attacking football but, in the second half as Charlton,

Reaney and Hunter tired, Sprake was at his agile best to retrieve the situation. With twenty minutes remaining he made two leaping saves to deny McClintock, before a breakaway goal from Bremner and a late Giles effort sealed the points.

As the Christmas fixtures came around there was a four-way battle for the title between Leeds, Liverpool, Manchester United and Burnley. After inflicting Liverpool's first home defeat of the season on 27 December courtesy of a Lorimer strike, Leeds were in fourth place, five points behind with four games in hand. The following day's fixture at home to Liverpool would go a long way to determining Leeds' title aspirations. In front of a 50,000 all-ticket crowd, Liverpool returned the favour, inflicting Leeds' first home defeat of the season. The next big test for Leeds was the visit of Manchester United, who were determined to keep the title that they had pipped the hosts to the season before. Another bumper 50,000 crowd witnessed, according to *The Times*, 'a hectic, exciting and balanced game'. After Storrie opened the scoring, Gary did exceptionally well to parry a Law shot, but Herd knocked in the rebound. Leeds had once more failed to beat one of their nearest rivals, having also failed to take maximum points from games involving Liverpool and Burnley. With fewer than ten games remaining Leeds were still in with a shout of the title, but a fifth team had entered the race, Chelsea, who had already beaten Leeds both in the League and FA Cup and who were to be the next visitors to Elland Road. Goals from Bremner and an own goal from Hinton ensured Leeds strolled to victory with Jack Charlton in commanding form, keeping Osgood quiet.

Osgood very rarely had a kick against us; if ever he got the better of Jack, which he seldom did, he then had Norman to contend with. He rarely troubled me footballing-wise because he could never get the better of those two. In his autobiography, Jack said Alf Ramsey had made a mistake not taking Osgood to the Mexico World Cup but maybe he was being a little bit tongue-in-cheek.

After losing at home to Fulham, Leeds couldn't afford to drop another point if they were to catch Liverpool at the top. Next up were Everton and fans were in for a shock as the teams ran out, for Everton had selected eleven reserves. What were the reasons for this decision? A cup match the following week against Manchester United? An easy two points for Leeds in their battle for the title with Everton's Merseyside rivals? Or the reason offered by the manager, Harry Catterick: that all his first-team players were injured? Whatever the reason, there was a Football League inquiry with an ensuing fine. Gary argues:

There were many fixtures over the years that threw up shock results. It was too much of a coincidence towards the end of the season that teams would be weakened and unusual results occurred in matches. I think the Premiership has gone a long way to ridding the game of this problem by awarding increasing cash amounts the higher up the league a team finishes.

Defeat at Newcastle in the penultimate game meant that Leeds had not only lost out in the title race but were in danger of losing the runner-up spot. The last game was against rivals Manchester United.

We needed a point to ensure we came second, while Manchester United needed a point to pip Chelsea for a place in next season's Fairs Cup. In an uninspiring game both sides played for the result needed, a 1-1 draw. It may have been a drab affair but it reaffirmed my opinion of United's players. Charlton and Law were terrific and scored wonderful goals with both feet, while the Lawman was also great in the air. For me though, one of the greatest players I ever saw play was George Best. He could dribble, cross with pinpoint accuracy, pass with either foot and score terrific goals, but he never liked playing against Leeds because Paul Reaney would mark him in more ways than one with his tackles. Some were good but others were perhaps not legal. I only met socially with George the once when we drank a bottle of vodka each on a one-hour flight from Belfast to Manchester. My wife Kathy was not amused when she picked me up at the airport!

So for the second year Leeds were runners-up in the First Division, having also reached the semi-final of the Fairs Cup in their debut season in Europe. A wonderful achievement, but this was not the only time a season was to end in relative disappointment and anti-climax. While bitter disappointment engulfed Elland Road, the players and staff could still take pride in their achievements, including Gary, whose statistical record had continued to improve along with the team. In the 1965/66 season he played forty League games, conceding only thirty-three goals and keeping seventeen clean sheets. In Europe he had been ever-present in the eleven games, conceding ten goals and keeping four clean sheets. Compared with the previous season, the young goalkeeper had played more games and conceded fewer goals.

As the new 1966/67 campaign got underway the Bank of England had ordered the banks to cut spending by limiting people's overdraft facilities. Perhaps the overdrafts were being spent on football; statistics showed that in the previous season £122 million was spent on the beautiful game, twice the amount spent on visits to the cinema. The banks' cautious approach was mirrored by the Elland Road board as Don Revie made no major signings in the close season. Football in England was on a high following the World Cup win two months previously and with English clubs competing successfully on the European stage – nine out of the victorious eleven players for England had furthered their football education by playing in European competition for their clubs. Such was the boom in football that the average First Division player was now earning £60 per week.

There was not so much an air of cautious optimism but one of real anticipation as the youngsters who were blossoming into world-class footballers took to the field for the start of the 1966/67 season. For Gary Sprake the world was at his feet, or rather in his hands. His wages had rocketed above the division's average to £70 per week and he was fast acquiring pop-star status with his blond hair and Adonis stature. Gone were the family-type cars, replaced by an Alfa Romeo sports convertible. Even though the trappings of a successful professional footballer were visible, minds were focused on the task ahead, which was to better the runners-up spot in the League and go one better than the European semi-final.

There was a wave of optimism pervading Elland Road at the start of the season; we all thought this would be our year. By mid-October the dreams were shattered, we had only won three games and were so far off the pace the boss called a team meeting. He told us we were going to focus on the cup competitions both at home and abroad. As the tables show, the decision was premature. At the end we were only five points behind the champions and only one point off being runners-up.

If Revie wanted to focus on the cup competitions then there was not going to be a treble. After disposing of Newcastle and Preston in the League Cup, an injury-hit Leeds crashed out of the competition, losing 7-0 away to West Ham. In goal, for a match that saw Leeds concede that amount for the first time since 1929, was Gary's understudy David Harvey. However, accounts such as that in *The Times* absolve Harvey of any responsibility.

No blame can be put on Leeds' young and relatively (to Gary Sprake) inexperienced 'keeper Harvey. He played bravely and sometimes brilliantly on the night. His nerves must have been shattered by the sight of men like Charlton, Hunter, Bremner and Reaney being taunted mercilessly by the West Ham forwards.

In their third season in the top flight Leeds were once again seeing their dreams fade as only two pieces of silverware remained within reach. The first two rounds of the FA Cup saw them easily dispose of Crystal Palace and West Bromwich Albion to set up a fifth-round clash with Sunderland. On the eve of the match there was a powerful lobby within the higher echelons of English football to set up a European Super League. There was optimism that the competition would get the green light as British clubs were excelling on the Continent. Talks were to founder, however, on the number of teams participating; the superpowers of England, Spain and Italy wanted more of their sides involved than those of lesser football nations. The game at Roker Park was ruined by gales and frayed tempers as the tie finished in a 1-1 stalemate, with Charlton scoring for Leeds. Even though the match had attracted almost 56,000 spectators, incredibly, the Leeds board did not insist that the replay be all-ticket.

In the previous season the directors had promised a stadium that would be the best in the North; within five minutes of the replay that dream was shattered as crush barriers broke under the weight of the crowd. There were almost 58,000 crammed inside and once the barriers gave way fans spilled onto the pitch. It was like a battlefield, injured bodies were lying everywhere, girls and women were hysterical and yet we were expected to carry on playing. I, like everyone in the ground, was concerned. After the game we all rushed to see if family and friends were okay. I met my brother Alfie who told me that ambulances couldn't get through because of the crowd. People were walking over parked cars to get to the ground – Wearsiders with big hobnail boots on. The board had wanted a 'Wembley of the North'. It was a miracle no one was killed.

When the game restarted, with the crowd almost covering the touch-line, Sunderland took the lead when, as *The Times* reported, 'Charlton was caught hopelessly out of position, which allowed Herd to flick on a clearance to O'Hare to beat Sprake as the 'keeper came out.' Two minutes later Leeds were level as Giles fired home from a Bremner free-kick. The tie moved into extra time and the game flowed from end to end with Montgomery, as he was to do in the 1973 final, breaking Leeds hearts with some magnificent saves. *The Times* reported the ebb and flow thus:

> Montgomery produced an outstanding save from a close-range Charlton shot, when it was 100 to 1 on that he would score. Then right at the death, Sprake ensured a second replay after punching out a slanting drive from Mulhall.

After the replay Revie withdrew Charlton, Hunter and Reaney from the Football League side managed by Alf Ramsay to face the Scottish League. It appears it wasn't only Gary that was withdrawn from international duty, although it is open to conjecture whether the same would have happened for a full England international.

For the second replay at neutral Boothferry Park, Hull, referee Tinkler was replaced by Ken Stokes. After Belfitt had given Leeds the lead, they were on top until twelve minutes from the end when a mistake by Bremner allowed Sunderland to equalise.

Billy, under no pressure, headed a clearance straight to them and they scored. I was shocked at what happened at Elland Road, but the last ten minutes of this game was something I had never witnessed before. Jimmy Greenhoff won a dubious penalty after being pushed. Before we had a chance to take it the Sunderland fans spilled onto the pitch and one punched Willie Bell. The referee had to be escorted off the pitch surrounded by policemen. When he came back on Giles converted the penalty and all hell broke loose. They had two players sent off after they lost their heads and in the five minutes or so that were added on we were playing with fans, players and cameramen on the pitch. After the game the Sunderland team were so incensed they wouldn't have a drink with us. When we played I don't think it mattered who the ref was, trouble was never very far away. After the game we were so relieved, if we had drawn again it meant we would have played two games on the same night, the replay and the away tie against Bologna in the Fairs Cup. The boss had assembled a squad of reserves to travel to Italy while the first team would have had to play the FA tie. As it was we flew straight from Hull to Luton and then on to Bologna. It was lucky no one was afraid of flying. It was little wonder we sometimes fell at the final hurdle; not many teams could play that amount of games. Season after season we were victims of our own success. Between August and April the boss was forced to make 140 positional changes and we were still a month or so away from May, the definitive part of the season.

In the next round against Manchester City *The Times* correspondent preferred to call Leeds 'lucky' rather than dirty as they were outplayed by a team belying their lowly League position. Charlton scored what proved to be Leeds' winner despite claims from his markers that he had fouled Dowd in the opposition goal before heading home. According to *The Times*, 'Man City played with verve while Leeds struggled, with Sprake making a firm save to deny Summerbee.' Not for the first time, Gary Sprake had produced a performance that took Leeds United to a cup semi-final, where their next opponents would be Chelsea, who had appeared at this stage in the previous two seasons. The tie, like those that were to follow over the years, was a brutal affair with *The Times* commenting, 'The tackling was ruthless with retaliation punished, but provocation escaped unseen. To be caught in possession was like standing in the path of a stampede.' In a footballing sense Leeds missed the aerial ability of the injured Charlton, with his replacement Madeley unable to cope with Tony Hateley. For what proved to be the winner, Cooke crossed for the England international, whose header, as *The Times* reported, 'left Sprake twisting helplessly like a fish out of water'. After Leeds brought on Lorimer the game changed as they found their rhythm.

We had two goals disallowed after we were camped in their penalty area. The first, from Cooper, was probably the right decision, but the second from Lash after Giles had rolled a free-kick to him was an unbelievable decision. How many times in the Premiership over the last few seasons has that type of goal been given? You've got to give the advantage to quick-thinking players, not let the kick be retaken. After all the controversies that surrounded our earlier ties I think maybe the referees had it in for us. I don't think they held meetings, but it could have been human nature; we gave them so much stick I sometimes wonder if they were looking for payback.

So the run had once again come to an end at the penultimate hurdle, while it had proved third time lucky for Chelsea and their manager, the tactless and impetuous Tommy Docherty.

Out of four competitions entered, Leeds' only hope of silverware was now the Inter-Cities Fairs Cup, where the fans wondered if their team could go one better than the previous year's semi-final. Their first-round opponents were DWS Amsterdam and Leeds raced into a three-goal lead in Holland before inexplicably settling into their old routine of sitting back on away soil. Then, as *The Times* reported, 'DWS tried hard to reduce the deficit and Boogaard took advantage of a blunder by Reaney to score.' Even allowing for Reaney's aberration, Leeds cruised to an aggregate 8-2 victory to set up a clash with opponents from the previous season. An air of caution abounded as Leeds once again faced Valencia. Forty thousand fans at Elland Road saw Leeds take and then lose an early lead with a goal from Greenhoff and an equaliser from Claramunt. Valencia had been the pre-match favourites and their performance demonstrated why. It was also thought that the match would be a repetition of the brutal affair served up the previous season but this fear proved unfounded as it was free-flowing football that ensued. Before Leeds scored, Valencia showed their potential with an incisive breakaway but, according to *The Times*, 'only a superb save from Sprake kept out a powerful header from Ansola, the Spanish international centre forward.' After the Spanish substitute goalkeeper performed heroics to keep Leeds at bay it was, according to Jarred & McDonald, 'Sprake that had to be at his best to block efforts by Ansola and Polinario.'

If Valencia were considered favourites before the tie in Leeds they were now odds-on, with the bookies refusing to take any further bets. Going into the match Gary Sprake, although only twenty-two, must have felt like an elder statesman as suspension and injury meant starting places for debutant Terry Hibbitt and youngsters Gray, Lorimer and Belfitt. The four were only a year or two younger than Gary, but they lacked his experience. Whether or not the Spaniards were overconfident, they soon had a reality check as Leeds went in front through Giles. From there on in it was a rearguard action, with Jarred & McDonald reporting that 'Valencia poured forward in search of an equaliser, but everything in the air was won by Jack Charlton and behind him Gary Sprake made four world-class saves.' Leeds had once again gone into their defensive shell, as the statistics confirmed, with Valencia winning fifteen corners compared to Leeds' five, but with three minutes left Spanish hearts were broken as Lorimer put the tie out of reach. Leeds had progressed against all odds to set up a meeting with Bologna.

After beating Sunderland Leeds had to travel through the night to Italy and after the eight-hour journey went straight to bed at lunchtime – not the ideal way to prepare for the quarter-final of a major European competition. Whether or not the journey had taken too much out of them, Leeds produced a lacklustre performance and for an hour Gary Sprake was, according to Jarred & McDonald, 'in first-class form' to keep the Bolognese at bay. On the hour, however, Neilsen scored the only goal of the tie to give the Italians a slender lead to take to Yorkshire. Inside Elland Road 42,000 fans roared Leeds on but Bologna's tactics mirrored those adopted by Leeds throughout every away tie; soak up the pressure and respond with swift counterattacks. Within nine minutes the away side's plans lay in disarray as Giles once again chipped in with a vital goal to put Leeds ahead and level on aggregate. *The Times* reported that

> After that it was absorbing stuff with both sides attacking relentlessly. Leeds without the absent Charlton were vulnerable and in the 13th minute Sprake twice saved at point-blank range with great reflex saves from Bulgarelli.

Following a goal-less period of extra time Leeds went through to an all-British semi-final after Bremner had called correctly on the toss of a coin.

Leeds entered the tie against Kilmarnock after securing another top-four spot after two wins in their last two League games. Whatever happened over the two-leg semi-final, Leeds had secured another European place for the following season.

For the first time in a long while we went into the match with carefree abandon. The domestic season had finished and we felt relaxed. The boss, though, was his usual methodical self; the night before the game we had the same old team meeting. Which opponent kicked with his left, who tried to beat a man on the inside, while all we wanted to do was go out and show the public that we could beat anyone on our day, or any other day come to that.

It appeared that both sides entered into the spirit of things as six goals were scored before forty minutes showed on the clock, with reserve striker Belfitt notching a hat-trick in just half an hour. That was the way it stayed, with Leeds taking a 4-2 advantage north of the border for the return leg.

We had defended ineptly in the first leg and the boss was none too pleased, so we knew what to expect when he unveiled the team and tactics. It was no surprise that we were going to operate with a lone striker and throw a blanket defence around our two-goal advantage.

These negative tactics incurred the wrath of the football media as Leeds produced a dour defensive display. The game was tough, fiery and often brutal. Neither side had conceded more than one goal in their previous away ties and with an eight-man defence Leeds were intent on more of the same. Whether they would succeed was in doubt as early as the third minute after Sprake had twice foiled Queen and McIlroy with brave saves that resulted in him being injured. Revie's defensive tactics enabled the Welsh custodian to demonstrate his breathtaking talents, with Frank Clough of *The Sun* reporting:

> Sprake produced one of the finest, if not the finest performance of his career, making five incredible saves and displaying reckless bravery. In fact, Sprake was truly magnificent, having an answer to everything that escaped the defenders in front of him.

Local reporter Alan Thompson argued that

> All of England can be proud of a Welshman today. The brilliance of Gary Sprake took Leeds through to the final of the Inter-Cities Fairs Cup. After the game the whole team celebrated his contribution with champagne.

For Gary, however, it was a bittersweet experience as his foolhardy bravery had left him injured. So the history books show that Leeds had gone a stage further than the previous season – but how many of those very same books have produced a balanced and objective account of Gary Sprake's contribution? These match reports from the time demonstrate that Gary performed way above the call of duty in nearly every tie, especially those away from home. Many believe that goalkeepers are paid to make saves; that it is their job, but the majority of Leeds fans who witnessed these performances would argue that Leeds were successful in Europe because of, not in spite of, Gary Sprake.

For the first time in their history Leeds had reached a major European final, but the Elland Road faithful had to wait as the final was moved to the forthcoming season. Going into the game Leeds were bottom of the table, without a win in the month of August. The first leg against Dynamo Zagreb was away and when the sides took the field there was a sense that the game was going to attract the attention of the football authorities. As the teams appeared the Leeds goalkeeper was kitted out in an all-black strip.

Call it a statement or whatever, I decided years before that if I ever reached a major final I would pay my respects to my goalkeeping idol, the legendary Russian 'keeper Lev Yashin, who always dressed in black. I had seen him a few times on television and was especially impressed with his performances in the 1966 World Cup finals. Gordon Banks was the best goalkeeper I played against at home, but I think Yashin was a better all-round 'keeper, he had everything. I sometimes incurred the wrath of the authorities at home because I wore an outfield jersey under my top with the white collar rolled over. A trivial thing to do but the powers that be thought it brought the game into disrepute. With all that was going on in the game, the violence on and off the pitch and the whispers of corruption, you would think they had more serious things to focus on. I was expecting a fine but nothing came of it.

Leeds took the field in sweltering temperatures against a team that had not conceded a goal on the way to the final and they were dealt a blow when Giles was ruled out through injury. In came Bates for his European debut in a cauldron of patriotic fervour. Once again Leeds adopted the usual tactics and according to Jarred & McDonald, 'Charlton and Sprake performed heroics in the United defence as Dynamo came forward at every opportunity.' Unfortunately, Leeds' most consistent performers in a gruelling season were unable to stop their opponents taking a two-goal lead back to Elland Road.

All roads led to Elland Road for the second leg, where expectations ran high that the deficit could be overturned. However, Leeds played poorly; a view endorsed by *The Times* correspondent, who stated:

> Leeds were thoughtless and unsubtle, which resulted in blind frustration. They were like automatons crushing themselves against an iron defensive fortress, with no effective methods to break down the citadel. Sprake was virtually an addition to the national unemployment figures.

We felt extremely confident going into the game but we were better suited to defending a lead than overturning one. We still sometimes lacked that creative guile and someone who could put the ball away on a regular basis – in fact, Johnny Giles was our top goalscorer. We were still too rigid in our tactics. Once again we remained trophy-less, failing at the last when the season had promised so much.

So Leeds had again finished a season trophy-less. They had run out of both ideas and luck against Zagreb; surely that luck would have to change. To help in the quest Revie would spend £100,000 to break the dearth of goals by raiding Yorkshire neighbours Sheffield United to sign the centre forward Mick Jones. Gary had been a model of consistency both at home and abroad. In a long and arduous season he had played a total of fifty-eight games, conceding forty-five goals and keeping twenty-nine clean sheets – hardly the record of a poor 'keeper.

FIVE

CHAMPIONS

A revolutionary atmosphere seemed to permeate the air in 1968, a remarkable year in both Europe and America. In Europe the invasion of Czechoslovakia resulted in increasing Cold War tensions and there was also student unrest in Paris and London. In the US the assassinations of Bobby Kennedy and Martin Luther King took place against a backdrop of inter-racial tension, anti-Vietnam protests and the drug-induced free love movement. Yet in traditional Yorkshire a more pragmatic turnaround was taking place as Don Revie's revolutionary aim of turning Leeds United from perpetual also-rans to domestic and European giants was finally coming to fruition. After seven long years of hard work, disappointment and sheer bad luck Leeds United were finally to become a winning club. In fact, from the spring of 1968 to the spring of the following year was to be the finest twelve months in the history of the club. In his book *1968* Mark Kurlansky argues, 'There has never been a year like 1968, and it is unlikely there ever will be one again.' These comments are equally applicable to Gary Sprake, for whom it was also a remarkable year and marked the zenith of his playing career. As Leeds picked up three trophies he was ever-present, seemingly blowing a gaping hole in the argument that he was the weakest link and that he cost them many trophies. Throughout this period he was, as Billy Bremner's earlier quote indicated, one of the world's greatest goalkeepers, with performances of the highest level demonstrating his class on numerous occasions at Wembley, Liege, Budapest, Old Trafford, Loftus Road, Upton Park, Goodison, Anfield and of course Elland Road during that phenomenally successful twelve months. Far from costing Leeds dear these performances enabled them to be so successful, with many of the precious points won during the championship season being solely down to Gary himself, not to mention three cup-final clean sheets.

The victory against Arsenal on 2 March 1968 in the League Cup final was a massive psychological breakthrough for the Leeds team. Despite being consistently among the best teams in the country during the previous three years they had little to show for this achievement in terms of silverware. In fact, they had earned more total League points than any other team during the three seasons they had been in the First Division since their return in 1964/65 and had been close to winning trophies on four separate occasions since their promotion. The League Cup win was vitally significant as United could finally shake off the tag of perpetual runners-up. The final itself against the Gunners was a dour affair punctuated by ugly scenes and tempers frayed during several flashpoints in which Gary played an integral part. *The Times* described the game as being 'as drab and cold as the afternoon itself'. The single goal came in the eighteenth minute from a favourite Leeds ploy as Jack Charlton knocked down Eddie Gray's corner for Terry Cooper to volley home the vital winner as Arsenal's players appealed in vain for a free-kick on 'keeper Jim Furnell. This tactic was not to the liking of reporter Geoffrey Green, who condemned it, suggesting it was a form of obstruction that referees needed to examine far more carefully. Terry Cooper himself after the match claimed, 'it's a funny thing but for the last three nights I have been dreaming that I have scored the winning goal at Wembley.'

After Leeds had scored, despite the fact that Arsenal had roughly three-quarters of the possession they did little to puncture the effective United defence. Although Gary was the busier of the two 'keepers he was never really troubled apart from turning a stinging left-foot shot from Radford around the post. Eric Stanger of the *Yorkshire Post* stated:

> Sprake, apart from hanging on to the usual number of crosses and corners, had only one save to make.

The national press were generally critical of both teams but, not surprisingly, of Leeds' tactics in particular. For Revie and his team this criticism was incidental; what was most significant was that they had won a trophy at last. Ultimately, this was all that really mattered to a team that had failed at the final hurdle so many times before. One constant theme of this final was the increasing confrontation between Gary and certain Arsenal players who were trying to niggle and unsettle him. Earlier in the game Gary had clashed with Frank McLintock, which resulted in a mass flare-up between both sets of players. The bitter rivalry between the two teams can be traced back to this game with the Leeds goalkeeper at the heart of the conflagration.

It was the first major trophy in the club's history and we were adamant that this would now be the first of many. I remember the match was tense and therefore became very dour and over-physical. There was very little football played at all during the match and this was not helped by the fact that the two teams didn't like each other. There were a few unsavory incidents but nothing major – even the incident with McLintock was nothing really, just a few handbags. However, the tension between the two teams was genuine and was similar to the hostility that had developed between us and Chelsea. The London press hated us and this certainly created a north/south divide. Revie really stoked us up to put one over the London clubs every time we played them. On a personal note the game was uneventful apart from a few routine saves, but I was very proud when I picked up my first major winners' medal for Leeds. It was also a great psychological relief for everybody as it finally ended our reputation of always being runners-up.

Gary was never far from controversy even at this, the zenith of his career, as he was sent off against Bristol City in the FA Cup only a week after Wembley, and almost six weeks after the success of the League Cup final there came the error at Old Trafford against Everton in the FA Cup semi-final. Although Gary gained a reputation for being temperamental he refutes the suggestion that this in any way undermined his performances or that it was an issue at the time.

Although I admit that I could be fiery and would never step back from a confrontation on the field I don't think this was a major problem. Goalkeepers today are well protected by referees but in my day you were a target and if you weren't fully committed you were in for a very hard time. If opposition centre forwards thought you were a soft touch they would exploit it fully. So yes, I did look after myself but no more or less than anybody else in our team – or any other team – at the time. Perhaps I got a reputation because I played for Leeds and the press didn't like us being so ultra-competitive. They called it gamesmanship, but we ignored them anyway. After a few years, when I was established, most opponents wouldn't bother trying to rile me as they knew what to expect if they did. After all, football is a physical game and if you dive at a striker's feet of course you are going to be annoyed if they stamp on you but most of the time you just get up and have to get on with it. Yes I did sometimes lose my temper but very rarely did this result in me being cautioned by the referee. Although the Bobby Gould incident is often cited I only actually ever got sent off twice; once in a competitive FA Cup tie against Bristol City in 1968 and in a so-called friendly against Grimsby. In the FA Cup tie against Bristol I was sent off for punching Chris Garland but I think anybody would do the same if they know what he did. As he challenged for the ball I won it in the air and we exchanged a few choice words and the next thing he has called me a Welsh so-and-so and spat in my face. Unfortunately the referee only saw me retaliate and I was sent off. When I attended the FA disciplinary hearing in Birmingham I was a little concerned when I was told there was a policeman waiting to see me. I was delighted, however, when he explained that he had seen the whole incident and was prepared to act as my witness. When he told the FA what had happened I was let off with a warning and my suspension for the next round was lifted.

As for the Everton mistake, history has remembered this very differently from the reality of the event itself as what is often overlooked in the recollection of what is listed as another Sprake clanger is that the goalkeeper was severely injured for the majority of the game and, in today's modern football with its full bench of substitutes, he would not have had to continue. The League campaign of 1967/68 itself fell apart as Leeds sustained four consecutive defeats at the end of the season, once again, it could be argued, victims of their own incessant quest for success on all fronts. In the final reckoning Leeds lost out on the title by five points to Manchester City, having lost consecutively to Stoke 2-3, Liverpool 1-2, Arsenal 3-4 and finally Burnley 0-3. An interesting aside to these results is that, due to his serious injury at Old Trafford, it was David Harvey and not Gary who kept goal for the last three games of the season. The Yorkshire club had lost six points and conceded nine goals during these games yet no fair-minded observer would possibly suggest that it was Harvey's goalkeeping that cost Leeds the title that year!

The high spot of a memorable twelve months for Gary Sprake came in the 1968 Inter-Cities Fairs Cup final against the famous Hungarian team Ferencvaros, which had been held over from the previous season because of fixture congestion. In earlier rounds they had had a comfortable 16-0 aggregate win over Spora Luxemburg but their eventual path to the final proved far tougher. In the second round they squeezed past Partizan Belgrade before encountering three consecutive Anglo-Scottish ties, the first resulting in a narrow

2-1 aggregate victory over Hibernian. In the quarter-finals they faced the might of Glasgow Rangers, overcoming them 2-0 in the home leg after a goalless draw in front of 80,000 at Ibrox. In the semi-final they defeated their third consecutive Scottish opponents Dundee, again by the aggregate score of 2-1. However, probably the hardest of all the matches on route to the 1968 Fairs Cup final was at Ibrox on 26 March. Leeds achieved a goal-less draw after inspirational performances from both Bremner and Madeley. In a swirling gale and on a quagmire of a pitch Gary excelled as Phil Brown of the *Yorkshire Evening Post* states:

> Sprake was as safe as a bank behind his defence, making his best save, a double parry from a shot by Ferguson, just when it was wanted late in the game.

While John Begg of the *Yorkshire Post* comments that:

> His handling was immaculate and eventually he broke the hearts of the Rangers attack.

It was also a result that stretched Leeds' unbeaten run to twenty-three games.

It was a slightly subdued early season feeling for the first leg of the Fairs Cup final on 7 August at Elland Road, especially as the League campaign itself had yet to kick off and the game was being televised live. This was reflected in the hugely disappointing crowd of only 25,268; poor attendances were a continual topic of conversation and perennial bugbear of manager Don Revie in this period.

We sometimes had disappointing attendances during these times despite our continued success. One possible reason was that Leeds had an excellent rugby league club and the area was a real hotbed of the game. It took quite a while for the football club to win these fans around. Also, Leeds was a very working-class area and so many people couldn't afford to take the family to both Elland Road and Headingley if fixtures clashed on the same weekend. It was understandable and no slight on the Leeds players themselves. In fact I don't really think it affected the players very much at all and they give it very little thought, although it did sometimes drive Don Revie to distraction as he felt that we deserved better crowds and could only continually compete with the Manchester Uniteds and Liverpools if we had their gates.

Peter Lorimer, commenting on the excellent support for Leeds during their relegation season from the Premiership in 2004, makes a different point:

> Leeds has outstanding supporters but fans these days are too forgiving towards the players as they applaud for simply winning a corner. In our day if we weren't 2-0 up at half-time at home we would be booed off.

The game itself was untidy and, in a muted atmosphere, was settled by a lone Mick Jones strike after Jack Charlton once again flicked on a near-post corner from Peter Lorimer. The hard-working Leeds style was in contrast to the showy continentals and the game was evenly poised with both teams having efforts cleared off the line. Phil Brown of the *Yorkshire Evening Post* was very critical of the lack of firepower in the Leeds team up front and especially the wasteful finishing of both Jones and Greenhoff in front of goal. The home crowd was very relieved to see Gary keep out an almost certain Rakoski equaliser in the dying minutes as he leaped to his left and brilliantly took the ball sideways in the air.

I had very little to do all game so it was really pleasing to keep out that shot, especially as if it had gone in we would have lost the advantage we had worked so hard for. Although my save in the Nep stadium has become more famous, the last-minute save at Elland Road probably turned out to be more important as it denied them a precious away goal.

The national media described the 1-0 advantage as precarious and generally agreed that the Hungarians would be the happier team and were now odds-on favourites for the trophy. Their manager Karoly Lakat stoked the fires for the second leg by criticising Leeds for an aggressive style of play and stating, 'One goal is not going to be enough in Budapest.'

The second leg was played a month later on 11 September. It was delayed due to increasing Cold War tensions within Eastern Europe as a result of the invasion of Czechoslovakia by Soviet troops earlier that year. This game was to be a vastly different proposition, especially without the injured midfield dominance and guile of Johnny Giles. In front of a fanatically partisan home crowd of 76,000 at the Nep stadium the Hungarians were clear favourites to overturn the narrow defeat they had suffered a month earlier at Elland Road. However, in a fantastic rearguard defensive performance, Leeds, against all the odds, displayed great steel and determination to hold out for a goal-less draw and become the first British winners of the trophy. In what was probably the most influential performance of his 500-plus appearances Gary Sprake was inspired in the Leeds goal. As the last line of defence he was unbelievable, making a series of crucial interceptions and vital blocks. However, in the dying minutes one save stood above all, as he tipped around the post a Novack shot that he could only have seen at the last split-second as it flew from behind the ten-man defensive wall. *Times* correspondent Geoffrey Green reported that

> In the second half Leeds were camped in their own half as the Hungarians threw all their efforts into trying to make the breakthrough. But Leeds held their lines superbly and twice were saved by dazzling saves by Sprake under his crossbar. First he kept out a close range effort from Szoke with his left foot, and then he dived with poetic grace to turn away a free-kick from the edge of the penalty area to his top corner from Novak. How the goalkeeper ever saw the ball at that moment was miraculous, since there was a solid wall of ten white shirts in front of him.

Phil Brown described the save thus:

> His lithe leap and powerful punch out sent the ball whirling away high around the post in what will be one of the saves of a lifetime however long he plays.

Colin McIntyre of the *Yorkshire Post* sums up his goalkeeping performance that night by stating 'Sprake was superb.'

Another eyewitness to the events in Budapest was Leeds fan Gary Edwards, who has watched every Leeds game for nearly forty years and who, in his book *Paint it White*, states:

> That night he produced probably one of the best goalkeeping performances ever seen. He pulled off a string of magnificent saves as Ferencvaros relentlessly bombarded the Leeds goal, looking for the vital equaliser.

Paul Madeley remembers that

> The second leg was a hard-fought rearguard action, and we were indebted to Gary who made a number of world-class saves. He was sensational and his performance won us the cup.

Even arch critic Eddie Gray admits:

> The Hungarians cut through our defence so often that it looked as if Gary
> was stopping them from putting the ball in the net virtually on his own. It
> was the best display I have ever seen from any Leeds 'keeper.

Gary's memories of the game are still vivid today.

*Although my recollection of some games is beginning to fade somewhat, the
game at the Nep stadium remains etched in my memory to this day. I remember walking out of the tunnel to be greeted by a crescendo of noise and the
atmosphere was unbelievably hostile. The political situation behind the Iron
Curtain was very tense at that time and for the 76,000 Hungarian fans in
Budapest it was one of the few chances they had to express and show their
feelings in public. They certainly did that with their hostility focused directly
towards us. Our defence that night was amazing and it was probably my
greatest performance for Leeds. Near the end of the game I made what I regard
as my best ever save. With minutes to go the Hungarians were awarded a
free-kick right outside the box in a very central position, to be taken by their
dead-ball ace Novak. I lined up the wall to my right-hand side and stood just
behind it to cover my left-hand post. He hit the ball as hard as he could and
you could feel the crowd trying to suck the ball into the net behind me. After
Novak hit the ball I had only a split second to see it as it dipped over the
wall and I managed to dive full length to my left and slightly behind me. It
was important that I got a full hand to it as it was hit so hard it rebounded
off me and ended up halfway up the stand. I was still feeling the pain in my
wrist when minutes later the referee blew for full-time and we had won our first
European trophy. Although I felt that I had more than helped us to win the
cup it was a fantastic defensive effort from every player and Terry Cooper had
a brilliant game. He was everywhere and even cleared one off the line. I think
this game was the only really consistently good report I got off the national
press who were especially complimentary of the Novak save. Looking back,
these two games still give me great memories but if push comes to shove I do
think that the away performance in Budapest was my best ever performance it
is certainly one that gives me immense pride.*

However, there was no time for Leeds to rest on their laurels as
within a week they were achieving a 0-0 draw against Standard Liege in
Belgium in defence of their hard-won trophy. It was a game in which
the Leeds 'keeper was again outstanding, a level he was to maintain

throughout the remainder of that memorable season. The *Yorkshire Evening Post* headline the following day proclaimed, 'Sprake is United Hero', with Phil Brown reporting that:

> The whole side could thank Sprake for the fact that they were not behind. He had a positively inspired twenty minutes getting him round after round of applause although he was frustrating the strong home attack. Sprake was just unbelievable. He had to face a barrage of shots from close range but his responses were electrifying. High and low he soared or dived in panther-like style and three times he kept the ball out of the angle only by brilliant acrobatics.

In defence of the trophy, after defeating first Napoli on the toss of a coin and then, comfortably, Hannover 96, Leeds lost 3-0 on aggregate to Ujpest Dosza in the fourth round. However, in reality, neither the team nor the manager shed too many tears about the cup exit. The emphasis was always to be on the big one – winning the League – that season. In fact in both domestic cup competitions during the 1968/69 season the team demonstrated a strange lethargy throughout. In the first round of their defence of the League Cup they struggled past Charlton 1-0 at home and were indebted to a Sprake save from a volley by Charlton striker Tees. They lost 2-1 away to Crystal Palace in the next round with both Gary and his teammates offering one of their rare under-par performances as an air of indifference was visible. This also seemed apparent in January when they lost at home to Sheffield Wednesday in the third round replay of the FA Cup. After two cup wins the previous season and so many previous near-misses in the championship it became obvious where the priority lay.

Although beneath the surface there may have been some subconscious focus on the League this was never stated openly. In fact, Don Revie wouldn't allow us to go out and give anything less than 100 per cent and we couldn't afford to relax as there were always other players eager to take our places, as in my case of course with David Harvey. We were beaten fair and square, 3-1 by Sheffield Wednesday and 2-1 by Crystal Palace in the League Cup, although once again Leeds showed the way for teams in later years as we fielded a weaker team in that competition, more so after having won it the year before. I don't think we ever deliberately tried to concentrate on the League but perhaps it was there at the back of our minds as the League Cup defeat wasn't seen as that traumatic.

There was an excellent start to the League campaign of 1968/69 as the team won seven of the first nine games between 10 August and 28 September. The scene was set for an exceptional year for the United goalkeeper as early as the second game of the season at home to First Division new boys QPR, with Phil Brown, the *Yorkshire Evening Post* correspondent, arguing that Leeds were very lucky as several outfield players had poor games and that 'Sprake twice saved Leeds superbly when he had no right to.' During this early season, apart from the brilliant Budapest performance, Gary was consistently excellent, undoubtedly helped by the usually ever-present resilience of the famous back four of Cooper, Charlton, Hunter and Reaney as Leeds conceded on average less than a goal a game. In that early season some outfield players were inconsistent and Phil Brown was particularly critical of the performance of the Leeds full-back duo after a disappointing draw against Sunderland, arguing that 'Reaney and Cooper have played much better and only Hunter and Sprake distinguished themselves.' Gary's best individual performance during this early season period came in the narrow 1-0 home victory over Liverpool on 31 August. In a dour game, dominated by long-ball tactics, he made two flying saves from Callaghan and Hunt. In fact, his early season performances were such that the *Yorkshire Evening Post* ran a back-page feature highlighting his consistently superb form. The paper reported that probably the biggest compliment to the Leeds 'keeper came from the Welsh FA, who had desperately tried to postpone the World Cup qualifier against Italy in Cardiff due to his lack of availability because of Leeds commitments.

During this early season another interesting game was against Leicester at Filbert Street on 14 September, a generally unremarkable match apart from two things: a Peter Shilton penalty save from Lorimer and the constant tussle between Gary and the Leicester centre forward and soon-to-be teammate Allan Clarke. Clarke deliberately challenged the Welsh 'keeper late, leaving his foot in and badly gashing Gary's ankle, leaving him hobbling for the remainder of the game. Despite this incident Gary refutes the suggestion that Allan Clarke was a dirty player.

Allan was a hard player and very competitive. Sometimes he would put his foot in where he shouldn't but that was the nature of the game in those days. I know that most people would expect me to slag Allan off, especially as it is open knowledge what he has said about me many times and even about the writing of this book. However, I am not going to let it affect my assessment of him as a player. He was an exceptional goalscorer and one of the most clinical finishers, up there with the likes of Jimmy Greaves and Denis Law. He scored goals wherever he played, for Fulham, Leicester and of course for Leeds. However, when he first came to Leeds he was very much a loner but eventually settled in well, striking up a strong friendship with Billy Bremner. Although I didn't socialise with him personally we got on fine but I am pleased to say he never scored a goal against me for England or when I played against Leeds at Birmingham.

In late September the team suffered a sharp rebuff in a 3–1 defeat to Manchester City and an even bigger 5–1 reverse came at Turf Moor against Burnley a month later. This match marked the worst performance of the season for both the team and the goalkeeper. However, these autumn blips were to prove the only blemish on an otherwise untainted season. After the Burnley shock, which was to be the last defeat of the campaign, Leeds temporarily withdrew into a defensive shell and confidence was restored with three consecutive goal-less draws, before a return to winning ways came as a result of a narrow 1–0 win over Coventry on 16 November. After the Coventry game Phil Brown praised the United goalkeeper, stating, 'It continues to surprise how he can go into the most difficult of saves after long periods of complete inactivity.' The middle game of the three goal-less draws was against trans-Pennine rivals Manchester United on 2 November at Old Trafford. Despite just shading the match, *Times* reporter Tom German stated that

> Leeds owed much to Sprake for not falling behind. Law almost scored twice, once with a hurtling header from Kidd's centre and then with a Law shot accurately dispatched. Each brought a lightning reaction and a splendid save from the brilliant Sprake.

This was a view reinforced by local reporter Eric Stanger of the *Yorkshire Post*, who commented on the breathtaking brilliance of both saves. In fact, in November 2005 Gary's performance in this game was featured in *The Times'* regular 'Saturday's Heroes' retrospective feature. His outstanding performance was given as the major reason that Leeds were able to keep Manchester United at bay, with the article quoting the famous Michael Parkinson match report in *The Sunday Times* at the time, describing the Leeds goalkeeper's performance as simply 'wondrous'. By early December, after the 2-0 home victory over Sheffield Wednesday, Leeds were holding down second place in the First Division, four points behind Liverpool but with two games in hand.

Many long-term Leeds fans have vivid memories of Gary Sprake's consistently excellent goalkeeping during their first championship season. There were few better than one on 14 December at Upton Park on a rock-hard pitch in front of a crowd of 27,418. Against the run of play Leeds had taken an early lead through winger Eddie Gray, which was virtually their last attack of the game. West Ham, with Hurst, Peters and Moore outstanding, dominated the game and bombarded the Leeds goal with shots and crosses. On a freezing day, without gloves, the track-suited Leeds 'keeper caught everything that came into the box, demonstrating exemplary defensive goalkeeping. Although West Ham equalised shortly before the end of the game from a Peters header, most in attendance would remember Gary's stunning save from a close-range Hurst volley. At the end of the game as the departing fans mingled all the talk was about the inspirational performance of the Welsh goalkeeper and the battling qualities of the Yorkshire outfit. Another interesting postscript from this game highlights Gary's brushes with authority as a month later he was fined £100 by the FA and given a warning with regards to his future conduct. This was as a result of an alleged foul and abusive remark to referee Mr P.R. Walters of Bridgwater. Despite the 6-1 revenge defeat of Burnley, as Christmas approached Leeds were still three points behind Liverpool. Geoffrey Green of *The Times* suggested that the title seemed to be tilting towards Liverpool but he continued to argue somewhat prophetically, 'I stick to my original instinct: Leeds United to win the title for the first time in their history.' This was a confidence that United were to justify while completing an unbeaten second half of the season.

At the end of January 1969 Leeds travelled to London to Loftus Road to face QPR. Unusually for the time this was to be a Friday night fixture as both teams had already been knocked out of the FA Cup. After Mick Jones had given Leeds a second-minute lead the United defence endured eighty-eight minutes of one-sided attacks from the relegation-threatened Rangers team. Match reporter Tom Freeman stated that

> The Leeds defence was bombarded with an almost non-stop assault in the second half as shots continued to rain in on Sprake from all angles.

Although the defence looked certain to crack under the pressure, Gary was outstanding and was evidently responsible for Leeds obtaining the two precious points. On a dreadful night for football with torrential rain and gale-force winds, Gary seemed insurmountable. QPR had probably two dozen corners and he caught virtually every one as they swung them further and further from away from the goal. He also made a string of fine saves, capped off by saving a forty-seventh-minute Bobby Keetch penalty. Barry Porter of the *Yoerkshire Post* commented that 'Sprake, who saved a penalty, was a hero in a cool Leeds defence,' while Terry Lofthouse of the *Yorkshire Evening Post* was even more complimentary:

> Sprake made many magnificent saves, caught everything confidently in the air and gave the overworked men in front of him the necessary confidence. He has played few better matches than this. His penalty save plus two wonderful point-blank stops gallantly made near the edge of the box in quick succession made him United's hero.

At the final whistle the entire Rangers team lined up as one to shake him by the hand for a performance described by many as equal to his remarkable performance in Budapest the previous autumn. After the heroic rearguard action at Loftus Road, Leeds went on to record seven consecutive victories, a run that took them towards the end of March. However, it would be April that would decide the fate of Leeds' title challenge as they faced eight vital League games with plenty of opportunity for the trophy to be once more snatched from their grasp, especially as they faced key trips to Highbury, Goodison and Anfield. The first game in April was a hard-fought goal-less draw against Sheffield Wednesday, a result obtained with the help of a brilliant save by Gary from a long-range effort by opposition full-back Burton. However, the major test of Leeds' nerves was to come as they faced fierce rivals and sparring partners Arsenal away on 12 April, a game that was once again to prove controversial, especially for Gary himself.

This was a vital fixture in the run-in to the championship but Gary's temperament seemed to get the better of him in another tempestuous clash with an Arsenal player, this time centre forward and future Wales manager Bobby Gould. These were continuing spats that had boiled over from the tension of the previous year's League Cup final. Barely four minutes had passed before the Gunners' centre forward flicked out with his heel as the Leeds 'keeper caught the ball and Gould was immediately poleaxed as Gary fitted him with a classic left hook. Brian Moore, reporting in *The Times*, states that

> After five minutes Sprake floored Gould with a left hook Henry Cooper would have been proud to include in his own formidable armour. A ball caught on the wind had eluded them both, Gould flicked out and may have caught the Leeds goalkeeper on the thigh, but Sprake was up at once and a moment later Gould was flat on his back.

Moore concludes his report by arguing that clearly the Welsh 'keeper should have been given his marching orders but amazingly referee Ken Burns allowed Gary to stay on the field as Leeds won the crucial game 2-1 due to Arsenal's defensive errors. The referee after the game stated that 'In this case of offences and retribution both offenders got the same justice. From what I saw I did not consider the offence serious enough to warrant a dismissal.'

For once luck had gone the way of Leeds as a refereeing decision seemed to do them a big favour. Peter Lorimer suggests in his memoirs that Burns's leniency had much to do with the controversial goal he disallowed in the 1967 FA Cup semi-final against Chelsea, as the referee was loath to court controversy again in such a crucial game in the championship run-in. Gary, however, suggests another possible explanation for the referee's leniency after the clash with Gould.

I caught a cross and as I fell Gould kicked me in the privates very hard. He then turned around and called me a fucking Welsh so-and-so and I lost it and felled him with a sharp left that I think knocked out a few teeth. I had started to walk towards the touchline and take off my jersey as the Arsenal centre forward still lay on the floor but, as the melee of players subsided, referee Burns (who was also Welsh) came up to me and said 'Everything will be okay Gareth. I heard what he called you.

For Gary this decision was crucial as another moment of temper could have undone a season of outstanding goalkeeping and possibly cost Leeds the title. Heaven knows what his many critics would have made of such a controversial event. Gary told Phil Brown at the time, 'Gould kicked me in the groin twice when I was down and it hurt. I got up and just let fly, but I didn't land on him anything like as hard as he tried to make out when he dropped.' Perhaps at the time of the interview Gary played down the punch just a little. Needless to say, the London press made a big meal of the incident but ultimately it was the result, a 2-1 win helped by two defensive errors from Arsenal's Ian Ure, that proved vital.

At the end of April Leeds faced another two vital fixtures as they travelled to Merseyside to face Everton on the 22nd and Liverpool on the 29th. In both games the Leeds defence, with goalkeeper Sprake at its heart, was outstanding as goal-less draws were achieved. After the Goodison game the table read Leeds played forty with sixty-four points and Liverpool played thirty-nine with fifty-nine points. A point at Anfield would be enough to bring the title to Elland Road for the first time. The 0-0 draw at Anfield was to become part of Leeds United folklore. It was during this period that Gary gave an interview to Mike Casey of the *Yorkshire Evening Post* sharing his thoughts on his reputation at the time. In the conclusion of the interview the 'keeper stated: 'When I go onto the pitch I know I have a job to do and I do it to the best of my ability. If I make a mistake I'm angered with myself but it doesn't worry me, otherwise I might make more.' Casey himself writes

Although often described as temperamental, this is a fault shared by most top-class performers and Sprake is dedicated to his club and colleagues.

Casey continues, pointing out that goalkeepers are the Aunt Sallies of soccer and it is a thankless job with the press and TV only interested in the 'keeper when he makes a mistake. The goalkeeper's job, Casey concludes, 'is one that most players wouldn't choose and couldn't cope with.' This is a perspective that many so-called experts since then would do well to consider.

The game against Liverpool was desperately tense as both teams pushed hard for the decisive breakthrough that would help decide the destiny of the title. As the tension became almost unbearable for spectators and players alike Gary dived full length in the last minutes to keep out a scorching effort by Ian Callaghan and seconds later Leeds had secured their first championship. Geoffrey Green, who had followed the championship race all season for *The Times*, superbly summarised the tension of the occasion:

What else could one expect with so much at stake in a madhouse of noise, which beat the senses like a hammer? Here was total entanglement of heart and body, complete involvement and identification. Liverpool had their fleeting vision of victory. It eluded them. Leeds survived magnificently. And now it's over.

Famously, Don Revie told Billy Bremner to take the team to the Kop, who demonstrated true sportsmanship and magnanimity in defeat by greeting the Leeds team with the resounding chant 'Champions! Champions!' It was a remarkable end to a remarkable season and it must have been a very sweet moment for Gary himself as the same crowd that had mocked him for his infamous 'own goal' two years earlier now applauded him. Derrick Watkins of the *Daily Mirror* summed up the feelings of all associated with Leeds when he said 'Leeds United are the Champions, the masters, the new kings of English football at last.'

The game itself was very tense and we defended so well I only had a few saves to make. The game was too important to be anything other than dour but at the end of the day a goal-less draw was good enough and we were champions. It may seem unusual for me to be saying this as the infamous mistake I made was at Anfield and the crowd gave me a lot of stick at the time. However, I never felt it was malicious and I never had a problem with playing at Anfield before or after that day. The 'Careless Hands' thing was mostly good humoured and after that game if I made a good save I would always get cheers and a round of applause from the Kop. Although they were always tough games and there was a great rivalry in that period between the two clubs there was never any bitterness between the players or the fans. In fact the reception that the Kop gave us after our winning the championship at their ground is legendary and is to the eternal credit of the Liverpool fans. At the end of the game we showed the trophy to the jubilant Leeds fans and then Don Revie stunned us by telling us we should take the trophy and show it to the Liverpool fans in the Kop. Billy (Bremner) was a little stunned but we did as we were told and, as we got near, our apprehensiveness turned to pure joy as the Kop started chanting as one 'Champions! Champions!' It just shows how fair-minded and knowledgeable about the game they were and I would often chat about this with some of the Liverpool players I was friendly with at the time, such as John Toshack, Peter Thompson, Chris Lawler and the late Emlyn Hughes.

As he stood in front of the Anfield Kop milking the plaudits with his teammates, Gary could only reflect on a fantastic achievement for the team and himself personally. Leeds United had won the title with an amazing record of only two defeats, with only twenty-six goals conceded and twenty-four clean sheets including a remarkable twenty-eight-game unbeaten run stretching back to mid–October. These statistics are not achieved with a goalkeeper who is either a liability or the weakest link. During the 1968/69 season Gary Sprake was a goalkeeper of immense class who played in a wonderful team, appearing in every one of the forty-seven League and cup games and every European tie. The consistency of goalkeeping performance, rarely matched by today's Premiership 'keepers, is mostly overlooked in the narrative history of Leeds United. The usual approach, that which has become commonplace, is displayed in Eddie Gray's autobiography, where he argues that 'Leeds' defensive record with Gary in our team was something of an anomaly and it was achieved in spite of his presence rather than because of it.' It is easy to create a myth and report it as fact but it is a lot harder to debunk such a viewpoint once it has been entrenched in people's minds. However, the numerous contemporary witnesses both from journalists and fans are not myth or conjecture tainted by personal animosity or agenda. It is remarkable how many times the contemporary journalists remark on the occasions that Gary was United's hero and this certainly doesn't suggest somebody being carried by his teammates. In fact the real truth is the complete opposite as he was continually excellent and a major contributor to Leeds' first championship success. For any objective observer the original reports speak for themselves and the Welsh goalkeeper deserves his share of the credit for what was a truly remarkable twelve months in the history of Leeds United AFC.

I think our first championship win was a remarkable team effort but I am confident that I played as big a role as any other player in our success. It was a remarkable achievement to only lose two games and I was proud that I played in every League and cup game, a total of fifty-five appearances, being the only player who was an ever present in all the games. I think the Leeds United team that season was the greatest in the club's history and certainly the most consistent. To play in every game in such a wonderfully successful team was a great honour and I feel very satisfied with the positive contribution I made, although it still perplexes me sometimes to read comments that the club achieved their success that season despite me being in goal. For a so-called liability I seemed to have been able to fool the manager over a long stretch of time and remarkably he still picked me for every one of the fifty-five games. He didn't select David Harvey once.

SIX

UPS AND DOWNS

In their anthemic song 'Marching on Together' Leeds fans sing about their loyalty to the club despite its 'ups and downs'. If ever there was a club that has experienced both the joys of winning and the despair of defeat and subsequent decline it is Leeds United. In the two seasons from 1969 to 1971 Gary and his teammates were to experience the full range of footballing emotions, from the joy of winning trophies to the utter despair of losing out on three trophies in a fortnight. This two-year period began with a trophy in August 1969 and ended with a trophy in May 1971 but in between saw some of the biggest disappointments in the club's history as they finished runners-up in the First Division twice. For Gary personally this was also a roller coaster of a time at Leeds, resulting in a series of exhilarating performances and also some high-profile mistakes, such as those at Wembley in May 1970 and at Selhurst Park in the November of the same year.

In the summer of 1969, before Leeds could begin their defence of the title they had so memorably won the previous year, they had to face FA Cup winners Manchester City in the Charity Shield. The match took place at Elland Road on 2 August 1969 and with Gary in goal Leeds picked up another trophy as they won 2-1 thanks to goals from Charlton and Gray. The 1969/70 League campaign saw the fixture list heavily concertina-ed as a result of the following summer's World Cup finals in Mexico. Leeds had already played six games in a month, resulting in four wins and two draws, before they faced championship rivals Everton on 30 August at Goodison Park. The match resulted in a 3-2 defeat and the end of Leeds' then-record thirty-four League match unbeaten run, despite the best efforts of the Leeds goalkeeper. Barry Foster of the *Yorkshire Post*, commenting on the excellent performance of Gary in goal, stated 'One save by Sprake, from a header by Royle, was superb.' This game was to mark Leeds' last League defeat before losing away to Newcastle at St James's Park on Boxing Day.

As the autumn progressed Leeds began to repeat their form of the previous season and after drawing 2-2 at home to Manchester United they won their next four games. In the same period they also recorded a record-breaking 10-0 home win over Norwegian side Lynn Oslo (16-0 on aggregate). One disappointing result was a loss to Chelsea in the League Cup after a replay. In the run up to the replay at Stamford Bridge, relations between both teams' management broke down as a there was argument over the date of the rematch due to fixture congestion. At one stage tension was very high as there was a distinct possibility that Leeds would be sending one side to play Chelsea in the League Cup and fielding a completely different team in Norway the following evening. In fact the game was played on Monday 6 October and Leeds lost 2-0. Gary missed the match through injury, with the *Yorkshire Evening Post* on the day of the match stating that David Harvey was 'to emerge from the huge shadow of Gary Sprake to play only his second game in sixteen months'. Gary remembers that his relationship with David Harvey was always good despite their intense competition for the 'keeper's jersey at Leeds.

While we were at Leeds David Harvey and I got on great and we were very friendly. I remember that we would go for a few pints after training and David introduced me to horse riding. We went quite a few times and I really enjoyed it. Every day we would stay behind for an extra training session with the coaches to work on our skills with either Les or Syd. When I was in the first team he supported and encouraged me and when he was picked I helped him as much as I could. We never had any problems even though David must have been very frustrated as he was reserve 'keeper to me for a lot of seasons. As a 'keeper he was very good and he deserved to play for Scotland. If I remember correctly he was voted best goalkeeper in the 1974 World Cup finals. He was a really good shot stopper and extremely brave. I don't think he was a natural 'keeper but he worked at his game with great dedication. His only fault technically was that cutting out crosses from wide areas wasn't his strongest point but he was still a class 'keeper. I have to say I was really disappointed that he wouldn't contribute a few comments to the book. He was my understudy for eight seasons yet we never had a cross word so I do think it's sad but at the end of the day it's David's choice. I do know that many of our other colleagues have stated that the team was better with him in goal than me but I do appreciate that David has never made such comments himself.

After the Chelsea defeat Leeds continued their impressive League form, going unbeaten through October and November with the highlight a 6-1 win at home to Nottingham Forest. They also made seamless progress through to the third round of the European Cup by beating 1968 Fairs Cup final rivals Ferencvaros 6-0 on aggregate. Leeds entered the crucial Christmas period on the back of four consecutive League victories but lost 2-1 away to Newcastle United. However, they bounced back in their next game to defeat title rivals Everton 2-1 at home with the game amazingly being played the very next afternoon. Gary had played every game and, apart from one goal against Liverpool, which he pushed onto the bar and in, he had been faultless.

It's really funny to look back and see that we played two crucial games in two days over the Christmas period but we never really thought about it at the time. We just got on with it. I have to say it was a great experience to play in such a wonderfully gifted team and I do regard myself as very lucky to have done so. We had a great team spirit and we enjoyed playing together and there were no cliques at the club. Looking back, the biggest shame is that we didn't win as many trophies as we should have. From 1965 onwards we were never out of the top four and for most of the seasons the top two and we were always in the semis or finals of the cup competitions. I never really felt pressurised playing for such a successful team and I don't think any of the other players did either. I enjoyed playing in a team with so many class players in front of me but I also feel that I made my contribution to making the team as successful as it was.

The start of the new decade saw Leeds drawn to face Gary's home club Swansea Town in the third round of the FA Cup at Elland Road. In a poor performance Leeds scraped home 2-1, even though Swansea had Mel Nurse sent off after a clash with Allan Clarke. In fact, the home team were indebted to their goalkeeper as Gary saved a one-on-one in the last minute from Swans striker Evans. Gary must have had mixed feelings as, although another unwanted game was avoided, he had also missed out on the chance of an unscheduled trip home. The first League game of 1970 saw the Yorkshire club visit Stamford Bridge to face Chelsea and, in a dress rehearsal for the later cup final clashes, Terry Brindle stated in the *Yorkshire Post*:

Leeds were as tough and uncompromising as only they can be, but dirty? Not by any yardstick acceptable in the north, and Chelsea were no saints.

Leeds were able to silence the jeers and taunts of the home crowd with a stunning 5-2 victory, with Gary playing his part with a series of fine saves as Leeds trailed 2-1 during the first half. Brindle continued:

> Chelsea might have had more goals if it wasn't for the fine positioning of Sprake.

In fact it was Chelsea's reserve goalkeeper Tommy Hughes who had a nightmare game, as Leeds scored four unanswered second-half goals. Three weeks later, the disappointment Gary was to suffer with the team in April of that year was put into perspective as his mother died. He took compassionate leave, missing the games against Sutton United and Manchester United. Gary's memories of his mother's support are still vivid today.

I remember that initially my mum didn't want me to leave Swansea to go to Leeds. I was only fifteen and, as a typical Welsh mam, I was her baby and she was really protective of me. It took all of my brothers in a family meeting to persuade her until she reluctantly agreed to let me go. My mother came to most of the Wales home games and always encouraged me a great deal. I still remember today how devastated I was when she died in January 1970 and that she never saw my daughter Julia. I used to go back to Swansea whenever I could to see her and the rest of my family and I had a great relationship with her. I was very proud of her and I know she was of me.

Despite David Harvey proving an able deputy Gary was back in the team for the next League game against Stoke, with Don Revie demonstrating that Gary was clearly still his number one 'keeper. By the time spring arrived Leeds were still in the hunt for three trophies but the fixtures had began to pile up. In March Leeds were due to face Standard Liege in the European Cup quarter-final and Manchester United in the FA Cup semi-final as well as four League games. It was the domestic semi-final against Manchester United that proved to be the most gruelling as Leeds eventually won a momentous tie after a second replay. After the first match, which was goal-less at Hillsborough, Leeds played the second leg of the European Cup quarter-final against Liege, winning the tie 2-0 on aggregate, and kept their League title ambitions alive with a 2-1 win over Wolves. In the European Cup semi-final Leeds were drawn to face Celtic in a tie dubbed the 'Battle of Britain', but before they could contemplate this game they had another semi-final to play; the first replay against Manchester United, their third game in five days. The first replay again ended goal-less after extra time, with Gary keeping his team in the cup in the final minutes. Barry Foster in the *Yorkshire Post* wrote: 'In the last breathtaking minute Sprake saved brilliantly from Kidd.' It took a third game to eventually settle the tie only three days later at Burnden Park, Bolton. An early Billy Bremner goal won the game for Leeds, with Gary making, according to Barry Foster, 'some sparkling saves'.

I remember that the three games against Manchester United were very tense and really close affairs. After three games there was only Billy's goal that separated the teams. I was really pleased to play my part in keeping three clean sheets, especially against a team containing the likes of Best, Charlton and Law. Although the games were great for the crowds it was very draining on the players and I do think it is a good thing that they have now done away with endless replays.

The Manchester United games had clearly taken their toll on the team and only two days later a much-depleted Leeds, including unfamiliar names such as Davey and Lumsden, lost their ground record and with it any chance of the League title in a 3-1 home defeat by lowly Southampton. As Everton went seven points clear Revie seemed to accept defeat and he fielded a reserve side against Derby two days later, with Leeds not surprisingly losing 4-1. The team were now forced to concentrate on the cup competitions but not before their manager was once again in hot water with the FA for fielding a weakened team. Revie remained adamant, saying that, given the same circumstances, 'I would do it again.' It was hardly surprising that Revie took the decision as the Celtic semi-final was scheduled to be played only forty-eight hours after the Derby fixture.

Looking back at this season it is frustrating to see just how close we were to making our mark and winning the treble, as we were still in with a shout for all three down to the last few games and then we lost everything. It was really tough. I think the boss thought that the League was slipping away from us so he sacrificed this by fielding weaker teams in the last four games. He wanted to concentrate on the cup competitions. Whether he was right to make this decision I'm not sure. At the end of the day he was the manager and it was his call. I am sure that he felt we would win at least one if not both cup competitions. In the end we won nothing and to cap it all I remember that the FA gleefully fined him heavily for fielding weakened sides.

The much anticipated home European Cup tie against Celtic was a major anticlimax and seemed almost over before it started as Leeds went 1-0 behind in the first minute to a Connelly goal. Leeds never really got going in this match; this could have been down to the shock of losing an early goal or from their general tiredness, or a mixture of both. Unfortunately the fixtures continued to pile up and Leeds had to face West Ham at Upton Park twenty-four hours later, showing great character to earn a 2-2 draw. However, Revie's problems mounted as Paul Reaney suffered a broken leg; the *Yorkshire Evening Post* reported that one of the first to visit him in hospital was 'Gary Sprake, Reaney's closest friend in the Leeds team'. Within two days Leeds were again in League action against Burnley at home, a game that Gary was rested for. Leeds won the game 2-1 but what was most memorable was a rare appearance from Albert Johanneson and two wonder goals from in-form Eddie Gray.

For Leeds supporters the real focus was now the following Saturday's FA Cup final against Chelsea. The game came to be synonymous for Gary with the mistake he made late in the first half when he failed to cover a shot from Houseman. In reality, despite Gary's error Leeds should have won the game easily, hitting the bar three times and conceding a sloppy late equaliser. For Gary this is the game that most people still approach him to discuss.

The 1970 ties against Chelsea are obviously classic confrontations and people still want to talk about them today. In the first game at Wembley we were winning 1-0 and then I was at fault for their equaliser as I should have saved Houseman's shot. I dived to my left and the ball landed and instead of bouncing into my body as it would have normally it skidded under me and into the goal. Although I should have done better and can't make excuses the pitch was terrible and the same happened for our first goal when their defender did exactly the same thing as I did. It was a disappointing mistake in a big match and I have to hold my hand up and say I should have saved it. What does annoy me though is that both Norman and Peter in their memoirs have blamed me for the second goal, which is a load of rubbish. With a few minutes to go the referee gave a controversial free-kick to Chelsea wide out and the ball was passed to me. As the referee had already blown for a free-kick, instead of picking it up I kicked it out of play to waste a bit of time. Instead of keeping their minds on the game some of the outfield players were still arguing with the ref when Chelsea took the free-kick quickly and crossed it to Hutchinson, who was unmarked to head their second equaliser. I am quite prepared to take my share of blame when I make a mistake but it annoys me when I see others try to pass their errors on to me. If the outfield players and especially the defenders concentrated on their game and marked their men instead of arguing with the ref they could have prevented a quick free-kick and cleared the danger. Ultimately if you look at the game we stuffed Chelsea and should have won by three or four, which is sometimes the case in football. The best team on the day doesn't always win.

For Leeds there was no time to contemplate their bad luck against Chelsea as four days later they faced Celtic in the return leg of the European Cup before an official crowd of 136,500. Leeds summoned up all their character to take a shock 1-0 lead through captain Bremner and were helped by a good confident performance from their goal-keeper, who was keen to make up for his Wembley disappointment. However, the home side's pressure eventually told and Hughes headed the equaliser in the forty-seventh minute and four minutes later Gary was stretchered off after bravely diving at the same player's feet to save. As the Leeds 'keeper was still being carried along the touchline to the dressing rooms Celtic scored, making the tie all but dead for the Yorkshire club. This injury kept Gary out of the frustrating and ultimately heartbreaking FA Cup final replay defeat against Chelsea. Gary states that the disappointments of the 1970 season still hurt.

I think 1970 was typical of our disappointments as we tried to go as far as we could in all competitions we played in. Over ten seasons or so we played over sixty-plus games every year and the boss picked nearly the same XI in every game. We were, to coin a cliché, 'victims of our own success'. Les Cocker's fitness regime ensured we were up to the task physically but mentally, towards the end of the season, especially so in 1970, we were drained. I think also that because we had been runners-up or close so many times this certainly added to the emotional pressure upon both the team and especially Don Revie.

1970/71 proved to be another roller-coaster season for both Leeds as a club and Gary personally. The season saw the 'keeper experience the lows of Selhurst Park, Layer Road and the controversial game against West Bromwich Albion at home but also the sheer joy of triumphing over the Italian giants Juventus in the Fairs Cup final. In the early weeks of the League campaign Leeds hit the ground running, achieving five con-secutive victories including four clean sheets for Gary in goal. The first game of the season was a hard-fought 1-0 victory away at Old Trafford with the *Yorkshire Post*'s Barry Foster commenting 'Gary Sprake was outstanding… making two magnificent saves from Best and Kidd.' The sequence of victories came to an end as a result of a goal-less draw away to Arsenal, which was disappointing as Leeds faced ten men for the majority of the game after home defender Kelly was sent off. The first real setback of the season came in the eighth game with a shock 3-0 defeat away at Stoke. The Whites were lucky to win the next game at home to Southampton, with the two points being achieved due in large part to a fine penalty save by Gary from Davies after Giles had brought down the same player in the box. So if goalkeepers can cost teams points in a League campaign it is also evident that they can play a large part in earning them, as Gary had demonstrated against both Southampton and Manchester United. Indeed, the very next game saw him again help the team pick up a crucial away point against Forest as he made a save in the final minutes with the *Yorkshire Post* stating that 'Sprake one-handed saved the day for Leeds', while the *Evening Post* commented, 'Sprake saved it for Leeds'. Although Leeds were knocked out of the League Cup by Sheffield United, they started their European campaign with a 6-0 aggregate victory over Sarpsburg.

After the Stoke game Leeds went fourteen games unbeaten in the League and also won through to the third round of the Fairs Cup on the away goals rule after a hard-fought 2-2 aggregate draw against Dynamo Dresden. In November Leeds won four games and drew one, ending the month with a 1-0 victory over Manchester City. Richard Ulyatt reported in the local evening paper that the points were saved for Leeds in the ninetieth minute when 'near the end Sprake needed all his agility to prevent what would have been a lucky equaliser.' Although the team remained unbeaten from 12 September 1970 to 9 January 1971 Gary's critics have ignored the goalkeeper's point-winning performances in the games against both Manchester clubs, Forest and Southampton, instead focusing on the mistake against Crystal Palace in the 1-1 draw at Selhurst Park as evidence of how he cost the team so dearly.

I struggle to remember many games I played in but I still remember my few mistakes, such as the one at Palace. Typically I had been playing really well and felt really confident, having made some good saves. I went to catch a routine cross-cum-shot and it slipped through my hands into the net. There's no getting away from the fact that it was a bad mistake on my behalf. As I had been playing so well my mind was on making a quick throw out to the full-back and starting the next attack and before I knew it I had dropped the ball. It's the nature of the game. If I had thrown it to the full-back and he had taken his eye off the ball it would have been a throw-in, but instead I did it and it cost us a goal. I can't make excuses as it's part and parcel of the 'keepers job, as you know you are vulnerable to the odd mistake and you are going to get slaughtered for it if you make one, but I knew that when I took the job.

Leeds continued through December unbeaten and also dispatched Sparta Prague 9-2 on aggregate in the Fairs Cup. Their second defeat of the season came away at Spurs on 9 January 1971 and they lost again at home to Liverpool 1-0 three weeks later. This game was decided by a single John Toshack goal after Paul Reaney clattered into Gary as he was about to collect the ball. The following week's defeat was even more embarrassing, as Leeds lost to Colchester at Layer Road in a famous FA Cup tie. Many Revie players have cited this game as a typical example of Gary's costly goalkeeping. However, the match reports at the time make no mention of Gary making mistakes. They collectively criticised the Leeds team performance and are especially critical of the back four. In fact Phil Brown in the *Yorkshire Evening Post* stated that 'For the second time running Reaney barged into Sprake at the vital moment of saving.' The only references to the Leeds goalkeeper were to several saves he made that kept the score from being even more embarrassing.

It's really funny how perceptions change over time and Colchester is one of those games that there has been some real mythology developed about which much is not true. Don't get me wrong, Colchester was a shocking team performance and our defending was woeful. In the memoirs of my colleagues it seems that I was the only one that played badly but I remember it differently. As I have already stated, when I made a mistake and it was costly I have held my hands up but against Colchester it was collectively a poor defensive performance. I should have done better on the first goal but it was certainly not a clear mistake that cost a goal and the other goals were down to poor defending by Jack and Paul. It has been said that after this game Revie blamed me and I was dropped but again this is not the truth. We were all bollocked by Revie and in training the following week it was really competitive and in one practice match I was caught on the hand and had to have several stitches, which put me out of the game for over a fortnight. As for the idea that I had lost my confidence, again this is rubbish as the following season I played in forty-four games. I hardly think that the boss would have picked me this many times if he thought my bottle had gone.

After the Colchester game Gary missed the next six League games and the fourth round Fairs Cup home leg victory over Victoria Setubal. David Harvey, who was at this stage still on the transfer list, replaced him in goal. Critics have claimed this as evidence that Don Revie had lost faith in Gary's goalkeeping. In fact once again the truth is somewhat different – a report by Don Warters in the *Yorkshire Evening Post* confirms that Gary had received a gash to his hand in training, which required a dozen stitches. Gary was not available for the next four games and for the first time it did seem that David Harvey posed a serious challenge for Gary's number one jersey. Just as the competition for the 'keeper's jersey seemed to be hotting up, fate and a great save from Gary intervened. In the away European tie against Setubal in Portugal Harvey was injured late into the game. Gary's case was helped in the final few minutes as Don Warters reported:

> Just before the end Sprake brought off an excellent save to a hard shot from Baptists, which saved Leeds the indignity of having to play extra time.

From this game on Gary retained the number one jersey for the rest of the season, even when Harvey recovered from his knee injury.

As Leeds approached the last seven crucial League games of the season they were competing neck and neck with Arsenal for the title and also faced Liverpool in a difficult tie in the semi-final of the Fairs Cup. The most infamous of the League games took place on 17 April 1971 at home to West Bromwich Albion. With the Yorkshire club losing 1-0 but pressing hard for the equaliser, the Baggies' Brown chased a ball into the Leeds half. The linesman flagged vigorously as Suggett was over twenty yards in front of the last Leeds defender but, as the linesman dropped his flag, referee Tinkler amazingly waved play on. Brown continued his run, passing the ball to the also offside Astle, who slotted the ball past the static Leeds goalkeeper. Richard Ulyatt in the *Yorkshire Post* wrote:

> In the forty-five years I have reported football, I have never seen a worse decision than the one Mr Tinkler gave at Elland Road on Saturday, which cost Leeds United a goal. Its repercussions were more important than that.

Don Revie lamented that it was 'nine months' hard work down the drain'. Despite Clarke pulling a goal back for Leeds the mood of the team and the fans was not helped by Tinkler controversially ruling out a potential equaliser from Jones. Leeds were subsequently fined for a pitch invasion and had to play several games away from Elland Road at the beginning of the next season. The game was to be crucial as Arsenal added the League title to their cup victory, defeating Leeds by a solitary point. Gary can still remember the controversy caused by Tinkler's decision.

Tinkler's decision in this game was an absolute disgrace and it was definitely a turning point in the season. Both Colin Suggett and Jeff Astle were a mile offside and the linesman flagged vigorously only for the referee to ignore him. As Jeff put the ball in the net our defence were still standing on halfway and I don't know who was most shocked, me or Jeff when he scored. Everybody expected the linesman to tell Tinkler to cancel the goal but amazingly it was allowed to stand. A few fans ran past me to get at Tinkler and he was a very lucky man that the police were so quick to react otherwise it could have got really unpleasant. The fans and players had had enough as this wasn't the first time we had lost out due to shocking refereeing decisions. The major one I can remember was when Ken Burns disallowed a perfectly good free-kick from Peter Lorimer against Chelsea in the 1967 FA Cup semi-final. The worst refereeing display I ever saw was when I was on the bench in the 1973 Cup-Winners' Cup final against AC Milan. The referee was a disgrace and never gave us one decision all night. I can remember looking about the stands and the local Greek crowd in Salonika who were furious as they all knew what was going on; the ref was had clearly been got at. I could never understand in these situations why the trophy wasn't taken away from the winners and given to the opposition in our case we deserved it. Especially as after the match the referee was banned by UEFA from refereeing for life.

Either side of the West Bromwich game was the Fairs Cup semi-final against Liverpool, with the first leg being played at Anfield in front of 52,877 fans on 14 April. Leeds won a tight encounter 1-0 thanks to a captain's goal from Billy Bremner. In an excellent team performance Gary played his part. In the first half he made key saves from Lawler, Lindsay and Heighway while in the second half the *Yorkshire Evening Post* reported:

Toshack also went near with a good header but Sprake saved well and also made a fine stop as Hughes burst through minutes from the end.

In the second leg, which was equally tense, Gary was again outstanding with Barry Foster of the *Yorkshire Post* stating, 'Fearless goalkeeping by Sprake kept the Liverpool forwards at bay', while Don Warters of the *Yorkshire Evening Post* wrote, 'Gary Sprake performed admirably in the Leeds goal.' Once again his goalkeeping had contributed to Leeds' success and helped Leeds through to their third Fairs Cup final. Leeds would now have to wait over a month before facing Italian giants Juventus in the two-legged final.

However, typically of the history of Leeds United, their search for the trophy was far from straightforward. Amazingly, the first leg at the Stadio Commuale in Turin was abandoned by referee Von Raus of Holland just before half-time due to torrential rain. This was especially frustrating for Gary as Barry Foster reported: 'Sprake had made some sparkling saves as the rain shuttered down.' After much reorganisation by the team and fans the match was replayed at the same venue two days later, where Leeds achieved a 2-2 draw thanks to goals from Madeley and Bates. It was therefore set up for a tense second leg the following week back in Yorkshire. After a nerve-racking game Leeds and Juventus drew 1-1 with Leeds winning the cup on the away goals rule. The national press reported on how richly Leeds had deserved their trophy, with the *Daily Express* summing up what everybody at Leeds felt:

> The champion chasers… finally won an important race after two seasons of heartache and near misses.

While the *Telegraph* stated:

> Leeds, England's most consistent side in recent years, were able to end a season of disappointment on a jubilant note.

Gary's was the last touch of the season; after pushing away a stinging long-range effort from Furinho, the referee blew his whistle and the cup belonged to Leeds.

I have fond memories of our games in the Fairs Cup and we always did very well. In 1971 we did brilliantly to win the trophy, especially as we had to beat two wonderful sides in Liverpool and Juventus in the last two rounds. I am very proud of my performances in these games, especially to keep two clean sheets against Liverpool in the semis. I remember that after the game against

Liverpool at Anfield in the first leg of the semi-final I got a massive round of applause from the Kop at the end of the game. I highly valued this as Liverpool fans were, and still are, some of the most knowledgeable in the game. As far as the final was concerned Juventus were a great side but my overriding memory was the abandoned first leg in Turin. At one stage I was really scared that I would dive for a ball and get drowned. The ref made the right decision to abandon the game but he should have never started it in the first place. I am really proud that I played my part in helping the club to reach three Fairs Cup finals and that we won the trophy twice. Although the European Cup was the prestige trophy you only had to win four games to get to the final. To reach the Fairs Cup final there were usually seven or eight rounds and the standard of competition was always very high.

If the 1968/69 season was to prove the zenith of Gary's career at Leeds and the campaign of 1970/71 saw both successes and disappointments, the seasons that followed the Juventus games were to mark the nadir of his time at the club.

SEVEN

THE END OF AN ERA

The 1970/71 season had once again been one of mixed emotions for those involved with Leeds United. The glory of the team winning their second Fairs Cup was tempered by the disappointment of seeing another title narrowly slip from their grasp, while also suffering the ignominy of being victims of a giant-killing act in the FA Cup. In the previous pre-season Gary Sprake had holidayed in Mexico watching the World Cup as a guest of the *TV Times*, whose readers had voted him in 'The Alternative Eleven', a side chosen by the magazine's readers comprising those they considered the best players from the Football League outside the twenty-two selected by Sir Alf Ramsey for his England squad. Gary's ability had once again been recognised on a wider scale as he mixed with players of the calibre of John Greig, Frank McLintock and Bobby Hope, while teammates Billy Bremner, Peter Lorimer and Johnny Giles also accompanied Gary on this once-in-a-lifetime opportunity to watch the world's finest ply their trade. This pre-season, however, Gary Sprake reported back early from his break so that he was in peak condition for the task ahead. Instead of a luxury break in Mexico with teammates Bremner, Giles and Lorimer there was a tour of Eire to negotiate.

During that summer the troubles in Ulster were escalating as the British government introduced internment without trial. The luxury car makers Rolls Royce had collapsed and in America NASA had announced the cancellation of their Apollo space missions. Back in Yorkshire the Elland Road faithful were optimistic that their own dream machine was going to produce many more sleek performances as the team once more reached for the stars. To do so it would have to overcome a severe handicap as the FA had banned Leeds from their own ground for the first four home games after their troubles the previous season in the infamous clash against West Bromwich Albion. Unfortunately, this decision changed the course of the season and ultimately, it could be argued, cost the club another championship title. It would not be until the ninth game of the season that football would return to Elland Road.

One of the things I remember is that every pre-season the boss set us targets. In our championship-winning season he told us he wanted to go through the whole season unbeaten. Although we won the title with a record number of points we still lost two games and for the boss that was still a big disappointment. The season before he wanted us to win the lot and we fell between three hurdles. For this campaign he made the League the priority as it meant European Cup football; that was Revie's burning desire, to compete once more with Europe's finest. The authorities had provided us with an inverse incentive by closing the ground. Once more we felt everyone was against us and how we revelled in the role of being the perceived bad guys! On a personal level I was aiming to go through the season without making any mistakes.

The season's opener against Manchester City at Maine Road would put Gary's plans to the ultimate test. With players like Young, Bell, Summerbee and Lee, City were renowned for their attacking flair. Within ten minutes of the kick-off the game was anything but entertaining as both sides became involved in a bitter battle to gain early ascendancy, with the match being littered with unnecessary fouls as tempers became frayed. Once the game settled down it was City who were on top .Welsh international centre forward Wyn Davies on his debut gave Jack Charlton a hectic afternoon, as City threatened the Leeds goal. As local reporter Peter Gardner commented:

> It took Manchester City half an hour to get geared up to full attacking power. And when they did only the brilliance of Gary Sprake robbed the Sky Blues, twice saving fierce drives from Young and then holding another fine full-length effort from Oakes. The brilliant Welsh international was in thrilling action as the home strikers suffered the same fate, with Sprake constantly getting his body between ball and goal. Sprake was once more in action towards the end of the first half when he again came to the rescue pushing away a fierce rising drive from Coleman. In the second half Bell thundered in a first-time shot, but the incredible Sprake made yet another fantastic save to foil City, who were soon back on the attack with Lee hammering in a low drive. Sprake, seemingly unbeatable, flung himself full length to make yet another grand save.

The *Sunday Mirror* the following day reinforced the local reports, leading with the headline 'Gary the Great', with reporter Vince Wilson describing Gary's performance thus:

> Even Don Revie will admit that Gary Sprake kept Leeds in the game as City built up enormous pressure. Three times in the space of three minutes he saved certain goals, the best of which left the 38,556 gasping with a wonder save when Lee connected with a vicious half volley.

The highlights of the match were shown on the ITV network with the commentator concurring with the papers, arguing that 'the save from Lee was within the compass of only three or four goalkeepers in the country.' In the following week's *Yorkshire Evening Post*, a letter was sent in by Leeds fan Allan Ryan, who wrote:

> It was a performance worthy of the finest goalkeeper in the world. Sprake earned the points; a thirty-yard piledriver from Oakes produced the greatest save the majority of the crowd have ever seen. Sprake is the best 'keeper in Britain.

Gary Sprake had again demonstrated his ability as a world-class goalkeeper. The first 'home' game of the season against Wolves was played at Huddersfield's Leeds Road ground with only 20,000 fans turning up, half the previous season's average. In a lacklustre performance Leeds could only manage a 0-0 draw, a point gained as the only goal threat came from Wolves, according to the *Yorkshire Evening Post*:

> Richards nearly scored but Sprake's excellent anticipation took the ball off his head after Charlton had misheaded.

As part of a clampdown against violent play both McCalliog and Sprake were given a severe lecture, McCalliog for a foul and Gary for his reaction to it. Just three games into the season the contemporary evidence states that Gary had helped gain three points for Leeds with his superb performances. Leeds were on their travels once more for the next 'home' fixture against Spurs, in front of 25,000 people at Boothferry Park, Hull. For the first time that season, Gary's colleagues performed to the same level as their goalkeeper in a fast and absorbing match, with Bremner scoring as Leeds shared the spoils in a 1-1 draw. In the next match, away to Ipswich, Leeds took both points in a 2–0 victory, although the scoreline flattered the visitors. The *Yorkshire Evening Post* reported that

> Sprake turned a ferocious shot from Robertson behind and then pulled off
> three great saves from Mills, Harper and Clarke.

Another new venue, Hillsborough, Sheffield, was used for the next 'home' game against Newcastle, with the pundits arguing that the ban was hindering Leeds' chances in the early quest for the title, even though they had taken six out of a possible ten points. They had already been written off in some quarters only a month into the new season and Leeds responded with a performance that few teams could have lived with, thrashing the Magpies 5–1, Gary keeping up his rich vein of form with a superb save from ex-teammate Hibbitt. However, even the Leeds goalkeeper, despite his brilliant form, could not prevent the Newcastle goal, which came from his own defender Norman Hunter. The last game of the enforced home ban saw United return to Huddersfield as Crystal Palace were beaten 2–0. In the week that saw Concorde make its first transatlantic flight the Leeds 'keeper was also flying high, defying the laws of gravity with three crucial saves.

Despite the difficulties imposed on us by the FA we had done remarkably well. After the game against Newcastle the referee Kirkpatrick applauded us off the park. Considering there was not much of an atmosphere created in these games, taking ten points from a possible fourteen was a remarkable achievement, but the ban did hit us. Our gates were down by about fifty per cent so we were financially disadvantaged, which meant the boss was hindered if he wanted to strengthen the squad. For my part I was very pleased with my form and looking forward to our first game back at Elland Road against our old adversaries Liverpool.

Normal service was resumed at the turnstiles with over 41,000 watching Leeds defeat Liverpool by a single Lorimer strike, with the Leeds goalkeeper's major contribution an excellent save from fellow Welshman John Toshack. The title was developing into a five-horse race between Manchester United, Leeds, Derby County, Liverpool and Manchester City. A disgruntled Don Revie went into the next few games without the services of his inspirational goalkeeper, furious that Gary had injured his knee while making a rare appearance for Wales. Gary was back for the visit of Everton and once again he helped his team to gain both points as he made a brilliant save from Morrissey that, at the time, would have doubled the visitors' lead. Leeds eventually ran out   3-2 winners. During that spell Leeds were involved in a gruelling 0-0 draw with Derby in the League Cup where Harvey deputised for Gary. Gary was back for the replay, Leeds' third game in eight days and the season still hadn't reached October. According to *The Times*, 'It was Sprake, demonstrating his alacrity', and a Lorimer hat-trick that ensured a safe passage into the next round. West Ham were the next opponents at Upton Park and Leeds once again earned a replay at home as West Ham were denied two goals after fouls on Gary. The press reported that West Ham caused a shock in the replay with the magnificent Bobby Moore inspiring the Hammers, who went through with the only goal of the game. However, for Don Revie and his Leeds team this was shrugged off as they once again showed their indifference to this competition.

The race for the title was taking on its usual look with Leeds pursuing the old enemy Manchester United, the next visitors to Elland Road. In a physical, sometimes violent encounter that saw Jack Charlton have his nose broken and Law and Hunter booked after a bout of fisticuffs it was Leeds who narrowed the gap, courtesy of a Lorimer strike. Leeds were, not for the first time, indebted to their blond-haired custodian, as *The Times* reported that: 'Sprake continued his rich vein of form with a series of good saves'.

I remember that, even though it was a vital top-of-the-table clash, the boss was not there to see it; he was away trying to strengthen the team. Rumours abounded that we were going to sign the Blackpool midfielder Tony Green, but the boss surprised everyone, including the players, when he announced he had signed the twenty-one-year-old Asa Hartford from West Brom for £155,000. We were introduced to Asa the next day when he trained with us and the first thing the boss did was to tell him about our code of conduct, which meant he had to get his hair cut. A pity the rule didn't apply to moustaches; Johnny Giles had one about that time and he looked absolutely ridiculous. He took a lot of stick off the lads for that. Before Asa had time to go to the hairdressers he had some devastating news. He had failed the medical because the scan had picked up a hole in his heart, which meant the deal was off. We were devastated for him and the boss was reduced to tears, although this diagnosis didn't stop Asa becoming a top player and a full international for many years. What it showed was that, even though we were never far from the top, the boss was always on the lookout for quality players to put the established players under pressure.

The following five games produced four wins and a defeat before the next big test, a visit to west London to face Chelsea. This was a fixture that was guaranteed to be both a bruising and violent encounter and a classic north/south confrontation, Yorkshire grit versus Kings Road chic. Old rivalries were once more renewed and the game was not for either the football purist or the faint-hearted. The match lived up to expectation and three times Osgood clattered into the Leeds goalkeeper, once from a Houseman cross and then from a corner by the same player. On the third occasion *The Times* reported how a 'frustrated Osgood once again fouled Sprake as he claimed a high ball and received a lecture from the referee'. The Leeds number one, not to be deterred by the physical confrontation, was once again in excellent form, making what the *Yorkshire Evening Post* described as 'a magnificent save from Hudson' to help secure another point in a scoreless draw. Peter Osgood recently recalled his confrontations with Leeds and Gary in particular:

> Gary Sprake was a very good goalkeeper but he will always be remembered for his few mistakes. However if he wasn't a top-class 'keeper Revie wouldn't have stuck by him for so long.

He concludes, somewhat tongue-in-cheek:

> He was loved at Chelsea because of his mistake in the 1970 cup final!

The next visitors to Elland Road on Boxing Day 1970 were fellow title contenders Derby County, who were left bewildered by the attacking genius of Leeds United, with the *Yorkshire Evening Post* reporting that:

> There were no weak links in a highly disciplined performance. Attacks that were started by Sprake flowed from one end to the other.

Derby did offer some resistance, with the paper also reporting that 'twice Sprake saved brilliantly and courageously at the feet of Hector.'

As they entered 1972 Leeds faced one of their most difficult games of any season, an away trip to in-form Liverpool, who boasted a proud record of thirty-four games unbeaten at home. Prior to the game it was announced that Paul Reaney had come off the transfer list. Reaney had requested a transfer after losing his first-team place to Paul Madeley the previous season, which had meant that he made only twenty appearances instead of the usual fifty-plus. For someone who has extensively criticised Gary Sprake over the last thirty years for his betrayal and lack of loyalty to the club it could be argued that loyalty to Leeds United was far from Reaney's own mind at the time. Don Revie was trying to build a large enough squad to continue the annual challenge for all the major honours, yet it could be argued that Reaney was thinking more of his own career than the wider interests of the club. It has become convenient to chastise Gary Sprake over the years but it appears that other former teammates have question marks surrounding their own commitment to the club, although these issues do seem to have faded with the passing of time. With Charlton injured, Madeley moved to centre half, which facilitated a return for Reaney. Goals by Clarke and Jones ensured Leeds kept up their fine record against Liverpool, and once again Gary played his part, with the *Yorkshire Evening Post* stating that

> Sprake inspired confidence when he leapt to tip a long-range effort from Hughes over the bar.

Gary's performances over the first half of the season had indeed been inspired. Leeds were sitting near the top of the table thanks, in no small measure, to his many match-winning performances. So consistent was he that his long-term understudy of seven years, David Harvey, was moved to put in for a transfer after the Anfield clash. As Don Revie told the *Yorkshire Evening Post* at the time:

> We at Leeds have reluctantly put David on the transfer list as there is little likelihood that he will replace Gary Sprake in the near future. David lacks Sprake's natural ability, but has compensated through remarkable dedication.

This contemporary view is a far cry from that presented by former colleagues such as Eddie Gray, who have constantly stated that Don Revie should have replaced Gary Sprake sooner than he did. Once again it seems that the facts of yesteryear have been forgotten by those that have their own agenda. Indeed, Gary's critics have argued over the years that Revie should have bought Gordon Banks when he became available in 1967, as well as replacing Gary with David Harvey long beforehe did. This is a view that not only criticises Gary, but also questions Revie's own managerial judgement. Such critics argue that the 1971/72 side that won the FA Cup was Leeds' best ever side. However, during that season it was Gary Sprake who dominated the Leeds 'keeper's jersey for the vast majority of that season, not Harvey. Gary played in thirty-five League games with the team suffering only four defeats, while Harvey played in the remaining seven games, of which Leeds also lost four. In the FA Cup Gary played in five ties of which Leeds won four and drew one. In fact, Revie went on record to say that although Harvey played in both the semi-final and final, if it were not for the displays of the Welshman in previous rounds Leeds would never have reached Wembley in the first place. Both 'keepers played in two League Cup ties. With Gary in goal, Leeds won one and drew one while with David Harvey in goal they won one and lost one. The Welsh 'keeper also played in three European games, including the play-off against Barcelona to determine who kept the Fairs Cup. Surely if that season's side is to be remembered as the greatest ever then Don Revie's consistency of selection throughout that season should be considered? Gary Sprake played forty-five games and was in a team that lost on only six occasions. Harvey played eleven games and was on the losing side on five occasions. Clear evidence, therefore, that Gary Sprake was very much part of the greatest Leeds United side ever, even though his critics seem to once again ignore these statistics.

February was going to be a defining month in Leeds' season in both cup and League. There was to be the visit of Manchester United in the League and, after comfortably disposing of Bristol Rovers in the previous round, the fourth round of the FA Cup. This brought yet another visit to Liverpool, over whom Leeds seemed to have had an Indian sign during those few seasons. After two League victories over The Reds, Don Revie and his players were in a confident mood of gaining a result as they prepared for the game, so much so that Revie cancelled a reserve team fixture at Elland Road against Bury on the same day to protect the pitch in case of a midweek replay. The gates were locked an hour before kick-off as Liverpool's biggest crowd of the season eagerly awaited what was going to be a fascinating encounter. Liverpool were on a high, having just recorded their highest win of the season, a stunning 4-1 demolition of Crystal Palace. Leeds' blanket defence nullified the home attack, with the *Yorkshire Evening Post* reporting that

> Sprake was competent under pressure, although only having to make one serious save from a Lloyd downward header.

The scoreless draw meant that Revie had predicted correctly, so it was back to Elland Road for an afternoon kick-off as the national miners' strike meant there were restrictions on the amount of electricity that could be used and there could be no floodlit games. The injured Charlton and Jones missed out for Leeds while Toshack was dropped for the Reds. The first half was a cut-and-thrust affair with Gary saving confidently from Keegan's swerving shot before Clarke gave the home side a goal advantage at the interval. The *Yorkshire Evening Post* reported that:

> After the break Sprake was quickly in action pulling down a cross, then making a fine save from Callaghan's rising shot. His finest moment came when he leapt across goal to keep out a header from Bobby Graham.

With Clarke adding the second the lights had gone out on Liverpool's cup aspirations as they went back across the Pennines after a 2–0 defeat. Gary remembers the positive rivalry with Shankly's team.

The most physical battles were against Chelsea, Arsenal and Sunderland; when we played Liverpool the focus was solely on football. We had some tremendous battles with them, and we had a profound respect for one another, but every game was always played in the right spirit. They had a great side: Ray Clemence was an excellent 'keeper; Tommy Smith was a real hard man but also a fine footballer; Tosh was a big old-fashioned type of centre forward, excellent in the air but also very good on the ground with, as he has since proved as a manager, excellent tactical acumen; Kevin Keegan was as quick as they come, although he wasn't as naturally gifted as Eddie Gray. He didn't have the same silky skills as Eddie. Many observers, myself included, thought that Eddie was a better player than George Best on his day but injuries always hampered him. After that cup tie the referee, Gordon Hill, clapped the teams off and after the game he came into both dressing rooms to thank us for two tremendous games. He said he had never done such a thing before but he felt it a privilege to be involved.

One keen observer of these conflicts between the two great sides was ex-Wolves and Birmingham City star Joe Gallagher who remembers that

> As a lad, between 1965 and 1971, I stood on the Kop and watched many games between Liverpool and Leeds and remember Gary producing many world-class performances. We both made our debuts together for Birmingham City and I remember looking up to Gary because he was a fantastic 'keeper and a fantastic guy.

After safely negotiating a passage into the next round of the cup it was back to the League, with the 'double' beginning to occupy the minds of those at Elland Road. The next game saw the visit of one-time League leaders Manchester United, who were in the midst of an appalling run, not having won for eight games. Leeds, with their new brand of attacking football, swept their opponents aside in a 5-1 win that ended the visitors' title aspirations and further narrowed the race for the First Division Trophy. If the supporters of Leeds United thought things couldn't get any better they were in for a shock, for in the next game they would produce a brand of football that has not been emulated since. The demolition of Southampton in a 7-0 thrashing is remembered by every football fan in the country regardless of which team they supported. Spectators will always recall the wonderful exhibition that humiliated the Saints that day. One spectator had a better view than those crammed into Elland Road and the millions watching the highlights on *Match of the Day* – Gary Sprake.

This was the finest display of football I and possibly everyone else will ever witness. We were magic. I saved an early speculative shot from Mick Channon and after that the lads put on a wonderful exhibition. I think this was the game where we dismissed that unfair assumption we were just a defensive side. To be honest, although people rave about the game and it is always repeated on classic Match of the Day, especially the sequence where Billy and Johnny play keep me up for what seems to be ages, I wasn't that excited. I had seen them both do it in training every day for years but this was the first time that the boss would let them get away with it in a match. Since we were promoted about eight years before we had built our success on solid foundations – the defence. As we progressed season by season we knew that if we scored one or two goals that would be enough to ensure us victory. There was never any need for an attacking strategy. When we became more successful we couldn't, or rather the boss wouldn't allow us to change our tactics or philosophy. There were many games, especially away from home, where we would set our stall out for a draw. When I did the pools on a Thursday night I nearly always put us down for an away draw and was usually proved right. Every year we were under intense pressure, but for some reason, in the 1971/72 season we were more relaxed and the boss trusted us a little bit more. For their part, however, the fans were as demanding as ever, we had to race into a lead and keep it before there was the slightest ripple of applause. People ask me what it was like to watch games like the Southampton one. In all honesty I was never a good spectator. My first love was playing the game and I thoroughly enjoyed that. However, as a spectator sport rugby was my game. At every opportunity I would go and watch Leeds rugby league

team with Big Jack and Billy. Even today I would watch rugby first, followed by
golf then football.

Leeds continued their winning ways with a 1-0 home win against
Coventry, where once again their goalkeeper was in superlative form,
with the *Yorkshire Evening Post* reporting that

> Sprake twice denied Coventry when saving a Carr wind-assisted shot and
> then denying a seventieth-minute equaliser from the same player with a
> brilliant tip over.

Leeds had taken another two points in a game that was a landmark
in the history of Leeds United Football Club; the 600th appearance
of Jack Charlton.

The statistics show that Billy Bremner and Jack Charlton jointly hold the record
for Leeds appearances with 772 each, but for me the title of 'Mr. Leeds United'
must go to Big Jack. The man was inspirational, a legend. Many have said he was
a one-man awkward squad, but that was because he believed so passionately in the
club. He wanted what was best for Leeds United and wasn't afraid to let everyone
know. He never suffered fools gladly and his gruffness perhaps alienated some people.
For me, he was a brilliant player, very much underrated. He could bring the ball out
of defence and play one-twos, or he could knock it into row Z. It was a privilege
to play with him and I would consider Jack to be one of the most sincere people I
have ever met, even though he owes me a fortune for all the babysitting I did for
him and his wife Pat! And of course he was the only player from the 'Legends'
team that made a success of management, perhaps because he was so single-minded,
but also because he was a great reader of the game. The only other player that had
success as a manager was Terry Cooper, when he turned Birmingham City from a
shambles into a well-run club that achieved relative success. It's amazing that the
side of the 1960s and 1970s was probably one of the best sides ever seen in English
football, but not many could make the transition from brilliant footballer to manager.
Billy, Eddie and Sniffer all had a go, without any success, although Johnny Giles
didn't do too badly at West Brom, albeit in a short space of time.

Sandwiched in between these displays of breathtaking football in the
League was the trip to Wales for the FA Cup tie with Cardiff City, which
was played on a pitch resembling nearby Barry Island with hundreds
of tons of sand laid to ensure the game would go ahead. While Leeds
were hammering Manchester United the Bluebirds had warmed up for

the game with a 1-0 win over Llanelli in a midweek Welsh Cup tie. Manager Jimmy Scoular named a full-strength side for the Welsh Cup tie just three days before a game against the team playing the best football in Britain at the time. West Bromwich Albion manager Bryan Robson put out a weakened team against champions Chelsea at the start of season 2005/06, arguing that his side were going to get beaten so it would be wiser to keep his better players for games they had a more realistic chance of winning. This was the philosophy of Scoular, who argued that beating Llanelli was a route into European football; beating Leeds was just a dream. He was proved right as Leeds comfortably moved into the next round courtesy of a 2-0 win. Spurs were their quarter-final opponents. Although Leeds conceded an unlucky goal against the run of play, this time there was to be no mistake as Clarke and Charlton put Leeds 2-1 in front before Sprake turned a Peters shot for a corner and then saved low down from Chivers. This is a game remembered for three things: Pat Jennings' brilliant goalkeeping display; the written account of Leeds' stunning play in the classic book by Hunter Davies *The Glory Game;* and the donning of named tracksuits, sock tags and that wave by the United team. Leeds were in the semi-final again but before that there was the title run-in on which to focus, and things were going well as they put together a four-match unbeaten run. With six games to go and a semi-final against Second Division Birmingham City to play, disaster struck for Gary as he badly injured his knee in the 3-1 win over Huddersfield Town.

When people read his teammates' memoirs of this period or people recount their memories of the glory years there is an assumption that Gary Sprake was dropped towards the end of the season, a victim of his below-par performances and a loss of confidence. The evidence dispels this argument as Gary's performances throughout two-thirds of the season were exemplary and some of the most consistent of his career. The *Yorkshire Evening Post* confirmed that rather than Don Revie dropping him Gary was indeed injured for the forthcoming game against Stoke City, reporting thus: .

> Sprake injury blow for Leeds. After two days of intensive treatment he failed a fitness test as his knee has remained swollen. David Harvey has been called up by Revie after only playing two league games all season. Sprake has remained in form and relatively free from injury.

Despite intensive treatment Gary was not fit enough to be selected for the semi-final, so Harvey kept his place. In the build-up to the game the *Yorkshire Evening Post* offered an analysis of the Blues and believed one of their strengths was the robust nature of centre forward Bob Latchford's play, citing that in previous games he had put both Huddersfield 'keepers Terry Poole and David Lawson out of action. This is a theme picked up on in Norman Hunter's autobiography *Biting Talk*. If anyone has been in the company of Hunter they will find a man who talks frankly and with some humour of his time within the game. Unfortunately he could never, with the best will in the world, be termed analytical and it could be argued he has been influenced over the years by the negative image portrayed of Gary. Hunter recalls that Gary was dropped because of the threat posed by Latchford. If he and many others were to recall the performances of Gary Sprake they would come swiftly to the conclusion that the 'keeper would never have shirked such a confrontation.

From a young age opponents had tried to intimidate me and I had to stand up for myself, so I was never afraid of a physical confrontation. In fact I used to thrive on it – ask Bobby Gould! The game was different back then, it was very physical and goalies were offered little protection. I played with Bob for Birmingham City and he was a superb footballer, but he was not a hard player. There were real hard players like Alex Dawson, Andy Lochhead, Jeff Astle, Wyn Davies and Osgood, although Big Jack and I always had the measure of him. There was also Joe Royle. He was hard but also fair and I had some right old battles with him over the years. So for people to offer that as a reason I missed the semi is a load of rubbish. I missed out because of injury and we won 3-0, David played well although he didn't have a great amount to do.

After three weeks out Gary made his comeback in the 4-0 thrashing of Blackburn Rovers in the Central League, which forced Revie into a dilemma for the penultimate game of the season against Chelsea and for the FA Cup final against Arsenal on the weekend, as both Sprake and Harvey were fit and playing well. As Revie told the *Yorkshire Evening Post*:

> The man selected in goal tonight is not necessarily the man that will keep goal on Saturday.

Unfortunately for Gary Sprake, Harvey got the nod and kept his place not only for the Chelsea match, but also for the journey to Wembley. After the game against Liverpool in an earlier round, Revie had gone on record stating that Gary had pulled off one of the best saves he had ever witnessed, a twenty-yard thunderbolt from Emlyn Hughes, and that he believed Gary Sprake was a better goalkeeper than the legendary Bert Trautmann, a teammate of Revie's from Manchester City. Sentiment played no part in Revie's decision, however, and Gary never regained his place even though he had consistently produced wonderful performances over a period of forty-four games that campaign. This was a decision that Gary still finds a little bemusing.

When I regained my fitness Revie told me I was still an excellent goalkeeper and I would have to fight to regain my first-team place. He said that David had played very well since he had taken over and he was going to keep him in for the final. He said it was great for the club to have two great 'keepers. I didn't make a fuss, or kick down his door to demand talks. I just accepted his decision, although I was bitterly disappointed. The other lads never mentioned it, we were all part of the family, team and squad and therefore we accepted the boss's decisions without question. After I lost my place some fans would shout my name if David made a mistake, but that was only natural, they also wanted what was best for Leeds United. The biggest issue with the cup final of 1972 was I just wish I had been told sooner that I wasn't playing as I was never informed until an hour or so before kick-off. I was playing really well that season and the boss could never really fully explain to me why I was dropped. All he said was that I was a great 'keeper but he wanted to make a change.

David Harvey played well on his Wembley debut, keeping a clean sheet as Leeds lifted the trophy for the first time, which meant that the double was still on two days later as Leeds would take on mid-table Wolves. Again there was disappointment for Gary as Harvey once more took his place between the sticks.

On a personal level I was disappointed, but that paled into insignificance as we lost 2-1 and never achieved the double. We almost overcame all the odds, the ban at the start of the season, injuries to key players and the perennial problem of fixture congestion. Every year we were victims of our own success. If there was one thing I could change it would be that Revie would have been more like Arsène Wenger and Alex Ferguson and played weaker teams in the perceived lesser competitions or in the earlier rounds of the cups. He wanted us to go as far as we could in all competitions, putting out as strong a team as possible in every game, which meant most of us played around sixty games a season. If he had done that my medal haul might have been much higher. In 1972 I feel the FA got their own back on the

boss for what they took to be his dismissive attitude towards them over the years.
If we had had another day or two to recover from the cup final there's no doubt
we would have won. Nearly every outfield player was suffering from some niggle
or twinge and twenty-four hours more would have made all the difference.

He had lost out on one of the biggest achievements in the game, but
Elland Road was almost full a week later as the team paraded the FA
Cup, and it seemed as if Gary Sprake was still held in high regard as
the *Yorkshire Evening Post* reported that, 'A young female fan rushed
up to Gary Sprake and planted a smacker on his lips'.

Revie, with perhaps some guilt, seems to have acknowledged the
Welsh goalkeeper's immense contribution to the season as on that day
he presented Gary with an additional cup final medal that the club had
had struck themselves. In what was to prove Gary's last full season there
was one more game to negotiate; the final of the West Riding Cup
against Halifax Town in front of 6,000 supporters at home. Leeds won 3-
2 with a Lorimer hat-trick, including one goal straight from the kick-off.
Gary's last cup final was an anti-climax, although he lined up with some
familiar faces as Revie sent out a strong side that lined up Sprake,
Reaney, O'Neil, Bremner, Saunders, Lorimer, Yorath, Bates, Galvin,
Mann and Jordan.

If the evidence available from the time is critically evaluated then
Gary Sprake, without a shadow of doubt, was one of the finest goalkeepers of his generation, comparing favourably with those before and
after his illustrious career with Leeds United. After Arsenal had lifted
the title in 2003/04 with an unprecedented season-long unbeaten run,
the former England manager Bobby Robson was asked by *The Sun*
newspaper who he thought ranked alongside such a talented team.
One of the sides he nominated was the Leeds side of the 1960s and
1970s: Sprake, Madeley, Cooper, Bremner, Charlton, Hunter, Giles,
Lorimer, Clarke, Jones and Gray – not a bad endorsement of Gary
Sprake's ability! What set Gary apart from the other goalkeepers at a
time when most top clubs had an international 'keeper on their books?
Gary had a bubbly personality and although shy in some situations
could also be a larger-than-life character. He was technically gifted
and had an acute awareness of the tactical side of the game. This was
evidenced by his ability to start swift attacking moves with quick
throw-outs or a precision kick. As a naturally gifted 'keeper he had
a belief and confidence in his own ability and had a strong physical
presence. One of Gary's prime assets was his speed of thought, allied

to balance and co-ordination that enabled him to react quickly to any situation. What set him apart from many of his contemporaries was his ability to command the whole of his eighteen-yard box, an art that is lost on today's 6ft 4in goalkeepers, who very rarely command the six-yard box. Gary dominated his box and, along with Pat Jennings, mastered the technique of the one-handed catch. Communication with fellow defenders is vital and over the years he developed an almost telepathic understanding with his back four. It could be argued, therefore, that Gary Sprake had all the physical attributes that only those at the very top of their profession possess, but there is more to the art of goalkeeping. There are also the psychological factors involved. He had many of the mental and psychological qualities that were needed to perform at the very pinnacle of his profession. The positive qualities were his bravery, decision-making ability and a dedication to training. One of the negative aspects, to which he would be the first to admit, was that he sometimes lacked concentration, probably because in some matches he would rarely touch the ball. Before every game he would be anxious, suffer stress and vomit. It could be argued, therefore, that these negative aspects might sometimes have manifested themselves in mistakes.

Looking back, I don't think I would have changed many things nor done anything differently. I enjoyed the experience immensely. My only real wish is that we could have had specialists to help us as goalkeepers as I was never coached once, nor had help with preparation, unlike today's 'keepers. If we had sports psychologists in those days I may not have made the five or six high-profile blunders but, inevitably, however well prepared you are mistakes still occur and over a period of 500-plus games I shouldn't be too highly critical of myself.

Being a professional footballer with Leeds United allowed me to experience a lifestyle I never believed possible. In the mid-1960s and 1970s I sometimes felt like I had pop-star status. I freely mixed with stars like Tom Jones, Rod Stewart and the Small Faces, Engelbert Humperdinck, Ronnie Hilton, Paul and Barry Ryan, Jimmy Saville and Peter Stringfellow. The legendary Dusty Springfield once asked me out on a date, but on the night we had arranged I stood her up. After that there were rumours that she was a lesbian – I don't know if it had anything to do with me letting her down! In the 1960s I judged many beauty contests, including Miss UK for a number of years, and sometimes I would give the winner a lift home afterwards and offer my personal congratulations!

As a team we had more than our fair share of laughs together and also a few scrapes. Sometimes we experienced both on the same night, like the time we went to Tiffany's nightclub. We'd had quite a few to drink and outside the club Billy decided to go for a pee, so he jumped over a wall. The only thing was that there was a drop of about ten feet on the other side and Billy bust his ankle and was out for a month or two.

When I signed in 1961 my wages were £2 a week and when I left in 1973 they had gone up to £200. I was also paid around £200 a year to wear Gola boots and I received a small amount from Typhoo for their famous football card series. It's really funny but somebody showed me ebay recently and these cards of me seem to be highly collectable, while at the time they were seen as a bit naff. In my last season I was also given a sponsored car by a local garage, but when I signed for Birmingham they took it back!

There were also some poignant moments as well, the injuries that meant I missed some big games and the occasional loss of form. We went through a rollercoaster of emotions together. One of the saddest things was the time we were waiting to start training and David Harvey arrived in a very emotional state. After we had comforted him, he told us tearfully that his pet monkey had committed suicide. The monkey had been watching David's wife doing the cooking over the years, putting on the gas and then lighting the oven. On that particular day, when both Mr and Mrs Harvey were out, the monkey turned the gas on but couldn't ignite it and had gassed himself. David was distraught and I was very sympathetic with him but some of the lads were more upset for his wife as they reckoned the monkey was better looking than Dave! All things considered the positives at the club far outweighed the negatives and I can only look back with fondness and a sense of pride at the things we achieved together. I had some disappointments and made a few mistakes but I wouldn't have wanted to have played anywhere else than at Leeds.'

EIGHT
PART-TIME INTERNATIONAL

On 19 November 2003 the authors attended the frustrating and ultimately demoralising Euro 2004 play-off second leg of Wales against Russia. It was, for all Welsh fans, yet another chapter in the sequence of near misses and failures that has all too often marred their fanatical support for their team. In conversation that week Gary Sprake, as a proud Welshman, was equally disappointed as he watched the game on national television in his Birmingham home. However one thing that he failed to mention was a ceremony at half-time when players who had represented Wales in over fifty games, including Leeds greats Brian Flynn and Terry Yorath, were awarded Gold Caps. It was only with some persuasion that Gary would talk about this aspect of his Wales career even though he won thirty-seven caps. When asked if he was disappointed that he had missed out on fifty caps he confessed:

Yes of course, but it was expected of you as a Leeds player that you put the club first, it was an unwritten law.

When this avenue of conversation was pursued he confirmed that during his Leeds career he probably missed nearly as many international games as he played and this was hardly ever through injury. In fact, research confirms that from his debut in November 1963 to his last game as a Leeds player in September eleven years later he missed twenty-six of a possible fifty-six caps. This is a fascinating statistic and clearly if he had been playing for another club he easily could have achieved the fifty appearances necessary to obtain the Golden Cap. Gary Sprake, chastised for his disloyalty in certain quarters, had constantly demonstrated his commitment to his club over his country. It begs the question as to why, if he cost Leeds so dearly with his performances over the years, was Don Revie so keen to keep him away from international duty, especially as Leeds had David Harvey in reserve? Gary did as he was asked by Revie despite these sacrifices being at the cost of his own international reputation in his homeland. With sixty-plus caps he could have become an even bigger legend of the Welsh game. The scenario once again demonstrates how another opportunity to gather the plaudits for his own career achievements had been lost.

Gary won his first international cap as the youngest ever Welsh goalkeeper in the Home International against Scotland on 20 November 1963. At that time the tournament was played throughout the year as opposed to the end of the season tournament it became in later years. He was one of four changes from the team that had lost 4-0 to England at Ninian Park a month earlier, when Dave Hollins of Newcastle United had kept goal. The *Western Mail* sports columnist argued on match day that

> The choice of young Gareth Sprake in goal is a popular one. He has played consistently well for Leeds United this season and did well in the Under-23 match at Ashton Gate, Bristol a week ago.

The newspaper's football reporter Dewi Lewis goes on to praise the young 'keeper's decisiveness when coming off his line, suggesting he was always 'after the ball in a flash'. Gary states:

Even though, as a youngster, I didn't really have ambitions to become a professional footballer, once I became one my desire was to represent Wales at the highest level. After my Leeds debut I played for the reserves until the 1962/63 season when I became a first-team regular. During this period Leeds visited the Principality twice and I had really good games at Ninian Park and the Vetch, keeping clean sheets on both occasions. The international set-up with Wales at the time was amateurish at best but this proved to work to my advantage, as the octogenarian selection committee didn't travel outside of Wales and therefore could only judge me on these two performances. Tommy Russell, the chairman of the FAW had seen the Cardiff game and the Welsh media were tipping me for my first cap. Although I wasn't picked for the full international against England in October 1963 I was selected for the Under-23 game at Ashton Gate, Bristol, with the proviso that if I played well I would make my full debut against Scotland the following week. Don Revie travelled down from Leeds to watch myself and Norman Hunter, who was playing for the opposition.

Joining the Leeds manager in the crowd were a large contingent of the Sprake family who had made the short journey across the border.

When Leeds had first secured my signature Don Revie had pledged that he would attend my debut at every level of the international pyramid. When I picked up the South Wales Evening Post *the following night at my parents he had told the paper that 'Gary looked understandably nervous as he lined up for the anthems, but he visibly relaxed as the game started. The game itself was played in atrocious conditions, the ball was very wet and muddy but he only mishandled once. He was especially good in the air, also bravely diving at opponents' feet on several occasions. Judging by this performance Gary has a great chance of playing against Scotland next week at Hampden.' In fact the telegram informing me that I had been selected arrived at Elland Road the following day and the club forwarded it to my parents' home in Winch Wen. I remember my brother Glyn taking me to celebrate in the Llansamlet Workingmen's club. I only had half a Hancock's beer but Glyn drunk my share as well, as it appeared the whole area was celebrating my success.*

As for the Scotland game itself, Gary remembers it vividly:

I travelled up alone the day before the match and was met by manager Jimmy Murphy at Glasgow station with the rest of the team. We then travelled on to Troon, about fifty miles away, where I had an early night and slept pretty well. The next day we left after lunch, arriving at the ground about two hours before kick-off after making our way through the throng of tartan-clad Scottish fans. I met Don Revie and Jack Pickard in the ground and entered the dressing room to find dozens of good luck messages awaiting me. Soon it was time to go out and face the famous Hampden roar. It was a full house and I felt very nervous.

This was not unusual for Gary, as fellow Welsh 'keeper Tony Millington points out Gary was worked up before every game and was often violently sick.

Once the game started, however, I did settle more quickly and I remember an early save from Jim Baxter's long-range effort. Even though they were extremely passionate the crowd were also very fair, warmly applauding any contributions I made. Unfortunately Denis Law and John White put good shots past me and even though my friend Barrie Jones from back home in Swansea pulled one back my debut had ended in defeat.

The performance on his international debut had matched the pre-match hype as he had an excellent game, being responsible for many fine saves, with the *Western Mail* stating that 'Sprake now looks as if he

is in the team to stay.' As the Hampden roar egged on the Scots, Gary
was not fazed as he made a series of excellent saves from Baxter, Law
and Mackay. As he looks back fondly on his debut he recalls:

*It was a great experience to win my first full cap with Wales, even though we
lost 2-1, especially being in the same team as such greats as Terry Hennessey,
Mike England, Cliff Jones, Ivor Allchurch and, of course, ex-teammate and
fellow Swan, the legendary John Charles.*

His second cap followed in the next international at home against
Northern Ireland in a 3-2 defeat. Wales' poor performance in dreadful
conditions was matched by an indifferent performance by Gary himself,
who was partially responsible for the opening Northern Ireland goal
when he failed to clear his box with a poor punch that resulted in a
McLoughlin goal. Wales finished bottom of the Home International table
without a win. It was a story of disappointing failure, a scenario he was to
become accustomed to at international level over the next eleven years.
This was in stark contrast to his experiences at club level. While Wales
continued to flounder Don Revie's Leeds United were to dominate the
British and European stage over the same period. Although kept far busier
in weaker teams at international level, the mistakes of his second cap were
rarely repeated as Gary realised that less was expected of him, which
contrasted markedly with the increasingly high-profile club games and
subsequent infamous errors at Leeds. Another thing that he also quickly
noticed was the sheer amateurishness of the Wales set-up compared to the
ultra professionalism he experienced at Leeds. This is a point reiterated in
John Toshack's autobiography *Tosh*, which comments that

> The whole set-up was a bit of a shambles in those days and some of the
> players with more fashionable clubs were not too concerned about turning
> up for the less glamorous games.

He also makes the interesting comment:

> I know for a fact that one particular player was paid the match fee by his
> club on more than one occasion and stayed away, feigning injury.

Gary's third and fourth caps came close together against Scotland (3-2)
and Denmark (0-1) in October 1964. The 1-0 defeat against the then
all-amateur Danish side would have been even more embarrassing,

apart from a string of fine saves from the Leeds goalkeeper, including an exceptional close-range stop from the Danish striker Madsen. Although he travelled to the next Wales gathering, against England, he withdrew after advice from the Leeds physio despite having played the full game carrying the alleged injury the previous Saturday. This was to be the first occasion of what was to become a regular experience of him being declared unfit at the last moment by the club. The *Western Mail* hoped at the time that Gary would be fit for the game the next day. The Leeds club already knew differently. In fact, after the 2–0 World Cup qualifying defeat against Greece in Athens, he missed the next four Wales games despite playing nearly every game for Leeds in the same period. Gary hardly ever played friendlies for Wales and Don Revie invented the 'friendly international withdrawal' thirty years before Alex Ferguson and Ryan Giggs became the source of much controversy among the Welsh media and supporters for exactly the same reason. So exactly why was Revie so insistent that he withdraw from these internationals? As Gary explains:

The reason I didn't play more international games was that Don Revie told me that Leeds needed me more than Wales and that the travelling and possibility of injury were far too great. He was very persistent, telling me that I was invaluable to the club and that he couldn't risk me with important games coming up. He would pay me the £50 international match fee and then phone the Welsh FA after the League match to tell them that I was injured, although I always recovered in time for the next Leeds game.

In fact, in his autobiography Norman Hunter confirms that Revie also offered him the match fee not to attend England games. Hunter stated that he declined Revie's proposal but he does suggest that several of his Scottish international colleagues at Leeds did take up their manager's offer.

Over the next five years, from November 1964 to April 1969, as Leeds United's rise to prominence as a domestic and European force became apparent, Gary played in only seven of the next twenty-three possible internationals. Despite having established himself as one of the top goalkeepers in the country he missed over three-quarters of Wales' games. This would be understandable if there was great competition such as that experienced by Clemence, Shilton, Corrigan et al for the England goalkeeping shirt in the 1970s. However, his understudy was Tony Millington, who plied his trade in the lower divisions with Peterborough United and then Swansea Town. Millington admits himself that most of his caps came from Don Revie withdrawing Gary, and states that:

Thanks to Don Revie I played three times at Wembley. He believed that it would be a hard game and wouldn't risk Gary playing. It was the same if it was a difficult away trip, like the time we spent hours going through Checkpoint Charlie before playing East Germany in Dresden.

Although experiencing niggling injuries like any other player Sprake played nearly every game for his club in the same period. Don Revie would pull Gary aside and encourage him persuasively not to play and as he wanted to please the boss and do the best for his new family he did what was required of him. This was to be the story of Gary Sprake's Wales career over the next ten years.

The dream of any proud Welshman is to represent his country at international level, especially against bitter rivals England, and Gary's first opportunity came at Cardiff on 2 October 1965. Wales were regarded as massive underdogs as the star-studded England team looked forward to an easy warm-up match for the following summer's World Cup finals. They arrived in Cardiff with Gary's Leeds teammates Jack Charlton, Alan Peacock and Norman Hunter all declaring themselves fit after the Fairs Cup game against Torino the preceding Wednesday, and both Peacock and Charlton made the starting line-up for England. In a memorable match in front of 29,000 spectators England were very lucky to escape with a goal-less draw. The *Western Mail* the following Monday praised the Welsh team, especially 'keeper Sprake who 'showed once more that he must remain the first choice as goalkeeper, for his play in the air in greasy going was a model of efficiency'. The paper concludes that England obtained a draw but Wales gained the honours. Gary remembers the game for a different reason, involving colleague and friend Jack Charlton who commented in his autobiography on how standing in front of the Welsh 'keeper would drive him mad.

When we played together at Leeds Jack used to stand in front of the opposing 'keeper at corners and cause massive problems, which resulted in several vital Leeds goals. I told him if he ever did that to me in a match I was playing against him I would do something about it and he just laughed and said 'we'll see'. During the game against England they got an early corner and predictably Big Jack stood right in front of me to try to flick on the cross. As the corner was swung over both Jack and myself went for the ball, which I punched away but followed through and caught him on the nose, which started to bleed heavily. Jack wasn't very pleased about this and called me a Welsh bastard, but I told him that he had been warned not to try it on with me. After the game we had a drink in the players' bar and it was all forgotten. I had a lot of respect for Jack Charlton and I still do.

Wales followed this impressive result against England with a famous 2-1 victory over the crack Soviet team at Ninian Park. Yet again Wales had shown themselves capable of one-off achievements of the greatest heights, but unfortunately it was another glimpse of what could have been as Wales were already out of the picture for qualification for the 1966 World Cup. Not only did Gary have the disappointment of missing out on World Cup qualification but he also missed the fantastic opportunity to tour South America with the Welsh squad, which would include two games against World Champions Brazil. This was because Leeds were once again competing on all fronts, having reached the semi-finals of the Fairs Cup, ultimately to miss out again over two legs to the Spanish side Real Zaragoza. Despite a fantastic personal performance Gary had missed out on a European final and the chance to pit his skills against the Brazilians and the great Pelé himself.

I missed the South America trip because of the Fairs Cup semi-final. At the time you just accepted the fact that Leeds were successful and that this took priority. In hindsight, when I really think about it I would have loved the experience of touring South America and playing against the Brazilians and of course Pelé. However, this scenario repeated itself every year as Leeds competed for every trophy and we played more games than anyone else, so summer tours with Wales were never an option.

As well as the three South American internationals he also missed two of the next three games against England and Northern Ireland, playing only in the 1-1 draw with Scotland on 27 October 1966. Despite a controversial late equaliser from Denis Law, which had more than a suggestion of handball, Gary could again be satisfied with another career-enhancing performance. Dewi Lewis of the *Western Mail* heaped praise upon him, arguing he had a great match, writing:

> Some of his saves brought gasps of admiration from the crowd and his brilliant anticipation got Wales out of trouble times without number.

The paper argued that he was clearly the natural successor to one-time neighbour Jack Kelsey in the Welsh goal. However, his chances of further enhancing this burgeoning reputation were partly lost as he missed six of the next nine internationals. His reputation in Wales had become so significant that the sports section of the national daily Welsh newspaper reported that when Sprake played Wales' chances of avoiding defeat increased markedly. Such praise seems to fly directly in the face of the image that has been created surrounding Gary's alleged liability as goalkeeper, which has been repeated and regurgitated so often since his retirement in 1975. In his next international, also against Scotland, on 22 November 1967, Gary maintained his high standards although Wales again proved themselves to be vulnerable in a 3-2 defeat in Glasgow, the highlight being a brilliant full-length save from Lennox that kept Wales in the game.

In March 1969 Gary broke one of the habits of his Wales career by making a rare friendly appearance against 1966 World Cup runners-up West Germany, despite having missed the previous three games. In fact, he didn't turn out once for his country in 1968 at a time when at club level Leeds were setting record after record on their way to winning their first championship during the 1968/69 season and both the League Cup and Inter City Fairs Cup of 1968. Wales turned up at Frankfurt's Wald stadium with only thirteen fit players, including reserve goalkeeper Tony Millington, and were ripe for a footballing lesson from the great West German side who were preparing themselves for their next World Cup qualifier against Scotland in April. However, once again Wales demonstrated their ability to occasionally shock the world's greats as the team took a deserved one-goal lead into half-time thanks to Cardiff City's Barrie Jones. The second half was a different story as Gary made a series of outstanding saves and brilliantly marshalled his all-Second Division defence. It was a great travesty that West Germany scored a controversial equaliser with the last kick of the game even though the ball had already gone well out of play. Despite vigorous Welsh protests led by Gary himself, Italian referee C. Lobello waved away protests. It was not the first or last time that disgraceful decisions would be made against British teams by European officials, as his Leeds colleagues could bitterly testify Gary was still fuming after the game when he told reporter Clive Phillips:

It was never a goal! The wind definitely swerved the vital cross from the right at least a yard over the line before it came back for Muller to score. It was disgraceful. I asked the linesman to go over to the referee and tell him but he wouldn't budge.

Despite this outstanding Man-of-the-Match performance he didn't play in the next game, a World Cup qualifier against the DDR, withdrawing through a shoulder injury obtained against Arsenal in a vital 2-1 win the previous Saturday. Once again Gary recovered to turn out for Leeds in the 2-0 win over Leicester the following weekend.

In May 1969 the Home International championship was to be played over a week from 3-10 May. With the League title safely in the bag and no European or domestic cup finals to worry about, Don Revie relaxed and allowed his players to fully participate fully in these fixtures. Gary was allowed the luxury of earning three caps in a week, having taken eighteen months to earn his previous three. On the first Saturday a depleted Wales team was hammered 5-3 by Scotland, and perhaps the goalkeeper's mind was elsewhere as he had a terrible game, probably his worst for Wales, being directly to blame for two of the Scottish goals. The lack of concentration and the poor performance is partly explained by John Toshack's observation in his autobiography that

> We conceded five, owing to the fact that Gary Sprake, our goalkeeper, had been up all night in Leeds at a dinner to celebrate their League Championship win.

It wasn't to be the first or last time that Gary had neglected the pre-match Wales preparations for the opportunity to party late into the night. However, the Welsh media seemed unwilling to dwell on Gary's aberrations too much, focusing on what they perceived to be the promising attacking roles of John Toshack and the two Davieses, Ron and Wyn. The regional media in Wales seemed to take a more rounded viewpoint that he was too much of an asset to the team to focus on one poor performance in an end-of-season match. This was in stark contrast to the record of the national media, who delighted in every mistake that both he and Leeds made. In fact, the *Western Mail* led their back page the following Thursday with the headline 'Sparkling Sprake' as the Wales number one was judged to be back to his best in a narrow 2-1 defeat to England at Wembley, and also played well in a disappointing 0-0 draw three days later against Northern Ireland in Belfast. Unfortunately, once again, Wales finished a distant fourth and bottom of the Home International championship table.

Throughout his international career the Welsh press were very complimentary of Gary and the relationship was always very positive, unlike those he experienced with the national press.

I was always very friendly with the Welsh media and happily gave interviews whenever they asked me. I built up a good relationship with them and never refused to answer their questions about Wales and Leeds and tended to be very honest about issues. In the 1960s and 1970s the Welsh players had a good relationship with the press, travelling away together and sharing a drink after the game. In this respect it was very different to today. Most importantly I believe that the Welsh media wanted to celebrate my success in playing for the best team in the country as it reflected positively on my homeland. Welsh people tend to celebrate success and fame and see it reflecting positively on their nation, while the national press in London generally hated Leeds and took every opportunity to criticise us, and I came in for a fair amount myself.

Gary's relationship with the Welsh fans was and still is fantastic. In September 2005 he attended the Wales *v.* England World Cup qualifier and throughout the day hundreds of fans still recognised him and wanted to shake his hand, have a few words or take a photo. Throughout the day not one person made a negative comment and the most common word used all day in addressing him was 'legend', a sharp contrast, it seems, with his perceived image in some of the footballing press.

In July 1969 an unusual international match took place as Wales took on the Rest of the United Kingdom as part of the Prince of Wales' Investiture celebrations. The strong UK squad included six Englishmen, six Scots and three Irishmen, including the legendary George Best. Leeds colleagues Terry Cooper, Billy Bremner and Jack Charlton all played. In a low-key pre-season atmosphere Wales lost 1-0, the goal being scored by Manchester City's Francis Lee. This wasn't the only time Gary was to compete internationally against his club colleagues.

At Leeds I played against Norman Hunter, Paul Madeley, Jack Charlton, Allan Clarke and Terry Cooper. It was a bit strange at first but once the banter had worn off we all wanted to win and I definitely didn't want any of them to score against me. One goal I remember vividly is Norman Hunter's strike at Wembley in the World Cup qualifier in 1973. It was an amazing shot from outside the box and the best goal he ever scored. Unfortunately the media tends to focus on his mistake against Poland but if it wasn't for his goal against us we would have put them out anyway. I also played against Peter Lorimer and Billy Bremner. Lorimer also scored a great goal against me and Lash was one of the hardest and best strikers of a football I have ever seen. Billy was simply world class, a very skilful player and very hard. I enjoyed playing against them. It inspired me and I generally did very well.

What was more important was the autumn campaign in which Wales faced East Germany and Italy for a place in the 1970 World Cup finals in Mexico. Once again Wales failed to qualify for a major tournament as they suffered an embarrassing 3-1 home defeat against the East Germans and a 4-1 defeat away to the Italians in Rome. Wales finished bottom of their qualifying group as Gary's chance of appearing on a major international stage seemed as distant as ever. Much like Wales greats Mark Hughes, Ian Rush and Ryan Giggs, Gary found that domestic and European success at club level was frustratingly far harder to replicate with Wales at international level. This was especially apparent with a squad of only fourteen or fifteen players, most of whom played outside the old First Division. In fact the Welsh team that played in Rome had a squad of fifteen including four players from club reserve teams and Fourth Division Wrexham's Gareth Davies, while the star-studded Italians had been in a training camp for ten days with a full squad of twenty-two, being pampered like kings. It's hardly surprising that Gary and some other colleagues found it increasingly difficult to take seriously the Welsh set-up, and on many occasions used the international scene as an excuse to visit foreign nightclubs and party until late.

A couple of nights before the game most of the players, including myself, went out in Rome. This was completely against the management's rules as we were not supposed to drink within forty-eight hours of the game itself. When we arrived back at the team hotel very late and a little worse for wear the manager, Dave Bowen, was waiting for us in the reception. He told us that we should all be sent home but as he didn't have enough players to make up the squad we were very lucky. Poor old Dave, it was a very difficult job for him as on many occasions we could only put out the bare eleven and under those circumstances a disciplinary management style was impossible. It wasn't only on away trips I used to enjoy the trappings of being a footballer. When we played in Cardiff I was friendly with a particular young lady and used to book her into the same hotel as the players, either in Cardiff or Porthcawl. I don't know about the other players, but I couldn't honestly say that my concentration was always on the international itself.

In the Italy match itself the Welsh team included two defenders from club reserves, Gary's own club colleague Terry Yorath and Cardiff City's Steve Derett, who had only played once for his side that season. It is no wonder that the Italian team, made up of the superstars of Serie A, routed Wales. Despite his late-night antics Gary was again outstanding, as was Derett, who made a series of fine last-gasp tackles to keep the score down to 4-1. The outstanding player for Italy that day was Italian Footballer of the Year Luigi Riva of Cagliari, who was touted in the Italian press as being the subject of a £860,000 bid from Inter Milan. The entire Welsh squad at that time would not have been worth that amount in total.

By late April 1970, while his international colleagues were achieving credible draws against England and Scotland, Gary was participating in a series of crucial club games as Leeds faced Chelsea and Celtic in the FA Cup final and European Cup semi-final. In what was probably the most disappointing few weeks of his career Gary made an infamous mistake in the cup final against Chelsea and this was then followed by a nasty injury in the semi-final first leg against Celtic. What had promised to be a momentous treble-chasing season had ultimately ended in bitter disappointment both for himself personally and for Leeds United as a club. The following domestic season (for differing reasons) was also a disappointing one for Leeds as, by the end of the season, they were out of contention for domestic honours. Therefore he was once again freed to represent Wales in what had become the annual end-of-season Home International Championships. Wales achieved goal-less draws against Scotland and a notable 0-0 draw at Wembley, but disappointed in a 1-0 defeat to Northern Ireland that, as manager Dave Bowen states, could have been a lot worse:

> It was fortunate for Wales that goalkeeper Sprake was once again in out-standing form.

Gary recalls:

George Best was a great player and he was idolised in Belfast and would always play up to the crowd at Windsor Park. During the first half George kept challenging my kick outs and threatened to kick the ball out of my hand, as he had famously done against Gordon Banks. As the half wore on he continued to do it and so finally, when I threw the ball up from my hands to kick it away, he tried to head it and as I cleared the ball I followed through and kicked him very hard in the privates, and he immediately collapsed in a heap. The referee missed it but the crowd knew exactly what I had done and gave me a real torrid time with a hail of coins and bottles for the remainder of the game. However, at the end of the game George was great and he shook my hand and laughed about it. In fact, before the game I had made my own travel arrangements to get back to Leeds and George and Wyn Davies asked if they could scrounge a lift back on the flight home to Manchester in a specially chartered plane.

1. Gary lines up for his first team photo with village side Winch Wen. Brother Dennis starts the family's goalkeeping dynasty.

2. Back to the unglamorous duties on the ground staff after Gary's dramatic first-team debut, when he became Leeds' youngest player at sixteen.

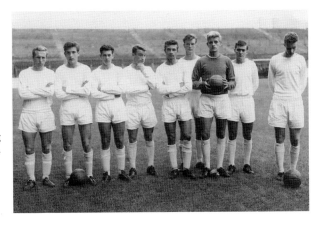

3. Gary in the Leeds second string that included soon-to-be-household names Greenhoff, Hunter, Reaney and Cooper.

4. Clowning around with best friend Paul Reaney before the Liverpool cup final.

5. Gary and Don Weston parade the West Riding Cup and Second Division championship trophy in 1964.

6. Gary demonstrating his skills, in a Man of the Match performance, against Liverpool in the 1965 FA Cup final.

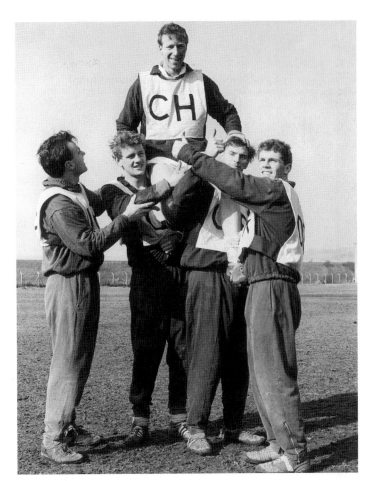

7. Gary holds aloft the player he regards as 'Mr Leeds United', Jack Charlton.

8. Gary receives his first Welsh cap from Leeds chairman Harry Reynolds, with a proud Don Revie looking on.

9. 'In safe hands!' Gary and Kathy O'Boyle at their wedding.

10. A pop-star lifestyle: one of the many beauty contests he was asked to judge.

11. 'You have to be mad to be a keeper!' Another physical battle with arch-rivals Chelsea.

12. 'United we stand!' Leeds' famous defence: Sprake, Reaney, Hunter (hidden on floor), Charlton and Cooper.

13. Gary in the classic style that won so many admirers.

14. Being introduced to Lord Montgomery in Gary's first season in the First Division.

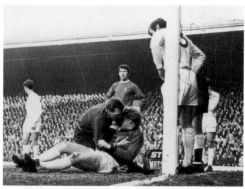

15. Suffering a knock after bravely defying Liverpool at Anfield.

16. Les Cocker once again in action to treat the injured 'keeper.

17. Leeds' smart-est-dressed player, Gary leads Leeds into another European adventure.

18. The trademark style copied by other 'keepers.

19. 'You, like the rest of your team-mates, are a pain in the neck, Mr Sprake.'

20. Leeds' first major trophy, the 1968 League Cup, held aloft by Billy Bremner as Gary receives his tankard from the royal guest.

21. Gary keeps an important clean sheet to help realise the dream.

22. 'All for one, one for all.' Gary, Cooper and Hunter adopt the famous siege mentality against Ure of Arsenal.

23. A confident Gary takes Leeds past Rangers in the Inter-Cities Fairs Cup.

24. Gary climbs high above Alex Ferguson in the European tie against Rangers. Not many have been able to say that since!

25. 'Don't tell the Wales man-ager!' Gary and Terry Yorath with Cardiff RFC's John Price, slightly the worse for wear, when they should have reported to the team's hotel six hours earlier.

26. One for the cameramen!

27. A pensive Gary awaits the start of the 1970 FA Cup final.

28. Celebrating the second Inter-Cities trophy after beating Juventus.

29. Gary denies he deliberately tried to injure an opponent. Seconds later Chelsea forward Boyle is carried off the pitch.

30. Gary relaxing after another Home International Championship with Ron Davies, Terry Hennessey and partners.

31. 'Where's Big Jack?' Leeds' team of full internationals pose for the camera without Jack Charlton, who forgot his kit.

32. In happier times. Gary and Norman Hunter share a joke in the Wales *v.* England clash at Ninian Park.

33. Old rivalries are forgotten as Gary and Kathy enjoy a summer break in Majorca with Liverpool's John Toshack and Emlyn Hughes and their wives.

34. Gary and daughter Julia at home in Leeds.

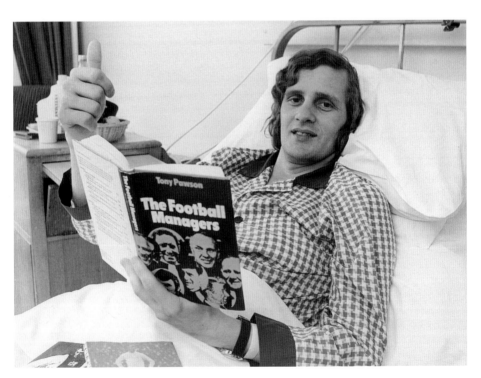

35. Gary recovers in a Birmingham hospital after life-saving surgery.

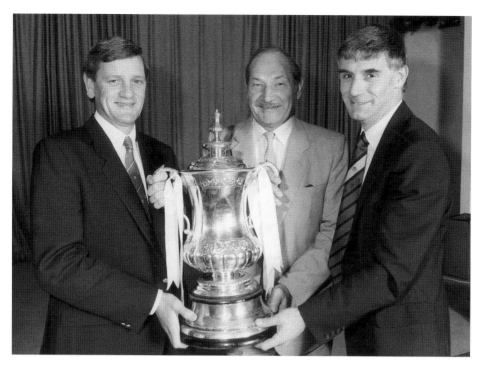

36. Gary belatedly holds the FA Cup with Birmingham City legend Gil Merrick and Ipswich Town's Roger Osborne.

37. *Above left:* Gary and partner Jackie relaxing in their West Midlands home.

38. *Above right:* Daughter Julia displays the Sprake pose.

39. Gary's greatest ever moment, holding aloft the Football League championship trophy with Billy Bremner.

*The only thing was it was not only George who enjoyed a drink; by the time we
touched down we were all pissed. If you look at videos of games in the 1960s and
1970s we all used to laugh and joke together coming off at half and full-time, despite
the importance of the occasion. We may have kicked lumps out of each other in the
Football League and in internationals, but usually, once the game was over, we were
the best of friends. George, despite being probably the best player in the world, was
a very down-to-earth lad, the only thing was he was easily led; sometimes even the
women would try to get him drunk. And George being George never refused the
offer of a drink. The problem was that the plane was allocated its slot for take-off
shortly after full-time, so I arranged for Tony Millington, the reserve 'keeper, to keep
an eye on the time. If there was to be time added on Tony would give the signal
and I would fake injury, have a quick shower and disappear. Luckily for Wyn and
George the game finished on time, otherwise I would have left them there!*

Although he was to withdraw, along with teammate Terry Yorath, from
the following week's European qualifier against Finland in Helsinki due
to club commitments, the *Western Mail* at the time reflects upon an
interesting story. Though Wales travelled to Helsinki with twenty-five
people only fifteen were actually players and the Finnish media sarcasti-
cally asked embarrassed Wales manager Bowen if he had brought along
the reserve team as well. Of the ten officials that travelled only two were
actually from the selection committee as the others enjoyed an early
summer vacation. This was the story of Welsh football during Gary's
twelve-year international career as officials were prioritised and players
received second-class treatment. Probably the most famous example of
this was when the late Gil Reece was asked to give up his seat and had to
leave the plane bound for a World Cup qualifier against East Germany in
Dresden for an official to travel. It would be unthinkable now that such an
embarrassing episode could occur, such has been the change in the profile
and power of professional footballers since Gary Sprake's heyday.

In October 1971, during a 3-0 win over Finland, for a change it was
Gary who had nothing to do as the Finnish goalkeeper Lars Nasman
withheld wave after wave of Welsh attacks. The Wales number one was
to come off at half-time due to an alleged knee injury, having only
touched the ball once during the whole first half. However, understudy Tony Millington remembers the incident very well:

We were playing Finland at the Vetch and were winning easily. It was a bitterly cold night and the wind and rain were driving over the old 'Double
Decker' stand. Gary kept trying to attract my attention and kept shouting

'It's too fucking cold.' I ignored him as I was grateful to be sat on the bench in those conditions. Finally he went down clutching his knee. The trainer went on to the pitch and Gary somehow convinced him he couldn't possibly play on. As he shook my hand he winked at me and said he would see me in the bar later. The bastard was on his third or fourth pint before I had thawed out. It was obvious that he didn't fancy standing out in the cold and rain for another half, especially as we were winning so easily.

At the end of the following season in May 1972 Gary again represented Wales in all three of the Home International Championship games, having missed the previous European qualifiers against Czechoslovakia and Romania. For the first time in his Wales career the Leeds 'keeper seemed at a crossroads, having been dropped two weeks previously for the FA Cup final, and his future club and even country situation was coming under severe scrutiny. However, only two weeks after the bitter personal disappointment of the FA Cup final Gary was more optimistic about his fortunes as he admitted to *Western Mail* reporter Clive Phillips at the time.

> I missed several First Division matches last month because of damaged knee ligaments and David Harvey took over. I was worried by regular newspaper reports saying that Peter Shilton was to sign for Leeds. I still had two years to go on my previous contract but decided to have a talk to the manager and to my delight I was offered a six-year contract – my biggest with the club – with an option after three years. I am really thrilled as it means I am almost certain to remain a Leeds player until I am thirty-two.

Although his personal fortunes seemed to be looking up, the Wales team progressed through another dismal campaign without a win, losing 3-0 to England and 1-0 to Scotland (with Leeds colleague Peter Lorimer scoring the winner) and obtaining the annual drab 0-0 result against Northern Ireland. In recent years there has been a call, especially from the Welsh and Northern Irish, for a return to some form of British Championship.

I thought the Championship was much better when it was played over the whole season as players were more enthusiastic and less tired after a long, hard season with their clubs. I am sure that a Home International Championship spread over the season would be very more beneficial to the home nations and of far more interest to the fans than some of the meaningless and farcical friendlies we have witnessed over the last few years. When they switched them to the end of the season they lost their appeal, especially to me, as Leeds had already played sixty-plus games every year. Although I missed many of these games due to being withdrawn or Leeds being involved in important games, when I did play I was desperate to do well. The Welsh team was always the underdog but despite some poor results we always gave our best as we only had a very small squad. I am a fiercely passionate Welshman and I always will be very proud that I represented my country. The only downside of playing for Wales was that bloody badge. It looked as though it came off a dodgy, second-hand blazer. And because it was so big when it rained my body would be covered in red dye and it would take forever to shower it off.

It is ironic that the draw for the qualifying groups for the 2006 World Cup in Germany once again pitted Wales with England and Poland, a repeat of the grouping the last time the World Cup took place in West Germany in 1974. The two crunch grudge matches against England were to take place at Cardiff and then Wembley in November 1972 and January 1973. In the first game at Ninian Park Wales were outclassed, although the 1–0 defeat could have been worse as the *Western Mail* stated:

> Only careless finishing and fine goalkeeping by Gary Sprake prevented England from winning far more convincingly.

England debutant Ray Clemence had barely a touch of the ball, while the Wales 'keeper was excellent, as the paper continues:

> Sprake once again was outstanding for Wales. A handful of saves from Bell in the first half and Hunter, Marsh and Chivers in the second half were of the highest international quality.

In the return leg at Wembley on 24 January he was equally outstanding in a 1–1 draw, with the England goal a wonder strike from clubmate Norman Hunter. Over the two legs Gary had been world class, yet historically the media has been fixated on the performance of Polish goalkeeper Tomaszewski in another 1–1 draw. In the same vein Norman Hunter's mistake against Poland is highlighted yet there is no mention of the wonder goal scored that saved England against Wales. Once again this highlights a selective memory and an emphasis on a certain version of events that some in the media want to have accepted as the truth. This view is endorsed by former Wales star and current BBC pundit Leighton James:

There are three perceptions of Gary Sprake; the one created by ex-teammates with an axe to grind, the one portrayed by the media that in turn influences people, but most importantly the opinion of Gary's contemporaries and those who played with or against him. For me and the rest of his Wales colleagues Gary Sprake was always regarded as a world-class goalkeeper. On his day, he was probably the best. There was a belief in the Wales camp that the more involved he was in the game, the better he became. With Leeds, I think his mistakes were down to loss of concentration rather than lack of ability. With Wales he didn't have the luxury of playing behind such a great defence, so he had to show what he could do and he did it really well! The one game that springs to mind is England at Wembley, that night he played the opposition on his own.

The two World Cup qualifiers against Poland in 1973 were equally memorable; while a clean sheet in the 2-0 home victory was significant, it was the away leg that was infamous for a variety of reasons. The preparations for the game itself were tortuous as the nineteen-hour trip included a twice-delayed flight from London and a nightmare flight within Poland itself. This was exacerbated by a fatal accident that involved the team in a huge and very long traffic jam.

We all reported to the hotel near Heathrow to catch the three-hour flight to Poland but as we boarded the plane petrol began to leak from the wings and BEA had to send for a replacement, which took several hours. As we approached Warsaw Airport the pilot stated that the conditions were very foggy and he would try to land anyway but, after two aborted attempts, we were diverted to Krakow instead. After landing we took a coach to Katowice but on route there was a fatal accident and the bus was delayed for hours. It was hardly ideal preparation for a vital qualifying game but this was often the case when you ventured to play games behind the Iron Curtain in those days. I am not saying it was all deliberate but sometimes it seemed far too much of a coincidence not to have been staged.

Leighton James also vividly remembers what he calls that 'nightmare game'.

I remember we landed on the grass by the side of the runway – a few of the lads including Gary Sprake were scared senseless. The Poles insisted on the game being played in Katowice because they wanted to make things difficult for us; the district was industrial, it was dominated by mining.

The game itself was equally controversial and memorable only 'for the fact that there were more accurate punches and deliberate kicks than passes' as Wales lost 3-0 and Trevor Hockey was sent off. It was evident that Swedish referee Ove Dahlberg had totally lost control in the face of a vociferous and partisan home crowd of 120,000 and the intimidating tactics of the home team at the Slaski Stadium, a typical Eastern Bloc arena surrounded by forests of tower blocks that pierced the leaden autumn skies. Leighton James recalls in the match programme for the 2004 World Cup qualifier against Poland in Cardiff:

> Poland were the reigning Olympic Champions, they were an excellent team. But I always felt the match officials weren't kind to us and on the night they seemed petrified of the hostile fans. Poland butchered our players; they certainly remembered Trevor Hockey's uncompromising style from Cardiff because they got him dismissed. We had no complaints about the result, but I'll always argue that there was nothing wrong with the goal Wyn Davies scored after three minutes. You could hear the ball going into the net, there was a deathly hush and then a deafening roar when the goal was unbelievably ruled out.

It was to be Gary's last chance to play in a major international tournament as once again Wales, with the inevitable hard-luck story, had failed to qualify. It also marked the end of another era as it marked his last international cap as a Leeds player. Although he had represented his country on thirty-two occasions, he had missed almost as many games from international withdrawals. He had played over 500 games for Leeds in same period and had missed less than twenty League games in ten seasons. In stark contrast, in his short stint as a Birmingham City player, Gary made only sixteen League appearances but won five Wales caps in the same time.

He was not selected for the Home International Championship's initial match against England in 1974, having played most of the season in the Birmingham reserve team due to after breaking his ankle against Chelsea the previous September, with John Phillips of Chelsea being Dave Bowen's preferred choice. However, Phillips had a nightmare match and his frequent fumbling, which cost both goals in a 2-0 defeat, prompted the Welsh media to call for Gary's recall to win his thirty-third cap against Scotland. The following Wednesday against Scotland Wales lost again, 2-0, although Gary kept his place against Northern Ireland as the players were to report to Cardiff the next day at 4 p.m.

Unfortunately Gary and Terry Yorath got a little waylaid on the way to reporting in, taking a little detour left into the Cardiff Athletic club rather than right into the Angel Hotel on Westgate street. They phoned manager Dave Bowen and told him that they had car trouble before strolling into the hotel nearer closing time. They explained that they had had a couple of pints while waiting for the breakdown van. Everything would have been fine except for the back page headline in the *Western Mail* the next day with a large photo of Gary, Terry Yorath and rugby international John Price drinking in Cardiff RFC clubhouse, obviously the worse for wear and being presented with a Cardiff RFC tie. The headline asked, 'Whoever Thought It Could Happen...?' Although both players had once again broken the rules Bowen kept them in the team and was rewarded by a 1–0 victory over Northern Ireland that Saturday.

Gary's last three caps came in the autumn of 1974 during the first half of the European qualifying programme. A 2–1 defeat by Austria in Vienna was followed by 2–0 victories over Hungary in Cardiff and a 5–0 win against Luxembourg at Swansea. In the home victory over Hungary he had a comparatively comfortable night although in the last few minutes he made a breathtaking save from Hungarian striker Nagy, only to suffer a very painful dislocated finger and be substituted for the last few minutes. Leighton James remembers not so much the injury but Gary's reaction to it.

> When we watched the highlights of the game Gary was led off holding his hand and limping. You'd swear he'd been the victim of the hardest tackle of all time. The other lads and I gave him a real ribbing, but Gary took it. We had a real team spirit in the Welsh camp at that time.

His thirty-seventh and final Wales cap came against Luxembourg on 20 November 1974, exactly eleven years on from his debut against Scotland as a raw eighteen year old. It was fitting that his home town Swansea, the scene of many significant games in the past, was to stage his final bow from the international arena. In an ironic comment, the significance of which was probably not realised at the time, Clive Phillips reported that:

> Gary Sprake was the cleanest player at the end of this mud bath and not once was he called on to make a save. It must have been the quietest of his thirty-seven games for his country.

For a goalkeeper so used to being the focal point of trying to keep the fragile Welsh defence together it must have been a strange epitaph to his international career. After all, for twelve years he had experienced the opposite, having to be consistently at his best to keep the opposition at bay, a fact that has continuously been positively remarked upon by the Welsh media as Gary still retains this affection and good reputation within the Principality, as Leeds and Wales great Brian Flynn comments:

> I made my international debut against Luxembourg in the European Championship at the Vetch in 1974. I remember looking nervously across the dressing room before the game and seeing Gary, who was to me a legend, a cornerstone of both the Leeds and Wales defence.

When he looks back at his international career it is with a mixture of pride and some regret. Apart from the mistakes against Northern Ireland in his second match and the disastrous game against Scotland after the over-exuberant celebrations of the 1968 championship win, he was consistently outstanding in a Welsh jersey. Despite the generally very poor record of the team Gary enjoyed hugely the experience of playing for his country, often without the burden and nerves that could sometimes haunt him at Leeds. Although often finding the team organisation frustratingly amateurish and sometimes turning a blind eye to the 'manager's rules', he had a great fondness for Wales managers Jimmy Murphy, Dave Bowen and Mike Smith. The Welsh public and media in return had a great regard for Gary and unlike the wider national media took him to their hearts, recognising that without him in goal Wales were a far inferior team. In return, their support was repaid with a high level of consistently excellent performances on the international stage, which once again seems to have been conveniently overlooked in some quarters. As he states today:

I am always proud that I was first picked to play for my country as an eighteen year old in 1963 and was proud every time I pulled on the Welsh jersey. I only wish I had played a lot more games for Wales, as when I look back I missed far too many games because Don Revie withdrew me from the squad. I did everything that Revie asked me because he was the boss and I respected him, but I do wish I had sometimes gone against his wishes and played more games than I did. Nevertheless it was a great honour and experience to represent Wales and I have nothing but fond memories of the occasions I did represent my country.

Leighton James, although loath to make comparisons with players from different eras, argues that Gary was one of Wales' finest.

> I wouldn't like to say if Sprakey was better than Neville Southall or vice versa because they played in teams where one group of players may have been better than the other. What I will say, however, is that Gary was more often than not world class. On the other hand big Nev also sometimes made mistakes. As you know Gary will always be remembered for his Leeds mistakes. No-one remembers Nev's, although he made a few, such as the vital one against Romania, but so has every goalie that has ever played.

A final comment on Gary's international career with Wales rests with colleague and fellow Welsh international 'keeper Tony Millington.

> Although Gary seemed very fresh faced and he was a bit of a character on and off the field, ultimately he was a brilliant 'keeper. My top two Welsh goalies would be Gary and Neville Southall; both were great shot stoppers but Gary was a better all round 'keeper and would just get my vote. In my opinion Gary Sprake was a class international goalkeeper for his country and deserves to be remembered as such.

Gary's Wales XI 1963-1974

Gary Sprake (Leeds United & Birmingham City) – Goalkeeper
Thirty-seven appearances for Wales between 1963 and 1974 would have been nearer seventy if it wasn't for the Leeds management and coaching staff wanting me to withdraw from so many games, which is still my only regret in football.

Peter Rodrigues (Cardiff City, Leicester, Sheffield Wednesday & Southampton) – Defender
Peter was a very quick and skilful full-back who was also an excellent passer of the ball. His pace allowed him to be a potent attacking threat and he would often support the attack effectively with well-timed overlapping runs.

Graham Williams (West Bromwich Albion) – Defender
He was another very attacking defender who also demonstrated great anticipation, enabling him to make many last-gasp goal-saving tackles. An excellent defender.

Terry Hennessey (Birmingham City, Nottingham Forest & Derby County) – Defender
Terry was a very confident defender whose reading of the game always gave him lots of time on the ball. He had the ability to break up the opponents' attack and his swift passing and movement would always set us up on the counter. An all-round defender of the highest standard.

Mike England (Blackburn Rovers, Tottenham Hotspur & Cardiff City) – Defender
Mike was an outstanding and commanding centre half who was a great header of the ball and a very strong tackler. For a big man he was also very skilful and a great passer of the ball. At his peak Mike would have got into any team in the country.

Barrie Jones (Swansea City, Plymouth Argyle & Cardiff City) – Midfield
Barry was a very quick and skilful midfielder who displayed great balance and excellent close ball control. He also had the ability to beat his man and put in penetrating crosses for the centre forwards.

Graham Moore (Cardiff City, Chelsea, Manchester United, Northampton Town & Charlton Athletic) – Midfield
Graham was also a very creative player and could spread the game with a range of long or short passes. He was a master of reading situations during the game and could also contribute useful goals.

Ivor Allchurch (Swansea Town, Newcastle United & Cardiff City) – Midfield
Ivor was an outstanding creative presence for Wales with a great left foot either passing or shooting, and he scored some great and very important goals for Wales. Ivor was a very skilful player who would also walk into any greatest ever Welsh XI. A legend of the Welsh game.

Cliff Jones (Swansea Town, Tottenham Hotspur & Fulham) – Midfield
A very quick and tricky winger with great dribbling skills and also fantastic crosser of the ball.

Ron Davies (Luton, Norwich City, Southampton, Portsmouth, Manchester United & Millwall) – Striker
Ron was a great target man to have in your team and he was a real handful

for opposition defenders. Although he was dominant in the air and scored some great goals with his head he was also very skilful on the ground. A very powerful and effective striker.

John Charles (Leeds United, Juventus, Roma & Cardiff City) – Striker
The word 'legend' in my opinion is too easily used these days to describe players from the past, but John Charles was a true giant of the British and European game. John would walk into any team as a centre half or centre forward. As a footballer he had it all. He was great in the air, the best header of a ball I've ever seen, and he also had a terrific shot with either foot. He was also very skilful and extremely powerful but never a dirty player. In my opinion he was both the greatest Leeds and Welsh player of all time and it was a privilege to know him and play with him for both my club and my country. If John wasn't born Welsh he would have been given far more credit for his achievements both at home and abroad. Every footballer, no matter how good they are, has their own hero and John was certainly mine. I only played with him a few times both for Leeds and Wales. I also played against him when he was with Cardiff and I consider it a great privilege. Like everyone else I was filled with awe in his presence and he was the one person I looked up to when I reached the top of my profession. It was an outrage that he didn't receive a knighthood when other much lesser players have been so rewarded.

NINE

SINGING THE BLUES

In October 1973, after almost two years in the Elland Road wilderness, Gary Sprake moved to Birmingham City for a then world-record fee for a goalkeeper of £100,000. After thirteen years of loyal service, which was synonymous with Leeds United's successes in the Don Revie era, Gary severed his ties with the club he called home. He said his fond farewells to teammates he regarded as brothers and said his goodbyes to backroom staff, from the tea lady and laundry women to the coaching staff he regarded as his extended family and especially to the 'boss', who had been a father figure to him since he arrived as a shy schoolboy from Wales. His legacy will long be remembered by the Elland Road faithful, being one of the youngest members of the team that helped lay the foundations for Leeds United's greatest ever achievements. Leeds fans remember him as one of the country's most consistently brilliant goalkeepers during his 507 games spanning twelve seasons. The record books also still show that he is the youngest goalkeeper to represent the club and his record number of appearances for a Leeds custodian is unlikely to be surpassed. As a seventeen year old Gary became a permanent fixture for the next ten years or so and he gave the club wonderful service. Without him Leeds wouldn't have been the team they were and he certainly played more than his part in ensuring that the club challenged for honours year in and year out.

Recalling two memorable saves in a career of outstanding saves, Don Revie paid glowing tribute to one of his favourite sons, the matchday programme after Gary's departure commenting that

> Gary pulled off two of the greatest saves I have ever seen from any goalkeeper anywhere in the world. The first was in the second leg of the Fairs Cup final when the opposition were awarded a free-kick that was thundered into the top corner. Everything from a goalkeeping perspective was wrong. The ball

was seen late and it was delivered at pace, but he saved it and that save won us the Fairs Cup for the first time. When we won the cup against Arsenal at Wembley, in 1972, we were only there because Gary had pulled off a miraculous save in an earlier round against Liverpool. Gary didn't play at Wembley, but I will always remember that save. Emlyn Hughes unleashed a terrific shot from eighteen yards. Gary was four yards off his line and the ball flew over his shoulder, but he dived backwards and tipped it over the bar.

Many if not all of Gary's contemporaries agreed with Revie's assessment, most notably Bill Shankly, who eulogised about Gary's performances on many occasions, believing him to be one of the finest goalkeepers in the world. After Leeds had won the championship, *Goal* magazine (May 1969) asked opponents how they hoped to overcome the champions in the forthcoming season. Tony Book, the title-winning captain of Manchester City, and Jimmy Adamson, the Burnley manager both came to the same conclusion: 'You hope that Gary Sprake has an off day' – evidence that if Gary Sprake was on form opponents had significantly less chance of winning.

The Leeds manager lamented at this time that the club had lost not only a brilliant goalkeeper but also one of the family, somebody he regarded like a son. Just four years later Revie would disown his favourite son and, until his death, even refuse to acknowledge Gary's existence. Yet at the time Revie argued that Birmingham had got themselves 'one of the greatest goalies that has ever lived'. Concluding his eulogy, Revie said 'We hope he and his family will be happy in the Midlands and they must remember that the door at Elland Road is always open to them.'

Unfortunately, that door has been firmly and officially shut for the last thirty years. During the research for the book Gary has been bewildered and very upset by many of the comments made by people he regarded as family. Paul Reaney, who Gary was particularly close to throughout his time at Leeds (in fact they were best men at each other's weddings), wrote to Gary expressing the disappointment he felt that Gary was thinking of writing his memoirs. Gary had written to Reaney to ask if he could help the authors with their research, perhaps by providing an anecdote or two. Reaney shocked him with his blunt reply including the sentence:

On this occasion I don't think I will be able to help, but I do hope things go well for you.

Mick Jones would not be interviewed unless he had discussed it with Clarke and Reaney and he then refused to comment. David Harvey would make no comment on Gary's career, 'for reasons you understand,' perhaps referring to the hostility shown to the Welshman by members of the 'Golden Era', while Clarke went a stage further by threatening, through his biographer, to take legal action if any quotes were taken from his book and included in this publication.

These attitudes are a far cry from the telegrams that were forwarded to Gary before his Birmingham City debut away to Arsenal at Highbury on 6 October 1973. Through the mists of time his former colleagues have obviously forgotten the high esteem in which they held their teammate when he left the club, as Billy Bremner forwarded Gary their best wishes:

> Good luck Gary, we will all be thinking of you today. Billy Bremner and players.

Perhaps the most telling of all were the greeting telegrams received from the two people closest to Gary in his years at Elland Road, Don Revie and Paul Reaney. Revie forwarded the message:

> Good luck, confidence and concentration. Hope you have very many happy years at Birmingham Gary. Love Kath also. The boss.

Revie told *The Times* in an interview on the day of the 'keeper's transfer:

> I'm very sorry to see him go. Gary has been a big part of the club and grew up as one of the family, but I understand his desire to play first-team football.

Before his untimely death Billy Bremner had been one of Gary's arch-critics, sullying Gary's reputation as both a player and person, obviously influenced by the latter's involvement in the exposé on Revie. At the time of the 'keeper's move to Birmingham he had a different perception, stating in his weekly column in the *Yorkshire Evening Post* that

> The move of Gary Sprake to Birmingham City is a move that saddened us all. Gary played a big part in making the club what it is today and I still rate him as one of the top six 'keepers in the country. We are lucky at Leeds to have two 'keepers in that bracket, but Gary wanted first-team football and

with Harvey playing so well the only way he believed he would get it was by moving on. Nevertheless, we will not forget what Gary has done for United and we wish him well with his new club. All the lads got together to give Gary a big send-off a couple of weeks ago when we arranged a private get-together for all the players and wives and it turned out to be quite an emotional time. Understandably really, for Gary had been at the club, like most of us, since he left school and it's a big wrench for him as it was for his wife Kath. There was a surprise for them at the party, a large cake from the gaffer decorated with the words 'Thanks Gary'. He was very impressed – what other manager would do that for a player who has just left his club?

If Gary was held in such high esteem why did he think of leaving what was probably the best side in the country?

The main reason I left Leeds was because I wanted to prolong my Wales career. I played the week before I asked for a move against Poland in a World Cup qualifier in Katowice in front of 120,000 spectators and Mike Smith (the Wales manager) had hinted I was in danger of losing my place in the squad if I wasn't playing regular first-team football. Also, after the buzz of first-team football I didn't want to go back to training with the youngsters. In those days if a senior professional was out of the side they didn't play reserve-team football very often, they just travelled around with the first team. In the days before substitute goalkeepers it meant I was sitting in the stands every week. In almost eighteen months I only played about eight reserve-team matches. I had played more games for Wales than for Leeds and I felt my life was wasting away. It was hard to face reserve-team football after ten or so seasons as first choice. I was sick of my existence in the stiffs and I often went home to my wife and family in a depressed state. I was short-tempered and did not have as much time for them as I should have. I loved the atmosphere of first-team football and was thrilled at starting all over again at Birmingham. I wanted first-team football so badly I would have taken a wage cut to sign. As it was, Freddie Goodwin made me an offer that was too good to refuse, I was on £200 per week basic at Leeds; Freddie offered £300 plus ten per cent of the transfer fee.

I approached the boss and said I wanted a transfer, even though I had just signed a three-year contract with a three-year option. So I could have bided my time and fought for my place, knowing I could pick up wages for the next six years. However, my confidence in my own abilities had been boosted even during my darkest days at Elland Road by two of the best managers in the country, Sir Alf Ramsey and Malcolm Allison, who had shown considerable faith in my ability. At the start of the year I had been selected by Sir Alf to represent Great Britain against Europe in a match to celebrate the formation of the Common Market. Four Leeds players were selected: myself, Bremner, Giles and Lorimer. The squad also included fantastic players like Bobby Charlton, Bobby Moore, Colin Bell, Steve Heighway, Pat Rice, Peter Storey and Colin Stein. It was a privilege to play with such great players and demonstrated to me that I could still play at the highest level, even though I hadn't appeared in Leeds' first team that season. It wasn't the first time I had represented the United Kingdom at Wembley. Ten years earlier I had shared the goalkeeping jersey with the legendary Pat Jennings, one of the greatest 'keepers ever, when we played against England Youth. My only appearance for Leeds that season was a substitute appearance in the Cup-Winners' Cup, and as I had played more games for Wales than Leeds I decided to look at my options in the close season. In the previous ten seasons my lowest number of appearances had been thirty-eight, which was in my first full season as a professional. I was understandably hurt that Revie was constantly overlooking me for first-team football and in the close season a wonderful opportunity arose. Durban City offered me a contract to play as a guest over the summer months in South Africa. I was put up, with my wife Kathy, in one of Durban's finest hotels. They were managed by the ex-West Ham and England forward John 'Budgie' Byrne. South Africa was and is a wonderful country. We were treated like royalty in glorious sunshine and I was being paid £1,000 for two months' work. While there, the Manchester City manager Malcolm Allison brought over a number of players to play in exhibition games. When he found out I was out there he contacted me to play in what was deemed three 'Tests'. I once again represented an unofficial Great Britain team, this time in the matches against South Africa.

There was some controversy about the trip as there was a sporting boycott at the time and I was very aware of the conditions in South Africa as I had discussed it several times with my friend Albert Johanneson, who had experienced apartheid first hand. I was pleased therefore that we would be coaching black youngsters and that our last game would be in Soweto. I was again going to be playing alongside some great players: Rodney Marsh, a very good player but a really arrogant man who was very close to the manager; Frank McClintock, an old adversary from his Arsenal days; John Greig, the Scotland captain; the legendary Johnny Haynes; and Alan Whittle, the Everton winger. The three 'Tests' were played in Cape Town, Johannesburg and Soweto in front of crowds of 50,000-plus. We won all three games and were praised by the South Africans for trying to break down the barriers of apartheid, because we used to go into the townships to coach the young kids. Unfortunately we did attract some criticism. Sir Stanley Matthews was also doing some coaching out there and he branded us a disgrace to the British game. He said we were only interested in fighting on the pitch and drinking off it. With Malcolm Allison as manager and Rodney Marsh alongside it was obvious we would have a drink or two. The two of them once drank twelve bottles of champagne between them back in England. They were second division when it came to beer, though. I was hewn from the South Wales' valleys where, at the time, drinking was part of the culture, especially for the men whose working lives were long and arduous. Our argument was that it was the close season and we were unwinding during our holidays. I was recharging my batteries for the battle that lay ahead; to regain my first-team spot from David Harvey.

Unfortunately for Gary, when the 1973/74 season kicked off, it was once again David Harvey who was first choice, with Gary making only one appearance. His last game for Leeds United was the away game against Stromgodset in the UEFA Cup, which ended in a 1-1 draw. Two months into the season Gary Sprake had to make a decision; to fight for his place or seek pastures new. Even in the days before agents there was to be no shortage of offers for the vastly experienced yet, at twenty-eight years old, still relatively young goalkeeper who had yet to reach his prime.

I had envisaged playing until I was thirty-five so there were many games left in me.

After some wonderful performances for Wales, especially when defying and frustrating England's World Cup hopes at Wembley, Gary had placed himself well and truly in the shop window. Revie had a fight on his hands to keep his goalkeeper as many teams were showing more than a passing interest. In fact it was Gary's excellent performances for Wales that played a significant part in his high valuation. David Lawson was the previous most expensive goalkeeper, having transferred from Huddersfield to Everton for £85,000, and, with all due respect to Lawson, he could never be considered in the same class as Gary.

Only once before had I considered leaving, when Harry Gregg tried to take me down to Swansea City on loan. The attraction of returning home for a few months was really appealing but Revie blocked the move, telling me that he didn't want me to leave but if I did it would be for a fee that was right for Leeds United. Over the previous eighteen months he refused many requests from other clubs, including one firm offer from Manchester City the previous season that fell short of his valuation.

Now, however, there were a few big clubs in for me, and after the confidence boosts provided by Ramsey and Allison I felt I could still do a more than satisfactory job. Throughout September I had talks with both Chelsea and Arsenal, but I really didn't want to sign for either. We had taken so much stick off the London media and we had some bruising battles with both. I couldn't see myself playing for a team that included the likes of Peter Osgood as we'd had some right old battles over the years. I was flattered by the interest but my choice had been narrowed to two clubs: Manchester City or Birmingham City. I had been impressed with what both clubs had to say and I had decided to sign for the Manchester club who were looking to replace Joe Corrigan. At the eleventh hour, on Tuesday 1 October, Freddie Goodwin the Birmingham manager drove up to Leeds to see me after Revie had alerted him to my availability as soon as I had left the boss's office. I had played a few games with Freddie at the start of my career. He sold the Birmingham area to me and promised me that the club had ambition and offered me a three-year deal. I hadn't shaken on any deal with the Sky Blues, but I did phone them to say I had decided against joining them. Within a few days they had signed Keith McRae from Scotland. Five days later I made my Blues debut. Some people have argued that the transfer took four days to complete because I kept dropping the pen when it was time to sign on the dotted line. That was completely untrue; the deal was completed in less than two hours!

Despite only having made two appearances for Leeds in eighteen months, Gary had now become the most expensive goalkeeper in the history of the game. In the week leading up to his signing the Blues' chairman Clifford Coombes had promised the fans a new signing after a 0–3 reverse against Ipswich Town, although nobody expected the previous season's player of the year, goalkeeper Dave Latchford, to be the man that was going to be replaced. The *Birmingham Post* reported that irate fans were jamming the St Andrews switchboard protesting against the signing, believing other areas of the team needed strengthening. Gary's Blues' debut was to be against his former team's arch rival Arsenal away at Highbury, which had been a particularly unlucky ground with Leeds. Before that, however, there were a few training sessions to fit in with his new teammates. Controversy seemed to follow him throughout his time at Leeds and if he was expecting things to be different in the next stage of his eventful career he was in for a shock.

When I went in for my first training session I was introduced to my new colleagues, got changed and went out for training. As I lined up for the first team the centre half Kenny Burns turned round and right up to my face said, 'Hundred thousand quid, what a waste of fucking money.' I don't know if he was the spokesperson for the rest of the squad but I just walked up to him and let him have my trademark, a classic right hook that floored him and, if I remember rightly, broke his nose, not that he was that good looking anyway! I looked down at him and reminded him that I had trained with real hard men. He never held a grudge and we became very good friends, even today we do some hospitality work together at St Andrews.

Unlike his Leeds' days, however, he was entering uncharted territory as Birmingham were in the relegation places. He was being introduced to the murkier end of the division after a decade of the rarefied atmosphere at the top. He joined a Birmingham side that had not won a game all season and the signs were that they were in serious danger of relegation, even at that early stage of the season. His first match at Highbury against the Gunners ended in a 0-1 defeat. Although having little to do throughout the match he did save a Peter Storey penalty near the end, with the local *Birmingham Post* reporting that 'Even a Sprake super save cannot save the Blues.'

I thoroughly enjoyed my debut but I was very much aware that while my new club had not won a game all season, the lads back in Leeds were embarking on a record unbeaten run. The first thing that stood out was the standard of defending. At best the Blues' defending could be described as shoddy, while at Leeds the defence was the cornerstone of all we achieved. Tactically the managers were very similar; both adopted a negative attitude away from home. Freddie broke his leg against Cardiff in the 1963/64 season and while out injured used to spy on opposing teams to help the boss and Syd Owen with their dossiers. He must have been influenced by his former manager's tactics but really could never achieve Revie's levels of man management.

Gary's second appearance was away to Second Division Blackpool in the League Cup, a trophy Gary rarely had the opportunity of winning at Leeds as it was rated as unimportant compared with the championship, FA Cup and European competitions, especially after their 1968 win. For the Blues it was their only realistic opportunity for silverware. Blackpool took the lead with a goal from Mickey Burns, only for his Blues namesake Kenny to grab an equaliser to take the tie to a replay. Even though there was still an air of pessimism surrounding the transfer Gary had an excellent match and was responsible for Blues having a second opportunity, with the *Birmingham Post* reporting that:

> Goalkeeper Sprake was constantly in action, showing the style and command that made him a record signing. He had to use all his experience throughout the first half as the Blackpool attack moved menacingly forward.

The *Daily Mirror* ran with the back page headline, 'Super Sprake, Gary is the hero as Blues earn a replay,' with reporter Ted Corbett arguing that

> Sprake kept his side in the League Cup with a brilliant display when producing a series of magnificent saves.

Gary had performed heroically in his first two outings away from home and should have been looking forward to his home debut against local rivals Wolverhampton Wanderers. However, in the run up to the match there were predictions that the match was going to be played amid a hostile climate for the new goalkeeper, which forced Freddie Goodwin to take the unprecedented step of contacting the local media on the eve of the game, telling the *Birmingham Post*:

> Sprake is the innocent victim of a hostile backlash by a minority of fans. I am furious at the situation that has been created. It puts Sprake under enormous pressure. If he makes a mistake he could be murdered for it and this would be grossly unfair. Gary has played exceptionally well for us since he has arrived. He saved a penalty against Arsenal last week and also did extremely well against Blackpool during the week. If any criticism is to be made it should be levelled at me, but I am delighted we have signed Gary. He is a world class 'keeper and I know he will do a wonderful job for us. He has a wealth of experience and I am sure the majority of supporters will be behind him all the way on his home debut.

The match itself was a typical local derby, abundant excitement, stirring physical challenges and some absorbing teamwork. Gary had a cruel home debut, not from the majority of the home fans, who gave him a warm reception, but from the opposition's Frank Munro, who came rumbling in to challenge him as he claimed a high ball, which resulted in him being stretchered off with a damaged thigh early in the first half. Although expected to return after the interval Gary failed to reappear, his place was taken by centre forward Bob Latchford, the brother of Dave whose place Gary had taken. While receiving treatment Gary was to miss the Blues' first win of the season.

Despite three days of extensive treatment Gary was unable to make the next match, so he had to wait another week for the home League game against Everton, a team that had provided some brutal encounters during his time with Leeds. With only one win to their credit and in danger of falling into the bottom three relegation places, which had been extended from two that season, the Blues sunk further into the relegation mire with a 0–2 defeat. And the major share of the blame, as far as the home fans were concerned, was laid at the feet of their new goalkeeper. For the first goal he palmed Harvey's waist-high cross into the net and then allowed a speculative Connolly shot to beat him on the near post. After the game Gary told the local *Mercury*:

> It makes me feel like hanging up my boots, I'm sick. I thought Connolly was going to centre, that's why I left my line. If I hadn't have stuck my hand out it wouldn't have been a goal.

Sprake's view was that the whole team were going through a bad patch when he told the *Birmingham Post* that

> The first was unlucky rather than an error. As far as that goal was concerned I thought I had made a fair save, but that was the kind of day it was, on another day the defender would have been back to clear after I had made the save. For the second [which was credited to Gary as an own goal] I misread the situation. I came off my line believing Connolly was going to cross it.

The *Birmingham Post* was more forgiving than the home support and offered a more balanced view:

> It would be unwise to crucify him [Sprake] without analysing the performance of the rest of the team and the defence in particular.

So the old football adage, 'You are only as good as the defence in front of you' was something that Gary Sprake was experiencing from both ends of the spectrum. At Leeds he was often shielded from opposing attacks by a full international line-up, while at Birmingham he was protected by some inexperienced defenders who were learning their trade and, in all honesty, would never reach the heights of Gary's former teammates.

Even though we were struggling at the wrong end of the table and I was never a fan of Freddie's tactics, especially away from home when he was totally defensive, he did give youngsters a chance, players like Joe Gallagher, Kenny Burns, Jimmy Calderwood and of course the wonderfully gifted Trevor Francis. That was the only way he could be compared to Don Revie, although Revie had the luxury of bringing youngsters into a side chasing trophies most of the time.

After his first poor home game Gary was desperate to impress and to redeem himself and, three days later, Birmingham faced Newcastle United in the League Cup. This game was to convince the terrace doubters that they had, in fact, signed a great goalkeeper who would be an asset in the fight against relegation and the quest to win the League Cup. It was their 'keeper, with his scintillating performance, that ensured the Blues earned a replay. After Malcolm MacDonald had burst through, Gary raced out of goal only to clatter the striker to the ground and unfortunately concede a penalty, a challenge that today would have resulted in an automatic red card. Both players got up and as MacDonald hit the penalty Sprake, according to *The Times*, 'redeemed himself by diving full length to his left to turn the ball around the post.' After Latchford had given the Blues the lead, their 'keeper 'twice had the best pulled out of him making excellent saves from a Newcastle attack trying desperately to stay in the competition'. Bob Latchford returned to goal-scoring ways with a brace, but for the *Birmingham Post* there was only one hero:

> The man who kept the Blues in the cup was Gary Sprake. The very same supporters who denigrated him against Everton hailed him as a hero after his penalty save, which was awarded after pulling down MacDonald to prevent a certain goal. He dived to his left to make a magnificent stop.

In the replay it was once again Sprake who played a prominent part as the Blues progressed to the next round. Immediately after Francis had converted a penalty, Sprake, according to the *Birmingham Post*, 'had a fine game making a wonderful point-blank save from a close-range Barrowclough shot. The Blues just about earned their success with Hynd and Sprake outstanding.'

The next games were vital in the battle against relegation and saw the Blues visit Sheffield United with Sprake, according to the *Mercury*, 'back to his sparkling best'.

> He was put under intense pressure but performed wonders, even though he faced wave after wave of attacks, finally conceding an equaliser two minutes from time which denied the Blues their first away win of the season.

After drawing the next game with Southampton, the following away game against Stoke City is remembered by Gary as one of the low points of his distinguished career.

We lost that game 5-2. I remember making a save within the first couple of minutes and after that I never had a save to make, even though I conceded five. It was the most woeful defending I had ever witnessed; to say we were shoddy was an understatement. Wayward back passes led to quite a few goals. It may have been entertaining for the fans, but from a professional perspective it was a disgrace. After the match I once again let Freddie know my feelings about his tactics. The lads were a great bunch, obviously not as talented as those at Leeds, but easily a good First Division side, it's just that Freddie was a useless tactician.

His next three games saw the Blues progress to the next round of the League Cup after beating Ipswich 3-1 and he also kept two clean sheets against Leicester and Coventry, as they gleaned four very important points in their quest for League survival. The Blues were on a high and feeling optimistic as they awaited their next opponents who, in a more than significant match for their new 'keeper, were Leeds United. Leeds went into the match on the back of a twenty-two match unbeaten run and were attracting more crowds to opponents' grounds with their newly found brand of attacking football than the perennial crowd favourites Manchester United. The last time they had tasted defeat was in the penultimate game of the previous season against the Blues. Since his move, Gary had kept close links with his old mates; training at Elland Road once or twice a week and going out for dinner every Saturday night with Terry Yorath, Paul Reaney and their wives after driving straight back from a game. Now it was the aim of their former colleague to end Leeds' remarkable run. In an interview with the *Birmingham Post* Gary gave his thoughts on the forthcoming game against those he regarded like family.

> I've mixed emotions, but no regrets. I'd rather be in the first team at Birmingham than watching at Elland Road. I was irritated last season, playing so few games meant I was an expert spectator. I still think Leeds are a great team and will go on to win the championship.

Gary Sprake had been carried off while making his home debut on the thirteenth and fate would decree this was now his thirteenth game for Birmingham against his old club. Like his former manager Gary was superstitious but was not going to be swayed by sentimentality. He entered the game with the same professional perspective as he had in over 500 games for Leeds. He was not going to give, nor was he expecting, any favours and after a very short time this was proven as he sought attention from the trainer after a foot-up challenge from Paul Madeley.

When I was receiving treatment it came across the tannoy that there was a bomb in the ground and the announcer asked if anyone wanted to leave could they do so while there was a break in play. It is incredible how both the game and society in general has changed since my playing days. No-one would dare contemplate issuing a statement like that in today's climate.

In a physical game that saw five players booked it was Birmingham who came within four minutes of ending Leeds' unbeaten record in a 1-1 stalemate. The Blues also had a legitimate winner cancelled out after the referee changed his mind after first signalling a goal. Apart from being injured Gary had a quiet game, making only one fine save from a Hunter long shot, while at the other end Harvey made many fine saves to deny Birmingham victory.

Before the game news filtered down to me from Elland Road that Revie had told the lads to give me a few kicks and to niggle me, hoping I'd lose my temper. I bet he included me in his pre-match dossier, even though I'd played over 500 games for him. I was aware of this and didn't react; my main focus was on trying to win the points for the Blues. It did feel strange playing against the lads, but we all shared a few pints together after the game. Though I was involved in a relegation battle with the Blues I drew as much satisfaction from that as chasing titles. I was not at all envious of the success they enjoyed that season. In fact, I still look out for their results first and foremost. You don't play that many games and not have an allegiance.

As Birmingham entered the new year they were in more optimistic mood as they had put together an unbeaten run of six games and next up was the visit of Cardiff City in the FA Cup. Gary was looking forward to meeting his fellow Welsh internationals Leighton Phillips and Gil Reece.

The game against Cardiff was the first time Freddie did what we always did at Leeds. We stayed the night before a home game in a hotel to focus on the match. Our unbeaten run had raised people's expectations of us doing well in the cup. I was really pleased that at last I was experiencing some professionalism with

Freddie. We stayed at the St John's Hotel in Solihull where I had been living since I arrived at the club. For the game, I was sharing with Bob Latchford and in the evening my thought that we were becoming more professional was dispelled. Bob walked in with twelve cans of beer and he said six were for me and six for him. It was like playing for Wales, where we always enjoyed a pint or two. When Jimmy Murphy and Dave Bowen were in charge they used to have a few with us, even before the game. One of my best games for Wales was against England at Wembley in the World Cup qualifiers. On the afternoon of the game, however, Ron Davies and I slipped into the hotel bar and had a few pints. We didn't do that after Mike Smith was appointed, although he once caught Terry Yorath and I breaking the curfew when we went to Mumbles before a game down at the Vetch. The squad was thin so he let us off with a rollicking and we still played the next night.

The few drinks the night before didn't affect the performance as the Blues moved into the next round courtesy of a 5-2 victory, although the scoreline flattered the hosts with the *Birmingham Post* reporting:

> If it had not been for some superb goalkeeping from Gary Sprake this could well have finished up as an embarrassing hiding.

The *Sunday Mercury* reported that

> The Blues held a two-goal lead, but if Sprake had not made a fine goal-line stop from Hynd's unintentional header things may have been different. This was his best game so far for the Blues and Cardiff should have managed at least a draw. Sprake drove winger Farrington to despair with three acrobatic saves.

Gary and his Birmingham teammates were in buoyant mood as they travelled to Anfield to try to overcome a Liverpool team that were still chasing Leeds for the title, with Gary receiving several messages of good luck from his erstwhile colleagues. All was in vain though as the home side triumphed 3-2 to keep up the pressure at the top of the table while plunging the Blues back into the relegation dogfight, with the *Sunday Mercury* reporting that 'Sprake was at times indecisive, but at other times he did extremely well.'

Even though I was an experienced professional there were times when there were misunderstandings with my defenders. We needed time to gel together, but unfortunately we didn't have that luxury, especially as three teams would be relegated at the end of the season. At Leeds we developed an understanding over ten or more years. Big Jack knew I would come for crosses, even to the edge of the eighteen-yard box, and if he got in my way I would clatter him. At the start of my career, however, Jack would defend deep to offer me protection. There was not that understanding with the Blues; that is developed over time, but that was at a premium.

The Blues' next game would prove whether or not the defensive unit was functioning properly when Manchester City were the visitors, boasting one of the finest attacks in the country: Summerbee, Bell, Lee, Marsh and the legendary Denis Law.

People talk about the 'fox in the box' that was Denis. You ignored him at your peril. If you didn't remain focused for ninety minutes he would stick one away. A great striker, but an equally nice guy; mean on the pitch but really nice off it.

The Blues gained another valuable point with Sprake needing to make only one save, a smothering effort at Donachie's feet. The following week it was the chance to progress in the FA Cup away to QPR. However, the Blues' hopes of progress were dashed, even though Gary Sprake was once more demonstrating the skills that took him to the top of his profession, with the *Sunday Mercury* reporting:

> But for the agility of Sprake, QPR would have won by a greater margin. He made three excellent saves as well as a fantastic stop to prevent a Clarke own goal.

The *Birmingham Post* commented that

> Gary Sprake made a number of fine saves trying to keep Birmingham in the competition.

The 2-0 defeat meant that the Blues could now focus on the fight against relegation, something Gary had never before experienced. For the last ten seasons, as the campaign entered the final straight he was involved in trying to win in two, three or even four competitions.

The battle started against fellow strugglers West Ham at Upton Park. The game was a predictable affair, a dour 0-0 draw and, with Welsh referee Clive Thomas officiating, there were a predictable number of bookings, including the name of G. Sprake for protesting after he gave away a penalty for bodychecking Holland as he burst into the area. Justice was done as Billy Bonds put the penalty wide. The *Birmingham Post* reported that

> Gallagher, Hynd and Sprake worked brilliantly to foil incessant attacking pressure.

The *Sunday Mercury* eulogised Gary's performance thus:

> Sprake pulled out a handful of top-class saves and by now must have convinced the Doubting Thomas's that Freddie Goodwin must have known what he was doing all along.

The Blues entered their next match against Wolves without centre forward Bob Latchford, who had been sensationally sold to Everton in a deal that saw Archie Styles and Howard Kendall move in the opposite direction. Once again the Blues 'keeper was at his sparkling best, producing a magnificent performance, although it wasn't enough to prevent the Blues slipping to a 1-0 defeat. Without the impressive Latchford the attack had very little to offer, as the *Sunday Mercury* pointed out.

> The Wolves 'keeper had one save to make, not so his opposite number, who had to be at his best to produce two sparkling saves to deny Daley and Parkin.

The *Birmingham Post* argued that Munro's solitary goal should have been disallowed after Sprake was impeded from reaching the corner kick. The report went on to argue that

> Sprake made the best save I have seen for a very long time; a spectacular reflex action to deflect Daley's shot. Then he pulled out another one nearly as good to deny Parkin.

In his first twenty games for Birmingham City, apart from one mistake against Everton, Gary Sprake had consistently demonstrated the form of a top-class goalkeeper. After a wonderful performance against Wolves, however, he was axed by Freddie Goodwin, who told the *Birmingham Post*:

Gary has been under a lot of pressure since he joined and the general position has not been helped by him not being able to settle into a new house yet. He could benefit from a rest.

Goodwin told the *Birmingham Evening Mail:*

I talked the matter over with him and he accepts the situation, accepting that he has not been playing well. He has been under a lot of pressure, not least not being able to settle down and being separated from his family. A lot of people do not understand this kind of thing in a professional footballer's life.

Gary has a different version to the 'party line' put out by his manager.

After the Wolves game I went to see him to tell him what a crap manager he was. He had just sold a player who would guarantee you goals as well as being a commanding presence on the pitch. Freddie didn't like what I had to say or the way I said it so he fined me a week's wages. I told him to fuck off so he added on another week. I told him again using the same industrial language. I got up to four weeks' fines, when Freddie said he would bring it back to two weeks' wages if I apologised. I told him I was fucking sorry and left his office.

The Welshman was once again cast into the football wilderness, missing the rest of the season because of Freddie Goodwin's intransigence. It would be thirteen months before he would make a first-team return. Gary knuckled down in an effort to not only regain his Birmingham first-team spot but also his place back in the national team. Even though he was unsuccessful in gaining the first-team jersey he was attracting rave reviews in the reserves. In fact, Goodwin praised his attitude and how hard he was training, although not recalling Gary until the following March when Gary appeared against West Ham in a 1-1 draw and in the 4-1 defeat of QPR.

The QPR game was the last time I appeared in a football match. I felt something go in my back and after the game the lads had to help me onto the coach. I was under treatment for months and then in January I exacerbated the injury doing a few jobs around the house. Within two weeks I underwent surgery and that was the end of my career.

In his short time with the Blues Gary Sprake had performed heroically, but there is still the perception today among some Blues fans that he was a waste of money. Research of the match reports, however, dispels that myth. It could be argued that the negative influence of the national media once again influenced people's views; many of the supporters who criticise Gary weren't even old enough to have seen him play. Those match reports unequivocally portray Gary Sprake as a top-class goalkeeper who in a short time had played consistently well. Lifelong Blues fan, and now one of Gary's closest friends, Joe Figg, recalls the memories he has of Gary Sprake:

> He arrived at Birmingham with the reputation of being a hard-drinking and fast-living character that got into scraps. That was a myth, he never once got into trouble on the pitch. Off it though, well! I once went to a fundraising event and Terry Cooper was the guest speaker. Someone from the floor asked Terry his memories of Gary Sprake. He said it went without saying what a great 'keeper he was. He said, however, he would remember Gary for three things, women, drinking and fighting. He said it was great to go on a night out. 'Sprakey would attract all the good-looking girls, choose his favourite then leave the rest for us.' Off the field Gary got into many scrapes during his time at the Blues, including the time he drove his car straight through a roundabout and ended up in an estate agent's window.

Controversy had indeed followed Gary Sprake from Leeds to the West Midlands, including the time a traffic warden accused Gary of trying to run him down after he issued him with a parking ticket and the time he injured a policeman's leg.

I'd been out for a few beers and foolishly drove home, which was only a couple of hundred yards away. There was a police station en route and as I was passing I had a puncture. As I was almost home I kept on driving. Two coppers were coming out of the station and chased after me. I ran up the drive and as I was slamming the door one of the policemen tried to put his leg in to stop me closing it. He was in agony so I opened it, although they never charged me with assaulting a police officer. At Leeds my best mate was Paul Reaney, but he never drank much so I used to go to watch the rugby and have a few pints with Billy and Big Jack. At Birmingham I used to enjoy a few pints with Alan Campbell and Howard Kendall. We would sometimes go for a few beers and a game of cards in one of the locals. During the late 1960s and early 1970s football became like show business, but most of us never forgot where we

*came from, a working-class background, so you would find most of us enjoying
a quiet pint, although I did sometimes go to nightclubs!*

Aston Villa supporter Andy Bessell remembers the down-to-earth
nature of the former Leeds and Birmingham 'keeper.

> When I was a teenager I was told Gary Sprake used to drink in Shirley
> Municipal club, but I couldn't believe it, a world-class footballer drinking in
> my local. I went up to him and asked if it was really him and got a strange
> look. He must have thought it was a windup. After that we became great
> friends and are to this day. He is a down-to-earth guy and we always meet
> up every Friday in the 'Pot' club in Olten. He is one of the lads even if we
> hear the same old football stories. Sorry Gazz!

Looking back at his Birmingham career Gary concludes:

*There were many reasons why my time at Birmingham City was not as successful
as I would have hoped, compared with my time at Leeds. When I arrived I took
the place of a local lad, Dave Latchford, and a section of the fans resented me for
that and never really gave me a fair chance. Another reason was that they thought
Freddie Goodwin was creating a Leeds-type dynasty. Freddie was an ex-Leeds
player and so was the coach, Willie Bell. As Leeds were hated throughout the
country for their tactics, professionalism and siege mentality the fans were sceptical
when I also joined. I'm just grateful there was not the technology around then
like there is today. Just before the 2005/06 season started, Steve Bruce tried to
sign Lee Bowyer from Newcastle, but the player opted out of the transfer because
the Blues' fans voiced their concerns on the internet. I would imagine the same
would have happened to me when I signed.*

*While at Leeds I had an excellent relationship with Don Revie. Freddie was
not in the same league as him as a manager, although having said that there were
not many managers that were! My relationship with Freddie broke down within
a week of me arriving because of his training methods. They were completely different to what I was used to at Leeds. We did a great deal of weight training at St
Andrews but I had never lifted a weight in all my time at Leeds. At the training
ground they had a weights machine with different exercises. The Birmingham lads
loved it and you could see the results – people like John Roberts, Bob Latchford
and Roger Hynd were like man-mountains but I was not used to it and it left
me knackered after every training session. This was the start of me getting back
pains. We also did a great deal of cross-country running and ran for miles each
day. All this meant that there was little time for any ball work; the only time*

we saw or played with a football was on a Friday morning when we practised free-kicks and corners for about half an hour. At Leeds we trained with a football most days, playing five-a-side and full-scale practice matches. In the 2005 rugby Test series against the British Lions, the New Zealand manager Darren Shand argued that players can be over-coached. To keep them at the cutting edge players should be allowed to get on with it, without any over-burdening interference from the coaching staff. That was one of Revie's strengths, apart from the dossiers, he just let us get on with it, although he could have showed more confidence in our ability a lot earlier than he did. The difference is, and this shows what an innovative manager Revie was, he did it forty years ago without all the technology available to the sports scientists of today. We enjoyed the training very much at Leeds, at Birmingham it was a chore. I had many arguments with Freddie and Willie about their methods. Sometimes the disputes would become really heated and once I was fined several weeks' wages for questioning the manager's authority. Not only were the training methods outdated but for a First Division club the facilities were second rate. We had a hut with very little hot water, so there was a mad rush to get into the showers after training and then we also had to take our training kit home with us to wash ourselves each day. I used to buy my own kit because the ones the club provided were a disgrace.

My time with the Blues was littered with arguments between the coaching staff and myself. Apart from the training we had constant rows over my living arrangements. I would travel from Leeds to Birmingham every week, after the game on the Saturday I used to travel back and return on the Sunday evening for training the next day. I asked on numerous occasions if I could sometimes travel back on the Monday morning to spend more time with my wife and young daughter Julia but Freddie always refused. On a few occasions I ignored his instructions and stayed an extra night with my family. When I arrived on the Monday afternoon I would be taken to the manager's office where Fred would fine me either a week or two weeks' wages. This only endorsed my view of Fred and I would tell him he was a crap manager and he wasn't fit to lace Revie's boots. The next thing I knew I'd lost another week's wages. For the first six months of my Blues career I lived in a hotel in Solihull because the family home in Leeds hadn't been sold. After six months Fred told me the club couldn't afford to pay for my stay any longer, so they moved me in with Trevor Francis in his house in Knowle. I agreed to this and I had to pay for my keep as well as pay for my home in Leeds. After four months with Trevor my house was sold and we moved as a family to Solihull. I had a very enjoyable time living with Trevor. Although he was only about nineteen at the time you could see he had both the skill and ambition to go to the very top, he was very single-minded. I would say he would have been the only player at Birmingham that would have got into the great

Leeds team. I could also see that he was starting to develop the characteristics of a manager. Sometimes after training Alan Campbell, Howard Kendall and I would nip down to one of the local pubs and have a game of cards and a couple of beers. If I was late home for tea Trevor would be straight in to Freddie's office the next morning grassing me up. After my first season with the Blues I was disillusioned with all the issues of training, travelling and living alone. I couldn't wait to go away and have a nice relaxing holiday with my family, get some sun on my back and have a few lazy beers by the pool. Unfortunately, when I got back for the first day of pre-season training I had put on a few pounds. Once again I was called into Fred's office, where he told me he thought I was taking the piss. I told him to fuck off and to fine me if he wanted, which he did. All the lads used to call Dave Latchford, who had also gained a few pounds in the close season, and me the 'Two Fatties'. After that Freddie put us on a strict diet. For every day we were above our ideal weight he would fine each of us a fiver. The pounds flew off, mostly from our wallets as we couldn't take Fred seriously. It took me two weeks to get my weight down, so it cost me seventy quid, about a quarter of my wages. In my short time at Birmingham I must have been fined around twelve weeks' wages for one thing or another. I didn't play much first-team football for a year but this had more to do with my arguments with Freddie than my performances for the team.

After a long drawn-out battle to overcome my back injury I finally accepted defeat and retired in December 1975. I am the first to admit the Blues' fans never saw the best of me, but that was down to the manager not playing me because of our soured relationship. The games I did play, with perhaps the exception of the Everton game, I played very well. When a player had to give up because of injury there was an unwritten law that the player would get around ten per cent of the insurance money. Birmingham had insured me for the cost of my transfer, £100,000, but when I finished they never gave me a penny. Whether they thought I hadn't given them good value is a matter of opinion, but it would not have cost them a penny to offer me some compensation.

This is a view endorsed by the *Birmingham Argos* at the time:

> Gary Sprake's long battle to recover from a back injury that culminated in a touch-and-go fight for life has been totally ignored by the directors and management of the Blues. The treatment of Gary is disgraceful. He has been moved from one hospital to another over several weeks and only when dangerously ill did he receive a phone call from Willie Bell. That was the first contact from the club, but the players have visited regularly. Don Revie wrote a long letter, Mike Smith phoned and Rod Thomas visited from Derby.

Despite all that happened to me I still do not hold any grudges towards the club, the fans or the people of the city. The major disappointment for me was that the injury robbed me of the opportunity of a lifetime. Just before my Blues contract was up I had an offer from the ex-Wolves 'keeper Dave McClaren to join him at a club he was managing in Sydney. I signed the contract and Dave got my family a flat overlooking Bondi Beach. Unfortunately my injury put paid to all that and they cancelled the contract.

After a turbulent time at Birmingham, Gary Sprake could look back with some regret over an unfulfilled part of his career. It could be perceived as a failure from a professional perspective, but in the wider scheme of things this was an irrelevance as, rather than fighting for a first-team place at a football club, Gary Sprake was about to embark on a fight of far more importance and significance: the fight for life.

TEN

A SECOND CHANCE

Gary Sprake's football career came to an abrupt end at 9 a.m. on 15 January 1976, when he died on an operating table at the Woodlands Orthopedic Hospital in Selly Oak, Birmingham. He had entered hospital to undergo an operation on his back to correct a spinal fusion. This was a problem that had been causing him increasingly excruciating pain and prevented him from training or playing for months. At that time such an operation was very complicated and involved taking some bone out of his hip and using it to separate the fusion in his back. Unfortunately the operation led to complications and several days afterwards he developed a terrible throbbing pain that had started in his leg but had now spread to his chest and lungs. He had developed an embolism or blood clot, which in ninety per cent of cases proves fatal. To their credit the medical staff acted quickly to put out a call for a heart specialist and with great luck one of the country's top surgeons, Tim Clarke, was within minutes of the hospital.

The staff were excellent and acted quickly and, after several phone calls, they contacted Mr Clarke who fortunately was close by. He arrived at Woodlands within minutes and I was immediately rushed into theatre where an operation was performed to remove the blood clot. The surgeon had to cut open my rib cage to get at the clot and I am still left with a ten-inch scar there today. During the operation my heart stopped for almost half a minute and the medical staff had to use electric shock treatment to restart it. I survived my operation, I believe, for two reasons: firstly due to the excellence of the surgeon and his staff and secondly due to my levels of fitness as a professional footballer. I will never forget the brilliance of Mr Clarke and his staff and will remain eternally grateful for their care and expertise. As a small thank you, over the last thirty years I have tried to raise money for the British Heart Foundation whenever I have been able.

Gary was to remain in hospital for nearly three months recovering from his operations and any thoughts of a return to his playing career now became out of the question. Although he recovered from this near-fatal operation a range of problems, which are partly related to these operations and also a legacy of his playing career, have beset his retirement.

I guess one of the consistent themes of my retirement has been ongoing medical problems. I have had several further back operations and attend Solihull Hospital on a regular basis for painkilling injections to my back and fingers, as I have arthritis in both my thumbs. My family has sadly been beset by a history of heart disease and I suffered a heart attack myself in 1996. A year later I was fortunate to undergo a successful triple heart bypass at Walsgrave Hospital in Coventry. I feel very lucky to have survived these operations and have been determined to enjoy the time I have been given. I also feel that overcoming these medical conditions has enabled me to put into perspective a lot of the criticism I have received about my footballing career since 1975.

Although Gary's heart condition could be hereditary, the other medical conditions he suffers from, such as the back pain and the arthritis in his hands, leads to an interesting debate about the impact of professional football on the medical health of players of a certain generation. These issues have come sharply into focus in recent years with the tragic death of West Bromwich Albion legend Jeff Astle and the terrible illness affecting Liverpool's famous full-back Tommy Smith that has meant he has to use crutches to walk. Over the last ten years or so Gary has been interviewed on a number of occasions by journalists and academics regarding these controversial issues with regards to the causes and impact of injuries in professional sport. During these interviews one question seems to crop up continually: 'Were you forced to receive cortisone injections as a player and what have been their effects?'

It is true that when I played at Leeds the medical staff, at the request of the manager or coaches, would regularly give us cortisone injections to enable us to play through injuries. I believe this was also a regular practice at other clubs and I know Tommy Smith has talked about similar experiences he had at Liverpool. To some extent the club's hands were forced as even the most successful teams only had very small squads compared with today's Premiership. The problem of injuries was also, I believe, worsened by the heavy or sometimes rock-hard pitches that put a great strain on players' bodies. The recent very sad death of

Jeff Astle, who was hugely popular in the Midlands where I live, led to a lot of controversy in both the national and local press over whether his brain haemorrhage was caused by continual heading of those old leather balls. I know that the Professional Footballers Association have found a large amount of footballers from my generation suffer from severe arthritis. However, at present the evidence is only circumstantial and the PFA medical staff are still investigating their findings. I am no medical expert so it is not for me to comment or make any assumptions about the impact of cortisone injections on the health of ex-players, but I will be very interested to read the final report when it is published.

Upon his retirement from professional football Gary initially faced the dilemma of many of his peers: what to do next? He had left school with no formal qualifications and had left his apprenticeship after only a few months. Although professional footballers in 1976 earned a good living they certainly couldn't retire on it. The two paths open to ex-players at that time seemed to be either back into football as a manager or coach or the well-trodden route of becoming a publican. Like many footballers of both his own and subsequent generations Gary found the sudden end to his career very hard to deal with.

It took me nearly a year to recuperate from my double operation and I'm afraid to say I did struggle to come to terms with life after football. I fell into a well-worn path of many ex-footballers and began to drink far too much and even got caught drink driving. I was banned from driving for a year. I realised that although I was in no way rich as a professional footballer I had still enjoyed a very privileged lifestyle. We only trained for a few hours a day and never really had to organise anything for ourselves. So yes, you could say that when it all came so abruptly to an end I was a little lost as to what to do. I didn't really want to stay in football and with my injuries that would have proved impractical anyway. Also I had no desire to run a pub, which is probably just as well as I was already tempted to drink far too much. The drink driving offence did open my eyes, however, to the path that I could be going down and I did sort myself out quite quickly after that. After a year of being a sports rep for Dunlop, which I didn't enjoy as it involved too much travelling, I was fortunate enough to obtain a job as a training officer at Solihull College, where I worked from 1978 to 1998.

Gary looks back at his twenty years at Solihull College with great fondness and he enjoyed the new challenges that this new post brought. His role was far removed from that of saving goals at Leeds United but he still enjoyed it immensely. His duties included organising training, interviews and work experience for students whose ages ranged from sixteen to sixty. People recognising his name also helped his initial transition into the job and it certainly enabled Gary to successfully organise job interviews for many students.

I was very happy at the college. I learnt many new skills and I hope that I also helped a lot of people get valuable training or jobs. I used to really enjoy finding placements or interviews for the students and company representatives who recognised me were always really positive. I am pleased that I decided to do this type of job and I was very sad when I had to retire from the college in 1998 because of my heart condition. I don't for one minute regret not staying in football at all. I loved playing the game but I had no desire to remain in football in any other capacity. I have to say that Ken Bates's opinion that goalkeepers don't make good managers does make me smile. Perhaps he thinks that we are too stupid or don't know much about the game? I don't think Dino Zoff did a bad job as the Italian national manager and I think that Kevin Blackwell did wonderfully well in his first year at my old club to keep them in the division and finish in a respectable mid-table position.

The subject of Leeds United and the club's attitude towards Gary has also been a recurrent theme of his retirement. There have generally been two distinct attitudes to him, the first being the overwhelmingly positive response he has received from the majority of Leeds United fans and the second being the less-than-positive response he has encountered from the club officially and of course from many of his former colleagues from the Revie era. How does Gary feel about the reaction towards him?

The majority of football fans and especially Leeds fans I meet today still recognise me and I am happy to reminisce with them about my time at the club. Some mention the 'Careless Hands' reputation but it is never malicious and I am always very pleasantly surprised when they tell me that they think that I have been very harshly treated by the press. I can honestly say that over last thirty years I can count the negative reactions I have got off fans on the fingers of one hand. I still get quite a few requests for autographs in the post each week and some Leeds fans travel to my home from miles away to meet me and get their books or photos signed. I am afraid that the positive reaction of the fans of Leeds has been in stark contrast to the club itself and of course some ex-teammates. I have never officially been invited back to Elland Road since I left in 1973. The club hasn't, as far as I know, actually banned me but it has been made more than clear that since the Revie story broke I have not been welcome at Elland Road. I certainly haven't received any invites to any of the Revie reunions. In fact, in February 2005 I wrote to the club asking why I hadn't received an invite for a big reunion evening the club were holding for the Revie team. I never received a reply.

While Peter Ridsdale was chairman of the club there was a contact opened between the club and myself for the first time. Ridsdale was being interviewed on Sky and he mentioned the fact that I was his boyhood hero and he thought I was a world-class goalie. After the interview I wrote to thank him for his kind comments and he wrote back inviting me to Leeds as a guest for a game. However, when I wrote back replying that I would love to come to a game as a guest I never heard anything else from him or the club. I'm not criticising Peter Ridsdale but I think that it was obvious that certain influential ex-players had got at him and vetoed the invite. I have been back to watch games at Elland Road with friends who are Birmingham and Villa fans and I have never had any problems. I was recognised a lot by the fans and there were no issues, although I never met any of my ex-colleagues when I went back to Leeds. In fact, since I left the club I have talked to very few of my former teammates. I did meet Terry Cooper and the late Terry Hibbett at Birmingham on several occasions and we had a few pints and got on fine. Since beginning to write my memoirs it has become apparent that some of my former colleagues such as Jack Charlton, Peter Lorimer, Mick Bates and Terry Yorath don't have any issues with me but there are some former players who are still very influential at the club who have never forgiven me for the Mirror *article on Revie* [The Mirror controversy surrounding Don Revie is discussed in chapter twelve]. *It doesn't really bother me that they don't want to invite me to Elland Road. It's their problem not mine because I know I told the truth. Even though I only played sixteen times for Birmingham my relationship with them is completely different and they have always been fantastic to me. I regularly attend the Blues' games as a guest and occasionally I have been asked to do some PR work for the corporate part of the club. This usually involves joining fans on their table for a meal or sometimes doing small question and answer sessions in hospitality boxes. I have to say I really enjoy doing them and that both Birmingham City as a club and their fans have always treated me really well.*

Although Gary's relationship with Leeds has been officially very strained, he still feels a strong affinity to the club.

I am of course very disappointed in the way the club has officially behaved towards me but it hasn't altered my attitude towards Leeds United as a team. I still regard myself as a fan and it is always the first result I look out for every week. I think the Leeds fans are fantastic and they have showed their loyalty and fanatical support despite the increasing on and off-field turmoil over the last few years. I thought the team under David O'Leary was very exciting and was reminiscent of the high tempo and aggressive pressing game that we developed in the mid-1960s under Don Revie's management. I think they were very unlucky not to win any trophies in those three years under O'Leary. In a way it was a lot like us in the 1960s. In our first three years in the First Division we were runners-up three times and got to several semi finals. The difference was that we were able to stick together as a team and we had our breakthrough win of three trophies close together in 1968/69. The major difference, I think, was that we were mostly all home-grown players who wanted to play for the club and the wages came second, so when we did sign players such as Johnny Giles, Mick Jones and Allan Clarke they all fitted into the existing wage structure. The tribulations under O'Leary, Venables and Reid are well publicised and the financial mess was sad to witness, although I think that Peter Ridsdale to an extent has been made a convenient scapegoat for the problems that the club suffered financially. I know the 'Living the Dream' cliché has been well worn but it is true to an extent as when Leeds were signing all those top-quality players the manager, board and fans didn't seem too unhappy. The club took a big gamble and unfortunately it didn't work out. Of course, Peter has some responsibility for the problems but the manager and the players themselves I feel were equally culpable. I hope they get back into the Premiership soon but I think they face a very tough task. Kevin Blackwell did a very good job with no money and lots of free transfer players in his first season in the Championship. It is a very strong league and I just hope it doesn't take them as long to get back to the top flight as it did in the 1980s.

Gary's profile since his retirement has been relatively quiet in comparison to many from his era, although he has still undertaken the odd newspaper or television interview. The number of requests for interviews has increased in recent years, especially as the press ask him to quote on the latest faux pas of today's top goalkeepers.

It is inevitable that when a 'keeper makes a high-profile mistake somewhere along the line my name gets mentioned and I have been asked a lot recently to comment on the perceived increase in mistakes made at international and Premiership level by today's 'keepers. I feel that it's inevitable that however good a goalkeeper is they eventually will make a few mistakes. Sometimes errors are caused by bad luck and sometimes by poor play but I still feel as individuals goalkeepers make far fewer key mistakes per season than outfield players. I think that although there are some very good goalkeepers today, such as Paul Robinson, Nigel Martyn,

Russell Hoult, David James and Robert Green, there was a far greater depth of goalkeeping talent in my day. When I played, the other 'keepers that I really rated included Peter Shilton, Ray Clemence, Pat Jennings, Alex Stepney, Peter Bonetti, Joe Corrigan and Jim Montgomery all of whom were British. The best of them all was, in my opinion, Gordon Banks, as he was a class 'keeper. He had such great positional sense and made saves look easy without ever resorting to being flashy. He was a lovely fellow as well and I enjoyed playing against him at both club and international level. The other 'keeper I really admired was the opposite of Gordon and was far more flamboyant and entertaining – that was the great Soviet 'keeper Lev Yashin. In my opinion the best 'keeper playing in the Premiership in the last few years has been Petr Cech of Chelsea. I know that some people may criticise my view for being far too nostalgic and may argue that with the back pass rule and new lighter balls goalkeepers face a harder job. I disagree that being a goalkeeper is any tougher today. I would have loved to play on the pitches that they have today with the wonderful protection goalkeepers now get from referees. Thirty years ago the pitches were bare by the end of September, frozen from November to March and rock hard again in April and May. I know 'keepers have to cope with lighter balls and the back pass rule today but I am sure that 'keepers of my generation would have adjusted well to these in training. I always fancied myself as an outfield player and during five-a-side training I was always up front anyway and never played in goal. If the present generation of 'keepers thinks they have it tough they should have tried marking some of the rugged centre forwards we faced with minimum protection from the officials, and played with leather balls that could break a finger with ease.

Despite the arguments regarding the merits of goalkeepers of different generations Gary is keen to point out that these views are not purely nostalgic and that he certainly doesn't think that everything was better in his day.

I am very pleased that many top-level footballers today earn such a good living. It is a very short life as a professional and you never know when it might end, so if they earn good wages good luck to them I say. Today there is much more money in the game, from television, sponsorship and the commercial aspects of the game than in our day, when buying a replica shirt was almost impossible. I am not jealous of the wages that current players earn, especially as being a professional footballer is far different today. Their lifestyle is now much more high profile and the media is far more intrusive, to the point of provocation in some cases. When I played we could mix more freely with supporters. I used to drink in many of the same pubs as them and most of the time we were left alone.

I think it was a much more working-class game than it is now as it has become big business and inevitably players' wages have risen, but so have the demands upon them. I was quite shocked recently when I saw that wages throughout the Football League topped over a billion pounds during the 2003/04 season and I am not sure how long the game can sustain such wage levels. Generally though, I think the players today are more professional in things like their diet, and the influx of foreign stars has seemed to dilute the drinking culture at many, but obviously not all, clubs. It is sad to note how loyalty to clubs has declined so dramatically and I was really angry when I heard Lucas Radebe's comments that during their relegation season some Leeds players were just turning up at training to collect their wages. I know that Don Revie would never have accepted such an attitude. When I started my career as a seventeen year old playing in the first team I was earning about £2 a week so there was really not much chance of me getting too carried away with myself and flaunting my money around town. By the end of my career in 1975 I was earning about £300 a week with bonuses, which was a very good wage but was never going to set me up for life. In fact, like all professional players, since I was thirty-five I have received a pension of £300 a week from my contributions to my pension scheme. I never received a penny from Birmingham when I was forced to retire though. I feel lucky I played when I did. I got paid very well, for the time, and I had a great life and to be honest even if I could change things I wouldn't. I would still choose to have played in the Leeds United team from 1962 to 1973 than play for any other team today or in the past.

Despite the initial twin traumas of the operations and coming to terms with the end of his footballing career Gary has been happy with his lifestyle.

Although I have had some major medical problems I still feel I am a lucky man to have had two such rewarding careers. In my personal life I am also very happy and have been in a loving relationship with my partner Jackie for over twenty years, and we are both very settled in the Birmingham area. It is nice to be remembered by people I meet today and they are always very friendly. I have come to terms with the negative reputation that some of the media have given me since I retired. I think it's unjust but worrying about it won't make them change it and anyway I'm not the first goalkeeper to come under such negative media spotlight and I'm sure I won't be the last. As I mentioned previously, the only thing that hurts me is the attitude of some of my former Revie colleagues. I don't have a problem with their not wanting anything to do with me. That's their choice and it doesn't really bother me. What does hurt, however, is that they have decided to use their memoirs not to deal with any of the issues raised by the Mirror *controversy but to attack me as some sort of scapegoat who somehow cost the team so many trophies. This is an accusation that I absolutely refute and will continue to do so until the day I die. I made mistakes but they were no more or less than any other of my colleagues and it was never raised as an issue at the time.*

One of the major issues that has been raised with Gary on many occasions has been why he has waited nearly thirty years to write his own memoirs.

To be honest over the years I have had quite a few journalists who have been very keen on writing my story but I have never felt quite comfortable with their motives. I feel many of them only wanted to open up old wounds between myself and other former Leeds players and use it as another platform to attack Don Revie's character. I was never prepared to go down that road, which I feel can only cause unnecessary bitterness and upset. I believe there was also the grave danger of defending myself too vigorously and coming across as arrogant or big headed, which is completely against my nature. So I was happy to go along with things as they were until I met my nephew Stu again three years ago and he mentioned the possibility of a book. We got talking about a pro-gramme that I did with Brian Moore that had been repeated on Sky at that time. Don't get me wrong, I think Brian Moore was a top commentator and a nice guy but during the interview for whatever reason he never moved on from my reputation for mistakes and it came across as quite negative. At this stage I thought that with someone I could trust perhaps it was now time to put the record straight and offer my own perspective. I have really enjoyed being involved in this process and although sometimes I have had to rack my brains very hard to remember all the games and incidents it's been great fun. There has been quite a lot of interest in the project and I have also done some interesting book-related interviews. I particularly enjoyed my interview on BBC Wales with Frances Donovan and on BBC Radio West Midlands with Tony Butler, and both were very positive compared to the Brian Moore interview. Recently I have also started to do some after-dinner work and particularly enjoyed the smaller and more intimate events I have done, such as at Bridgend Cricket Club. I can't see me making a third career out of these events but I certainly wouldn't mind doing a few more as I have enjoyed them immensely. I also hope people will enjoy reading about my career and maybe it might allow them to read what I feel is the real truth about Gary Sprake.

ELEVEN

THE MISTAKES:
A REPUTATION TARNISHED

Over the last few years the increasingly frequent and high-profile mistakes made by goalkeepers at both domestic and international level have found the much-maligned role of goalkeeper central to rigorous debate, and there have been many interesting articles on the issue in the national press. In one of many such articles Rick Broadbent in *The Times* of February 2004 quotes the Uruguayan novelist Eduardo Galeano, who wrote of the goalkeeper that 'Damnation will follow him to the end of his days.' Broadbent goes on to argue that it is the goalkeeper's lot to be judged on his failings rather than his success, and that supporters inevitably only remember their high-profile mistakes. Although the *Times* article was focusing on the mistakes and reputation of modern England 'keepers David Seaman, David James and Nigel Martyn, it could quite easily have been applicable to a Leeds goalkeeper of a different era. The reputation of Gary Sprake as an error-prone and fundamentally flawed goalkeeper whose mistakes cost his team dearly is taken for granted by commentators and many casual observers of the game. The image of the temperamental and gaffe-prone Welsh 'keeper is part of football folklore and has been well honed in football literature, especially in the autobiographies of some of his former Leeds colleagues.

Former Glamorgan and England cricketer Steve James recalls in his autobiography *Third Man to Fatty's Leg* that his cricketing colleagues at Cambridge University, including former England captain Michael Atherton, would enthusiastically shout out 'Sprake' at anything remotely resembling a fielding error made by their teammates. Michael Atherton himself, commenting on television during a Test match in 2004, described a dropped catch by an England fielder as being worse than Gary Sprake. In fairness to these two cricketers, there is probably little malice in their actions; as Francis Hodgson, in his book on goalkeeping, states, every schoolboy and Sunday league footballer knows what is meant by a goalkeeper doing a Sprake. Gary has become an iconic figure, the image of a hapless tragi-comi goalkeeper who constantly lost the plot, especially in vital games. It has now become an integral image in the annals of football mythology, a reputation written in stone, but to what extent is this image really true? Was Gary Sprake an error-prone goalkeeper who let Leeds down on many occasions? Or were the mistakes simply the goalkeeping errors that happen every Saturday to goalkeepers from the local parks to the international stage? As his image and reputation are so intrinsically linked to the concept of mistakes, any biography of Gary would be incomplete without analysing them and their impact on somebody with a reputation for 'Careless Hands'.

At one time or another we have all had that compelling desire to kick the cat or aim a well-placed kick at the telly, and Gary, throughout his career, may have felt the desire to undertake one or more of these activities more often than most. Nearly every game that the highly successful Leeds team played was under the media spotlight, with a vindictive press eagerly waiting to pounce on any signs of a chink in the well-crafted Leeds armour. By the very nature of their position goalkeepers have a pedestal of their own especially in front of the camera's piercing eye. If you believe many football commentators Gary Sprake was an accumulator of prize gaffes, with few other sportsmen in Britain being pilloried so much. The mistakes have been shown, replayed, slowed down, dissected and analysed by commentators and ex-teammates alike. Gary, along with the public at large, has endured this misconception that it was a common occurrence, an inherent part of his game. In reality there were only a handful of genuine gaffes, which included famously throwing the ball into his own net playing against Liverpool at Anfield, stubbing a soft left-footed clearance to an Everton player in an FA Cup semi-final, diving over a shot he should have gobbled up in the FA Cup final against Chelsea, dropping a simple lob in an away game against Crystal Palace and also being part of an abject defensive performance in the famous FA Cup giant-killing defeat away to Colchester United in 1971. The problem for his reputation is obvious. It is not the number of mistakes he made but their perceived significance that has served to add fuel to the anti-Sprake flames and has characterised his subsequent image.

Gary recalls, in the staccato accent that alternates between a broad Yorkshire brogue and a Welsh lilt traceable back to his native Swansea, how he would sometimes sit at home and ponder on the real impact of these mistakes, reckoning that throughout his whole career they added up to no more than single figures. One particularly vivid memory he has is of the team's hotel before the FA Cup tie against Cardiff, en route to the 1972 final. The players were watching the football preview of the day's ties when the commentator got round to the Leeds game. He started by saying, 'If Leeds has a weakness in their team it is...' Gary beat him to it by saying, 'It will probably be me!' The programme makers then showed the 1970 final goal against Chelsea and the slip against Palace. It was all played over again with the rest of the team sitting in silence. Although such incidents hardened his own personal resolve and determination to go out and continue to perform at the highest level and dispel this image, to what extent did the constant media criticism affect the relationship between Gary and some of his colleagues? Did some teammates indirectly vent on to him their own disappointments and frustrations at the seemingly endless close calls and sheer bad luck that saw the team so often end up empty handed? Although much of the banter directed at Gary was obviously good natured and typical of football dressing rooms, did it serve only to sow further seeds of doubt in his own mind about his teammates' confidence in him? Did his teammates really believe the media hype that he was the team's weakest link? This is a point that both Jack Charlton and Mick Bates have recently picked up on, arguing that Gary did have a tendency to becoming increasingly paranoid that he was the focus of the conversation. As Big Jack states:

> Gary was a great goalie but he always thought people were talking about him; he would come over and ask what we were talking about, so all the lads would lead him on but there was nothing malicious about it.

Another major issue that nearly every ex-Revie player has commented on was Gary's supposed problem of keeping focused during games. Because he played in such a great team he would often not touch the ball for long periods, especially at home, where he would patrol his area following the ball, but when it was forever at the other end of the pitch this would prove difficult. Did his mind wander and drift into thinking of other things? Perhaps his family, friends or jobs around the house? To what extent did the image, encouraged by the media, of a 'keeper who made spectacular mistakes fuel opposing fans' attempts to rile Gary and undermine his confidence? To what extent were they successful? Mick Bates argues that as soon as Gary ran out of the tunnel the crowd would try to get at him straight away in an attempt to undermine his confidence. Catcalls and booing were the least of the Leeds 'keeper's worries. There were the occasional spanners, apple cores and the inevitable coins that used to come in very handy for a few pints after the game. The worst moment, however, was when a billiard ball crashed onto the crossbar during a League game at Burnley. On the whole though, he did attempt to build up a good rapport with opposing fans, cracking jokes and handing out chewing gum. The only way to unravel the complexities of his reputation and whether it is justified is to examine the infamous mistakes themselves. Were they simply goalkeeping errors that could happen to any goalie, or were they unique to Gary himself, part of an inherent weakness in his own game?

Probably the most talked-about mistake ever made by a goalkeeper occurred at Anfield on 9 December 1967, a miserable wintry day. Nearly every football supporter in the land, whether they were present that day or not, still chuckles with glee as they remember or visualise that split-second of horrifying drama when Gary famously tossed the ball into his own net. Indeed, in the November 2000 edition of the *Observer Sports Monthly* reporter Jon Henderson choose this incident as one of his ten greatest sporting mishaps of all time. The worldly-wise Liverpool manager Bill Shankly, who had seen and done it all, commented at the time that this was 'an utter freak, never seen before'. While attempting at the time to find words of comfort for his disconsolate goalkeeper, Don Revie argued that 'if he played for another fifty years he would never do that again'. Even though Gary attempted to take on board the advice there was no real consolation, as he was probably more critical of himself than others were at the time. Gary had picked up a back pass from Jack Charlton and was trying to set up a quick counterattack, as he so often did, by quickly throwing the ball out to Terry Cooper who was, however, rapisdly closed down. Changing his mind, the Leeds 'keeper decided to check the throw and pull the ball back into the safety of his chest. But as a result of the icy conditions the ball slipped, went over his shoulder and everyone in the ground knew where it landed. This was probably with the exception of the referee, who was said to have turned to Jack Charlton and asked what had happened and what he should do. With typical dry humour

Jack replied, 'I think the silly so-and-so has thrown it in his own net; you'll have to give a goal.'

Mention the name Gary Sprake to the majority of non-Wales or non-Leeds fans and their reaction is still to immediately shout out 'Careless Hands', referring of course to the famous mistake in 1967. This association came about as a result of the DJ playing the Des O'Connor hit of the same name at half-time, much to the delight of the Kop, which was perhaps a more significant event than the error itself. However, eyewitnesses present that day agree that the error, although horrific for any goalkeeper, had no real bearing on the overall result of the game. Liverpool showed far more menace in front of goal than the Leeds attack, which was easily shackled by Smith and Strong. As Tom German of The Times reported, 'I can remember Lawrence [Liverpool's goalkeeper] in urgent action only once.'

As a result the Leeds defence was constantly under pressure, with Tony Hateley and Roger Hunt receiving a constant supply from the wingers Thompson and Callaghan, who were excelling in conditions that full-backs hate. In the second half the Leeds defence kept the score to a respectable level, given the footballing lesson they received that day. They covered, tackled and worked tirelessly trying to stop the Liverpool juggernaut with the not-so-small contribution of the goalkeeper, who was excellent in the second half. Inevitably, however, this will always be overshadowed by his incredible own goal.

In fact, what most people don't know or have simply chosen to forget is just how atrocious conditions were at Anfield on 9 December 1967. In the UK that weekend forty-seven counties were in the grip of snow and ice and twenty-one other matches in the League programme had already been postponed, falling victim to the terrible conditions. Eric Stinger reported in the following Monday's Yorkshire Post that

Gary Sprake of Leeds United almost achieved immortality at Anfield on Saturday when the ball slipped into his own net. It was not a silly mistake but a freakish happening, caused by the slippery ball on the snowbound pitch. Two minutes before half-time a Liverpool raid was checked and at Anfield Sprake prepared to throw the ball out to Cooper, a situation that arises a thousand times or more in any goalkeeper's career. This time it was shatteringly different. Sprake checked momentarily but when he carried on with his throw, the ball, instead of leaving the gloved palm near the top of the arc stayed there for one split-second and on being released it sailed over his left shoulder into the net. I doubt if Sprake could repeat it if he tried. I did not blame him for a moment, nor did his colleagues or manager Don Revie. Indeed, during the second half Sprake turned the ribald jeers of the notorious Spion Kop to cheers by his display.

In fact, by this time Leeds were already one down as a result of a defensive mix-up between Reaney and Hunter, who had both slipped to allow Hunt to squeeze between them and put the ball into the net. Stanger concludes his report by analysing the cost of Gary's mistake:

> Even without the second freakish goal I feel Liverpool would have won comfortably as Leeds never looked like scoring. Freak goal or not, Leeds could have no complaints. Liverpool won well.

Terry Lofthouse of the *Yorkshire Evening Post* reported that

> Although Gary Sprake gave away perhaps the most amazing goal seen on a soccer pitch in the defeat at Anfield, nobody on United's staff could blame him or did. Up to that point Sprake had made several good saves and in the second half, to his great credit, he never allowed the incident to upset him and his excellent effort brought admiration.

As for the impact on the result he agrees with Stanger's opinion:

> I believe they [Leeds] would still have lost, for Liverpool were far happier on the snow-covered surface than United.

Tom German of *The Times* agreed:

> Carelessness or sheer misfortune, one could only sympathise with Sprake, who later regained his undoubted stature with some characteristic saves. The remainder was an almost unrelieved chapter of Liverpool swift and precise in spite of the conditions, searching with accustomed power and urgency for further openings.

The 2-0 defeat therefore highlights the fact that the mistake was more significant for Gary's reputation than the actual outcome of this particular match. If 'Careless Hands' is an apt moniker it seems to reflect more on the humorous reaction of the home DJ and the Anfield crowd, and to the myth that has developed around this infamous incident, than it does the actual mistake. What actually happened was that a goalkeeper, on a terrible day for 'keeping, made a miscalculation lasting only a split-second that resulted in an amusing error for the crowd present and a unique own goal. For most 'keepers that would be a terrible error soon forgotten. Unfortunately what Gary Sprake found, to his cost, is that, much like modern 'keepers David James, Roy Carroll and Jerzy Dudek, once your reputation is made, whatever moniker you are given as a goalkeeper, it is almost impossible to shake off that perception. For Gary's own reputation the problem was that when he did make a mistake it was usually televised, as every game Leeds played in was important in their annual hunt for major honours.

Even when his career was at its zenith during the period 1968/69 Gary could never quite shake off that tag that he was somehow error prone. Only six weeks after the success of the first trophy win against Arsenal, at Wembley in March 1968, the Welsh 'keeper was blamed for the error that led to Everton's winner in a 1-0 defeat at Old Trafford in the FA Cup semi-final. This mistake is often recalled by critics to suggest how vulnerable Gary's temperament was during the big occasions and to illustrate his unreliability in tense situations. However, in no recollection or memoir of that match has there been any reference to the fact that for the majority of the game Gary was severely injured and today, with goalkeeping substitutes, would have immediately left the field before the actual incident occurred. Phil Brown of the *Yorkshire Evening Post* made this very point in his match report at the time. What did make the difference on the scoresheet was Royle's challenge – ruled a fair one – that sent the goalkeeper down hard on his right shoulder, leaving him unable to throw the ball. When Royle challenged again, unable to throw, Gary was forced to kick with his weaker foot.

As Don Revie himself told the paper at the time, the mistake would never have happened without the injury:

> Gary was unlucky in being forced into a position where he could not throw
> because of his injured shoulder.

In fact, the *Yorkshire Post* also reinforced this opinion on its back page, which led not with negative headlines about Gary but 'Shoulder injury leads to vital goal in cup-tie', with their reporter Richard Ulyatt stating that

> When Sprake hurt his shoulder after a clash with Royle early in the first
> half there was no free-kick, but the incident was significant because Sprake

could not thereafter throw the ball as he usually does when ending an attack. Royle challenged Sprake again after forty minutes and, not able to throw the ball, he was forced to kick with his weaker foot. Caught in two minds, his kick went to the menacing Hubbard whose lob was prevented only by Charlton deflecting the ball with a hand and Morrissey subsequently scoring from the spot. The question arises, would a fully fit Sprake have erred? My answer to this question is no.

Unsurprisingly, this viewpoint of the mistake has manifested itself somewhat differently over the years and in their memoirs Gary's ex-colleagues remember it as another example of a 'typical' error by the temperamental Welshman. An interesting aside to this mistake was recently made by Paul Reaney in an interview with the official Leeds magazine in April 2005, when he recalled:

> When the left winger put the ball over I'm going across the line towards it – but Big Jack's coming back and handballed it. I'm yelling at him going 'What you doing?' I could have got it off the line, but instead it was a penalty, and they scored. I gave Jack some stick for that.

If the mistake at Anfield is the most infamous, in reality the most important for Gary personally was perhaps that which took place in the FA Cup final in 1970. Coming towards the last few weeks of the 1969/70 season Leeds were still on course for a remarkable treble. However, within a short space of time they had narrowly lost out on all three trophies and the team were once again to bemoan how fate seemed to be conspiring against them. The Leeds 'keeper must have felt this as much if not more than his colleagues, as not only had he made the mistake in front of millions of viewers in the FA Cup final but he also suffered a serious injury against Celtic in the European Cup semi-final on 15 April. After a long, hard season of training, matches and excellent performances in all conditions, the Welsh goalkeeper should have been looking forward to demonstrating his skills on the biggest stage of all, the FA Cup final at Wembley. Any football fan of a certain age will tell you exactly what cup final day represented to them, and the particular order of that exciting day. Firstly in the morning came *It's a Knockout*, between the two sets of cup final supporters, hosted by Eddie Waring and Stuart Hall, and then possibly a special *Question of Sport*. This was followed at 2.45 p.m. by the two managers leading the players out onto a sun-drenched Wembley with every inch of grass perfectly manicured like a bowling green. This image is mostly true, except in 1970 when Wembley resembled more of a quagmire than a football field. The authorities had, in their infinite wisdom, decided to hold the Horse of the Year show at Wembley days earlier, which, unfortunately, also coincided with a torrential thunderstorm. As left-back Terry Cooper stated, 'It was the worst pitch I ever played on.' Phil Brown of the local *Yorkshire Evening Post* argued that 'The diabolical pitch had a leading if malevolent part in swaying the drama.' United skipper Billy Bremner described the pitch as being in a terrible state:

> You found yourself almost ankle deep in mud at times. The ball came at you from awkward angles, bouncing and bobbling about.

Chelsea began the game itself very poorly and were behind early as they conceded a soft goal of their own. Jack Charlton had managed to flick his head at a cross and looped the ball innocuously towards goal, where it landed about a foot short of the Chelsea line. The Chelsea defender on the line was Eddie McReadie, who seemed to have all the time in the world to launch the ball into row Z but, in almost comically slow motion, the ball trickled under his foot as he swung his boot into thin air. As Leeds continued to dominate, Gary's nightmare moment came in the forty-third minute, as he dived over a shoot from Houseman to let Chelsea back into the game. Peter Lorimer recently argued this was the decisive moment of the game, which cost Leeds the trophy. Geoffrey Green of *The Times* reported at the time:

> As half-time approached it was their [Leeds] turn to blunder as Houseman hit Hutchinson's side header first time from the edge of the box. Sprake looked to have the low ball well covered. But again the pitch proved to be the villain of the piece. The shot skidded then slowed up to creep through under the goalkeeper's dive inside the post. It was tragic as Sprake hung his head in disbelief. Yet soon enough he made amends at the change of ends with two point-blank saves from Hutchinson.

If anyone actually watches the DVD of the 1970 cup final it makes interesting viewing and puts Gary's mistake into the wider context of his performance throughout the game. In the second half of normal time Gary made four crucial saves, including two one-on-ones with the Chelsea strikers and a save from Houseman which had seen commentator Kenneth Wolstenhome already pronounce a goal. Gary arched himself backwards and, one-handed, clawed the ball, which was already behind him and going into the goal, back into his arms. In the ninetieth minute he made a brilliant and brave save to keep Leeds in the tie at 2-2. In extra time, as both teams tired, Gary made a wonderful reflex save to palm the ball from Dempsey over the bar, with Wolstenhome stating, 'Dempsey did fantastically well, but Sprake did even better.' The last kick of the game saw Gary once again save well from his nemesis Houseman, which again reinforces the view that sometimes it is necessary to actually revisit the games themselves, as the truth can easily be overlooked and forgotten.

In a winning performance goalkeeping errors are soon forgotten, as would have this one been if Leeds had turned their second half dominance into goals and not hit the post three times, nor conceded a soft equaliser from Hutchinson almost at the final whistle as Jack Charlton missed his clearing header. Green continued:

> It was a well-researched tactic that now caught Leeds flat footed at the last breath, their concentration perhaps already deflected by the thoughts of their approaching celebrations

If Leeds had enjoyed a little more of the luck that their performance deserved people would have remembered the game as the Eddie Gray final, the Scottish winger being outstanding and at his mesmerising best. In the replay at Old Trafford on 29 April, despite going a goal up early on, the season culminated in calamity when Webb scored Chelsea's winner in extra time. This game, which Gary missed through injury, was probably best known for its notoriety and Harris's diabolical early tackle on Wembley hero Gray, who became a virtual passenger for the remainder of the replay. Interestingly, the winning Chelsea goal in extra time came from a mistake by the Leeds defence. As Hutchinson launched his long throw into the box Jack Charlton mistimed his header and it went backwards across the goal, where David Harvey subsequently missed his clearance punch for Webb to head the Londoners' winner. For Leeds it had proved a game too far in a season in which, by that time, they had played ten games more than Chelsea.

Six months later on 9 November a tough-looking away fixture at Crystal Palace was going well for Leeds, who were leading 1-0 through a fifty-second-minute header from Peter Lorimer. This was until the eighty-seventh minute, when an innocent-looking thirty-yard lob from Palace skipper Sewell slipped through Gary's hands and into the net. Unsurprisingly, given his reputation in some quarters, Barry Foster in the following Monday's *Yorkshire Post* brought up the 'keeper's alleged reputation for errors with Leeds manager Don Revie, who replied, 'Gary Sprake is still the best goalkeeper in Europe for me.' The reporter himself adds:

> Mr Revie, like everyone else who has seen Leeds play regularly, knows that Sprake has made errors in the past but his goalkeeping this season is once again a key factor in Leeds' domination of the league. If anything stands in the way of Sprake's showing the command of his area in cutting out high crosses, which has been a feature of his work for Leeds, and displaying courage when under severe pressure, then it could be a great blow for his team. On Saturday Sprake gave a faultless display until the eighty-seventh minute although several mistakes had been made in the 'holding' conditions by the defensive players around him.

But as Don Revie told Foster at the time, unfortunately, 'when a goalkeeper makes a mistake everybody sees it.'

Don Warters of the *Yorkshire Evening Post* argued that

> Up to the mistake Palace's failure to break through had been much due to Sprake's command of the area. It would be easy to criticise Sprake but in this instance it would be unfair in view of the command and authority he had shown up to the fatal eighty-seventh minute. He had not put a foot or a hand for that matter wrong.

Warters suggested that, although many Leeds fans leaving Selhurst Park were disappointed, the majority were prepared to concede and comment on 'how many times have brilliant saves he has made won us games?' Mick Bates recalled:

> That this was one of the few times I witnessed Revie losing his temper. We had fought a rearguard action for almost ninety minutes before the late equaliser and he was clearly very frustrated, but he did acknowledge that Gary had very much been part of keeping Palace at bay until his unfortunate mistake.

At the time Gary refused to comment. Perhaps he had already realised that goalkeeping can sometimes be an unrewarding activity and however much you argue that the mistakes of 'keepers are always emphasised more than outfield players some people will never budge from their opinion of you. It is to their great credit that these local reporters who saw Leeds play hundreds of games over many years were able to form a far more rounded overview of Gary Sprake's contribution to Leeds United.

The other infamous game often cited as an example of Gary's propensity to make mistakes took place on a windy day at Layer Road against lower-league Colchester in February 1971. It was a dreadful day on a sloping, rock-hard pitch, with the ball bouncing everywhere, the sort of nightmare conditions every 'keeper dreads. Before they knew it, Leeds were 3-0 down to a team that consisted of a mixture of rejects, hand-me-downs and veterans who were affectionately dubbed 'Grandad's Army'. Leeds were the leaders of the First Division and strongly fancied to add the FA Cup and the UEFA Cup to the silverware cupboard. Although Peter Lorimer recently stated that Gary made mistakes for two of the goals it is Jack Charlton who once again makes a very astute point:

> It wasn't so much that Gary made mistakes, they happen to all 'keepers. This was the only game I ever actually saw Gary play badly.

Colchester stormed into a three-goal lead thanks to a brace from Crawford and then one from Simmons early in the second half. Gary and his defence should have done better on all three. However, Barry Foster of the *Yorkshire Post* suggests that the goalkeeper wasn't the only one who played badly.

> Leeds could not settle on the small ground and did not size up the dangerous situation until the match was an hour old.

At the centre of the Colchester effort was veteran former England striker Ray Crawford, who was then thirty-five years old. In the nineteenth minute Gary misjudged a swirling cross, only to see an unmarked Crawford head in at the far post. Only two minutes later Crawford out-jumped Reaney at the far post and, as Gary raced towards the bouncing ball, the prone striker stuck out a leg and the ball fortuitously hit the Leeds post and went in. Colchester were 2-0 up. In the fifty-fifth minute Leeds went 3-0 down as both Gary and Paul Reaney watched the ball bounce, only for Colchester's Dave Simmons to score. Crawford later claimed that

Dick Graham, our manager, reckoned Sprake was vulnerable coming to crosses and basically that's what we tried to exploit.

It's evident that Gary played badly but so did the rest of the defence, who were supposed to prevent such crosses. In fact Paul Reaney had a real stinker, which the match reports comment upon, especially Phil Brown, who argues after Leeds went 3-0 down it could have been even worse:

Gary Sprake made two saves from Hall and Crawford after Reaney had twice made further errors. The score could have been even worse.

Now, Reaney himself has a favourite joke he tells at after-dinner speeches. When asked why he didn't score more goals, he argue:

I couldn't be up at one end of the field scoring and at the same time continually saving Sprakey's arse at the other end of the pitch.

Maybe he overlooked this particular game and his own performance when he reminisces about Gary's alleged failings.

Although Gary would admit this was hardly his greatest performance, the local match reports at the time don't really make much of his goal-keeping, but focus more on the poor effort of the team as a whole. The national papers were also quick to criticise Leeds and celebrate Colchester's win, with the *Daily Telegraph* arguing that 'Leeds had used familiar tactics, tackles had been ruthless, fouls stealthy and sophisticated.'

They seemed happy, though, not to comment on the long-ball tactics and physicality of the home team. Geoffrey Green in *The Times* also comments on how poorly Leeds played as a team.

It was an heroic all-out performance in which certain men played key parts – Crawford and Simmons the strikers, who between them reduced the lanky Charlton to a dithering novice. Lewis, for the clever way he organised attacks and turned elusive Pimpernel as he constantly switched wings to confuse England full-backs Reaney and Cooper. Gilchrist, for reducing the Leeds commander-in-chief to a mere name in the programme; and finally Garvey and Kurila, for shackling Jones and Clarke down the middle. It is no exaggeration to say Colchester might have scored five or six.

If the goalkeeper was to blame for this defeat then it was no more so than any of the rest of his colleagues, although again this is not how it is reflected in the memoirs of his ex-colleagues. Gary clearly should have done better on the first goal but also Crawford should have been more closely marked and not had a free header. As far as the other goals go, they were as much down to poor defending from the Leeds team and defence, especially Reaney. If you actually watch the game it is a poor team performance from everybody except possibly Paul Madeley. Yet, once again, it is Gary's reputation that seems to have suffered the most with the brunt of the blame being shifted onto him. It has now become evident that some of his colleagues have seized the opportunity to deny some of their own responsibility for the mistakes and failings made during this period and the many disappointing close calls of the glory years, and found themselves a convenient scapegoat.

David Saffer, in his biography of popular Leeds star Paul Madeley, *Leeds United's Rolls Royce*, continues this approach, stating that by 1971 Revie's team were consistent performers with 'the only downside being the occasional gaffe from Gary Sprake'. He then goes on to cite the Anfield error in 1967, the 1970 cup final and the missed lob against Palace in the same year. This quote seems to sum up the very paradox with regard to the debate about Gary's reputation. Although Saffer uses the term 'occasional', his statement reinforces the Welshman's negative image. The very point is, however, that the mistakes were relatively rare occurrences with the three mistakes he refers to, plus the Everton and Colchester games, which make it five. How many of the Leeds legends who have pilloried Gary in their memoirs could honestly admit to making less than five mistakes in this period and how many of today's Premiership 'keepers would gladly accept a record of only one mistake a year? This is a point that BBC Yorkshire's John Boyd picked up on in March 2005 when he argued that

> Despite his mistakes Sprake would nevertheless stand up very well against the current cream of the crop, with Manchester United and Arsenal in particular struggling to find a 'keeper who can catch the ball, let alone who can command his area and marshal his defenders. Indeed, if you rolled all their goalies into one and chucked in the likes of Liverpool's Jerzy Dudek into the equation you would still be struggling to find a reliable 'keeper... come back Gary Sprake.

Unfortunately, until now this reputation has remained unchallenged and mud sticks – Gary Sprake made high-profile mistakes, therefore he was a liability. This is not true. He made mistakes and some, it could be argued, cost the team, although their significance has clearly been exaggerated over time. This book attempts to discuss the mistakes in a far more open manner than previous analysis, although both the authors and Gary himself believe the tag of 'Careless Hands' to be grossly unfair.

It would be interesting to compare this discussion of Gary's mistakes and try to identify how many others of the ex-Revie team have admitted to making key mistakes in their memoirs. During Gary's twelve-year tenure at Leeds between 1962 and 1973 he played over 500 games. In the same period a study of the match reports for Leeds games would, if compiled as an error count, make interesting reading. Bearing in mind that if goalkeeping mistakes were high profile as a result of the importance of every game, then so would be any other players' errors as the team consistently challenged for honours. How would the records of Gary's teammates look if we were to assess their game on the grounds of their mistakes only – the missed penalties, crucial missed tackles, poor back passes, bookings or missed open goals? Indeed, Billy Bremner made this very point in his *Yorkshire Evening Post* article in August 1969:

> A goalkeeping error is nearly always magnified because he rarely gets two chances. Nine out of ten 'boobs' result in a goal. Yet think of all the mistakes the rest of us make. I've made a lot of mistakes in my time but usually I have been able to make up for them. So too have the other lads. Gary, however, is wide open in goal and the mistakes can look really bad. Yet before you judge don't forget all the brilliant saves he has made. There have been many occasions which we have marvelled at his keeping. In the Fairs Cup last September you wouldn't believe the save he made when Novac bent a free-kick around our defensive wall. I believe Gary is Britain's best 'keeper.

Since Gary left Leeds it is not surprising that only one Leeds player of the period has continued this theme and given the most honest appraisal of these issues. That is Jack Charlton, who stated recently:

> Football is a team game and no one player can be blamed. Gary made mistakes but so did everyone else. In the end you win or lose together as a team.

Another ex-colleague who has consistently defended Gary's reputation and refuses to fall into the trap of blaming him for the team's failings is Terry Yorath, who stated in the February 2000 issue of the Leeds official magazine *Leeds Leeds Leeds!*:

> Poor Gary is unfairly remembered for his mistakes. A lot of matches weren't televised back then, but when Sprakey made a mistake the cameras were always there.

The mistakes inevitably then drag our focus away from the other long months of competent, often staggeringly brilliant, demonstrations of goalkeeping that made Gary Sprake one of the finest craftsmen during this period. As Yorath continues to argue:

> He was the most natural goalie for club and country that you ever saw, he really didn't have to work too hard at his game. His technique and reflexes were almost superhuman at times.

Yorath develops this positive theme in his excellent recent hard-hitting autobiography *Hard Man: Hard Knocks*:

> Gary Sprake's miraculous save against Ferencvaros was one of many he pulled off during his ten years at Elland Road. He was a natural goalkeeper and an excellent shot stopper but I am worried he'll always be remembered for some of the high-profile mistakes he made... I will defend Gary against anybody who criticises him because football is littered with brilliant goal-keepers who all made the odd mistake.

This argument was presented perfectly in conversation recently with one of the heroes of Manchester United's 1968 European Cup win, Alex Stepney:

> Gary was a tremendous 'keeper, but like the rest of us at the time he made some mistakes. In our day only the top teams appeared on TV so if we made a mistake it was highlighted. With today's exposure every 'keeper is seen to make mistakes week in and week out. Unfortunately for Gary the few mistakes he made were all on telly.

Terry Cooper, the left-back in the Leeds dynasty under Revie, in a recent interview was loath to select Gary's best game for Leeds United, arguing that he was consistently brilliant throughout his career:

> It is sad that people remember the occasional blunder and forget that many of Gary's performances kept us in key games that enabled us to snatch a point or to go on and win the game. In fact, even when Gary did make a

rare mistake it had no impact on our view of him as a world-class 'keeper or affected the team's relationship with him. We all made mistakes; the only difference was that, as Gary was near the goal, it was obviously more costly, but that's the nature of goalkeeping. As far as I am concerned, although I fully understand the reasons he did it, the only mistake he made is the comments about Revie after he left Leeds.

Having researched hundreds of articles, books and magazines that have been written since he retired in 1975, one mostly finds the same common theme to describe Gary Sprake: an error-prone 'keeper who made key mistakes. The reality of this reputation is not as clear-cut as some observers would like to make out. Gary has obviously been disappointed that his image is so closely intertwined with a reputation for errors but he has accepted that if you make mistakes, as a professional sportsman and especially as a football goalkeeper, your reputation will suffer as a consequence. However, what frustrates him and what he finds very hard to accept is the premise that his mistakes cost Leeds so many trophies and that, even though he played over 500 games, that the club would have somehow been better off if he hadn't played for them. To be criticised for making mistakes is one argument but to suggest that one player is to blame for the team's failure to win trophies is quite another. Therefore, to what extent his mistakes cost Leeds is a question that must be addressed and the truth established.

If we look at the mistakes, how costly were they in reality? The infamous Liverpool incident had no impact on that game or the championship as Leeds finished fourth, five points behind the winners Manchester City. In 1970/71 the Crystal Palace point was important but whether it was the crucial point that cost the title depends on whether Leeds' home defeats against Liverpool, Spurs and infamously West Bromwich Albion are discounted, and if away defeats against Stoke and Chelsea or draws against Blackpool and Huddersfield are ignored. To start attributing blame for losing a championship to one incident in a season is a hazardous business that most commentators and fans are very wary of involving themselves in. In fact, Charlie George recently made this very point in his autobiography:

Some of the Leeds players who were involved then have said the difference between the two sides was we had a great goalkeeper and they didn't. I don't see the point of blaming others: you can't pin down the loss of a championship to one poor soul. If a 'keeper blows it in a cup final, for example, then he has to shoulder the blame but this is shared in a long championship campaign. They found a scapegoat or thought they had, and missed the fact that their own inadequacies at times contributed to the crucial defeats.

If individual mistakes are significant, they tend to be more important in one-off games like cup ties where by the very nature of the competition they are harder to redeem. Although the Colchester defeat in 1971 was embarrassing, it was collectively a poor team effort and blame can be apportioned equally across all the defence. If we are to identify the key mistakes that could have cost Leeds trophies they seem to point towards the 1968 and 1970 FA Cup matches. In 1968 the semi-final mistake was undeniably vital in a 1-0 defeat but Gary was carrying an injury that in later years, with substitute goalkeepers on the bench, would have seen him immediately leave the field. This leaves the cup final of 1970, when Gary's mistake was, it can be argued, very important in letting Chelsea back into the game. However, even disregarding the dreadful nature of the pitch, a presumption that Gary cost Leeds the cup that year would then have to ignore the other 197 minutes of the game, 120 minutes of which he didn't even play. If Gary Sprake's goalkeeping cost Leeds trophies then a comparison with David Harvey's record would only be fair. Both 'keepers won a championship medal; Gary played in six finals, winning three, losing two and drawing one, while Harvey played in four finals, winning one and losing three. It is also generally accepted that in the 1965 FA Cup final defeat Leeds would never have reached the final, nor made it to extra time on the day if it wasn't for Gary's performances in that cup run. It could also be pointed out that if it were not for his goalkeeping against Liverpool in the earlier rounds of the 1971/72 cup run Leeds may not have even made the final itself. It is interesting that these arguments seem to be missing in many of the previous comparisons of the two 'keepers.

The reputation of Gary Sprake as a fatally flawed and error-prone goalkeeper who cost Leeds United many trophies is not the real truth. He made mistakes, as do all 'keepers, and some were more important than others. However, what the actual match reports demonstrate is that these were all individual errors and not part of any inherent flaw in his goalkeeping. The most important argument that still frustrates him to this day is that somehow his goalkeeping cost Leeds trophies, a myth that has remained unchallenged until now. Some perceptive observers, such as Bagchi and Rogerson, are very aware of the flaws in this argument.

> Revie was ungracious in stating that Leeds would have won more if
> Gary had been replaced earlier. Unfortunately Sprake... continues to
> be remembered more for his occasional failures than his considerable
> achievements.

In fact recently Terry Yorath has reinforced Peter Lorimer's criticisms
of Don Revie's own conservative nature and the extent that this negativity had on Leeds' quest for trophies.

> Sometimes we were restrained by Don. He let his caution get the better of
> him. If he'd let us express ourselves individually a little more, then it could
> have been different. Everyone had to play within the team structure and
> although I'm sure he didn't restrict the flair players intentionally, if he'd
> realised just how talented his footballers were then I think we would have
> won more trophies.

This is an interesting perspective and one that gives a different take on
the the blame that can be apportioned to Leeds' relative failings.

A recent example of the culture of blame attached to goalkeepers
came on the *Match of the Day* game between Charlton and Birmingham
in 2004. Birmingham defender Tebily made a terrible defensive
blunder that led to a goal, then immediately turned to berate his
'keeper, Maik Taylor. When asked to comment on this the ex-Liverpool
defender and pundit Alan Hansen stated, 'it's a well-known rule of
thumb as a defender: if in doubt blame the 'keeper.'

Perhaps some of Gary's former Leeds colleagues have been too
quick to apply this rule of thumb to themselves. Gordon Banks once
stated:

> I think it was President Truman who kept a sign in his White House office
> that read: 'The buck stops here.' Goalkeepers could have that carved on
> their backs.

For Gary Sprake this is a very apt analogy as for thirty years he has
borne the brunt of the criticism for the disappointments and failings
of Revie's team. Perhaps now some critical commentators will be
forced to reappraise this perception and consider his career record in
its entirety, and not based just upon the mistakes he made.

The analogy of the goalkeeper made by Banks is one that Gary
reinforces in his own interpretation of his reputation.

I certainly don't think I was more error prone than any other 'keeper at the time or since and I don't believe that I was the liability to the team that some people have tried to make out. I have no problems with accepting that I made a handful of significant mistakes but I feel that this should be put into context as I played over 500 games for Leeds. The probability of making mistakes is an occupational hazard for goalkeepers and it is part and parcel of the job. This is especially so if you play for a highly successful team, such as Leeds United in the 1960s and 1970s. Any football fan who watches the Premiership or Championship on television today can testify that mistakes by goalkeepers are as rife as ever. I gained a reputation and a nickname in some quarters as 'Careless Hands', but this is still going on today as England 'keeper David James is always referred to by the press as 'Calamity James'. At the end of the day this has always been the case as goalkeepers are the most vulnerable target for criticism in any team. Any fan today could give a comprehensive list of goalkeepers who have made high-profile mistakes: David Seaman, Jerzy Dudek, Roy Carroll, Tim Howard, Ian Walker, Jens Lehmann… the list could go on. I am especially pleased that David Seaman has been able to turn the tables on the media and has exploited the negative comments and turned them into fun, and also made a lot of money out of this image. Good for him!

I think that I have received more criticism than many other goalkeepers for two reasons. Firstly, the general dislike of Leeds by some commentators meant that my mistakes were always going to be emphasised compared to those of other teams' 'keepers, and secondly my mistakes at the time were all televised, while other 'keepers' mistakes weren't. Whereas today Match of the Day and Sky show every goal from all the leagues, in our day televised games were rare and when they were on they inevitably featured Leeds. If you watch Sky Sports News on a Saturday evening you can now see every goal from over forty games in one hour and inevitably there will be four or five real goalkeeping howlers, but this has the effect of sanitising their impact as people now seem to more readily accept them as part of the game. During my playing career only a handful of games were shown on the box so if you made a mistake it became big news, and I think that my mistakes stick in peoples' minds more because of this fact.

Unfortunately I feel the whole mistakes reputation has also been reinforced by the negative comments of some of my former Leeds colleagues who, I believe, have unfairly targeted me for criticism in their memoirs. I have to admit that of all the criticism that I have received since my retirement I have found that directed at me by some of my ex-colleagues to be the most personal and upsetting. This is because when I played for Leeds the issue of me being error prone was never mentioned. A dressing room at a football club is a small place and even if they had not told me to my face any criticism would have got back to me, but at the time the issue was never emphasised. Although during my time at Leeds we had several high-profile disappointments and frustrations nobody at the club used me as a reason for these failures. In fact the manager Don Revie, the coaching staff and all my teammates were very supportive and they accepted that all goalkeepers made the odd mistake. Their comments were always along the lines that everybody makes mistakes in a team and we win or lose together as a family. At the time everybody at the club was excellent to me and they never believed the media hype that I was somehow the weakest link. We were very supportive of each other and although I would sometimes worry if I made a mistake that it could become a big issue, in fairness to my colleagues it never did. It has only been since the Revie controversy with the newspapers that some of them have changed their interpretation of me, which, as I mentioned, does still upset me.

Keith M. Edwards, who was on the Leeds playing staff from 1967 to 1972 before going on to a successful career captaining Cork City in the League of Ireland to many League and cup triumphs, recently commented on both the excellent team spirit at Elland Road and the issue of Gary's reputation at that time:

> Gary was a nice guy and easy to get on with. If he made a mistake he was obviously disappointed but he never let it put him off his game. Under Don Revie we had a squad of eighteen players and we were all one big family. Every player made mistakes and during the game there may have been some arguments, especially from Big Jack or Billy, but afterwards it was immediately forgotten. All the squad were mates and not one player was disliked, and I never saw or heard anybody make an issue of Gary's abilities all the time I was at the club.

Obviously I wish I hadn't made any mistakes but it is an inevitable part of being a goalkeeper. I have read lots of comments that I was nervous and that I somehow lost my confidence due to the mistakes but this was never the case. I openly admit that before a game I would be terribly nervous and sometimes be physically sick but I had been like that since the start of my career. Once I started the game I would be fine and although I would be angry at myself and disappointed if I made an error I can honestly say it never affected my confidence. If I made a mistake, I would put it behind me and get on with the game. I think the games where I made mistakes prove that, such as at Anfield. Even though I scored the own goal, during the second half I played really well and it was the same in the second half against Chelsea and Colchester. I accept the argument that sometimes I was so well protected I never had to make a save but I was always ready and fully concentrated in case I was to be called into action. At the end of the day it was my job. I was paid to concentrate for ninety minutes and with David Harvey competing for my place I wouldn't have been allowed or got away with being able to switch off. Don Revie was no fool and he was a very astute manager who would never put up with less than 100 per cent from any member of the team. Also, the mistakes I made were well spread out over time and I never went through a period like some of today's Premiership 'keepers of making three or four mistakes in a row, or even multiple mistakes in one game, and so no, I don't think I had an issue of loss of confidence.

Although I got a lot of stick and some very humorous banter from opposition fans, calling me 'Careless Hands' or worse, it never affected me or put me off my game. At the end of the day all fans give the opposition players stick and being stuck right in front of them for most of the game the goalkeeper gets his fair share. However, when the crowd shouted at me or tried to put me off it only served to encourage me to be more determined to do well and if you look at our away record over the years and the number of clean sheets we kept I didn't do too badly. When I watch football on television today and attend the odd game at St Andrews, even at the highest level goalkeepers still make mistakes on a regular basis. Every goalkeeper at international, European, Premiership or League level makes mistakes. This has always been the case and always will be. Unlike outfield players, however, the goalkeeper's errors always stick out because they inevitably lead to a goal being scored by the opposition. If a striker misses an open goal or a penalty or a defender misses a tackle or a crucial header it tends to be overlooked, but for goalkeepers there can be no hiding place. I wholeheartedly agree with Gordon Banks' (in my opinion the best ever British goalkeeper) comments on the goalkeeper's lot. I believed he had it spot on.

TWELVE

THE MAN WITH A PLAN

Don Revie was regarded as an astute tactician of the game even in his playing days, particularly during his time with Manchester City. At the Maine Road club he introduced the forward-thinking 'Revie Plan'. He had been heavily influenced by the wonderful Hungarian national side of the 1950s, whose tactics were passing and then moving into space, a seemingly simple tactical ploy but nonetheless innovative at the time. The plan was that the centre forward Revie, who was a mobile striker, would come deep off his striking partners, lay the ball off and then find space for the return pass. The oppositions' answer was man-to-man marking, whereby an opponent would follow Revie wherever he went and in turn Revie would drift into wider positions to create space for his teammates. When the opposition eventually worked out how to play against this style of football some contemporary football commentators argued that Revie had no answer and was reluctant to try anything new, a criticism that was also later levelled at him for not allowing his talented Leeds squad to play with the more carefree approached that their talents warranted. However, it was this innovation that first brought Revie to the attention of the Leeds directors and influenced their decision to offer Revie the position of player-manager in the early 1960s. Like every new manager Revie had a vision of making his young protégés at Leeds United the most successful team in Europe. One of his first acts as manager was to change the blue and gold strip to all white in the hope of emulating the great Real Madrid team of the time. While Madrid had swept away all before them in Europe, winning five consecutive European Cups between 1956 and 1960, Leeds United were perennial also-rans of the English game. By changing the strip Revie hoped he would also change the club's fortunes, but this was not the only method he adopted to give Leeds an advantage over their rivals. Some were within the laws of the game, others perhaps more questionable and some commentators have deemed illegal.

Revie surrounded himself with trusted lieutenants at Leeds, delegating responsibility while keeping a firm grip on overall affairs on and off the field. He fostered a family atmosphere for players and staff whereby the players became more like brothers than teammates. Revie ensured that birthdays of wives and girlfriends were never forgotten and a bouquet of flowers would duly arrive on special occasions. Relatives would be given access to the players' lounge on match days and friends would also be found precious tickets for both home and away matches. To help with the team's preparations were the coaching staff and backroom team of Maurice Lindley, Les Cocker, Cyril Partridge and Syd Owen. Revie also recruited others who would make the players' lives more bearable in the lonely hours between games and on away trips, not only in the Football League but also in far-flung arenas of Europe; people such as Harold Warner, who would entertain the players with his anecdotes, jokes and bingo calling. Advice on any topic was also available to players with a team of experts or counsellors on hand to help if it was required. If a player had relationship troubles or found the attention of some female fans over-bearing they only had to see the staff, who would offer advice on anything, from sex education to buying a car. Nothing was too much trouble. One of the favourite members of the 'family' was Gary Sprake, whom Don Revie had treated like a son since his move from the Welsh valleys a decade or so before.

I always had a special relationship with the boss. He watched me at every level of the international scene and I was the only player whose wedding he attended. He had a rule of not attending players' functions, but he was there the day I married Kath, although he didn't stay for the photographs or reception.

Gary remembers Revie as a great manager although he also recalls he could have some really odd ideas.

The boss was highly superstitious and would follow the same routine week in, week out. One of his most remarkable actions was the hiring of a Romany gypsy to lift a supposed curse around Elland Road. Even though he believed in these rituals wholeheartedly the national press ridiculed both him and the club and on occasions we became a laughing stock. Revie would wear the same lucky blue suit for every game even when it became shabby, and he would go for the same walk around the ground before a match, following the route with military precision. In fact, when I first started playing he borrowed my coat during one game when it started raining. We won easily and after that he wore it for the rest of the season. He also did some other bizarre things, such as changing the club's badge, removing the peacock because he didn't like birds as he thought they were unlucky. Also, whether we played home or away we always stayed four nights a week in a hotel so that we could focus on the job in hand. We would play bingo and carpet bowls to relieve the stress of playing against opponents who inevitably raised their game for what was, for many, their cup final. We always obeyed the boss, but with hindsight I think we could have vented our disapproval of some of the things we did. Can you imagine, grown men who were professional footballers, probably the best in the country, playing carpet bowls? – although the money from the bingo did come in handy! Whoever called 'house' would be the caller for the next game so if Paul Reaney or I won we would try to memorise each other's numbers and call out those numbers whether they came out or not and for some reason the other lads never cottoned on to our little scam. What it did though was engender a family spirit. You don't share more than half a week with people and not form close bonds, although some would say it manifested itself in a siege mentality.

Despite Revie's superstitions and idiosyncrasies Gary believes that he couldn't have played for a better manager as, professionally, Revie was light years ahead of all bar a few of his contemporaries. There has been much made of his infamous dossiers, with many ex-Revie players since commenting on how they found them to be no more than mind numbing. However, in today's Premiership much of Revie's astute management style can be reflected in the use of 'Prozone' by many clubs to analyse performance and also the employment of psychologists, nutritionists and vast scouting networks. Apart from the nutritional advice Gary recalls that Revie had used most of these tactics forty years previously.

Our diet in those days was far from scientific as on the morning of the match we could have a cooked breakfast if we wanted, and most of us did. A couple of hours before the game we would all sit down together and have a steak, while the boss would 'fine tune' the tactics. However, in later years Revie did begin to pay more attention to our diets and was especially careful in European games when we started to take our own food with us. In the dressing room before the game we would be prepared psychologically by the coaching staff, who would tell us how great we were and build up our confidence. One far-from-scientific ritual was that before running out one of the coaches would open a bottle of whisky, which we would all have a sip of. Perhaps that's why Revie played Albert Johanneson as number eleven as we used to have a tot in numerical order. If Albert had played right-back there may not have been any left, because he used to have a real swig. Much has since been made of the dossiers and for me much of it was pointless, as I felt they paid the opposition far too much respect. Without them we could have just gone out and imposed ourselves on the opposition. In fact, I believe the best thing the boss could have done was throw us the ball before the match and tell us to go out and enjoy ourselves, as our team full of internationals could have beaten anyone. Even after playing in the top division for a decade he would still analyse players we had played against for years or even played with at international level. The only time they were really of use was when we played European teams for the first time. We were told which player would try to beat a man on the inside, who would try to get to the byline before crossing and for me as a goalkeeper which penalty taker would favour which side of the goal. I remember one game being briefed about the opposition's penalty taker and during the game had to face two penalties. However, I ignored the advice I had been given and on both occasions dived the opposite way and ended up saving both penalties. At the final whistle the boss and Syd Owen, who was the inspiration, if you could call it that, behind the dossiers, gave me a right dressing down for ignoring their orders. Despite the over-emphasis on the dossiers Revie's more forward-thinking style contrasted widely with my experiences on the international scene and showed me just how much thought he put into his management. When I played for Wales it only reinforced my opinion of the boss and how great a manager he was as he left nothing to chance in his preparations. In comparison, when I was with Wales I had to travel by train, changing three times between Leeds and Cardiff. I then had to catch a train to Bridgend and then get a bus to the team's hotel in Porthcawl. On the return journey I had to inform the secretary of the FAW on the Sunday morning whether or not I needed sandwiches for the train. As well as that we had to provide our own training kit and even our own towels. I read recently that Ryan Giggs in his autobiography was scathing about the conditions that the Welsh squad had to put up with. It's a good job he didn't play thirty years earlier!

Gary also argues that Leeds were way ahead of most of the other teams in their preparations and this could also extend to their use of what became known as professionalism or, some would argue, gamesmanship.

When people mention Leeds and Don Revie today they immediately associate us with professionalism. The boss created a team that would use every tactic at our disposal to gain an advantage. We were a hard team and would sometimes indulge in foul play and gamesmanship. We would feign injuries to disrupt the flow of a game if things weren't going our way and if we wanted some tactical advice we would get the trainer on and he would pass some tips on from the boss. We were possibly the first team in England to waste time by keeping the ball in the corner, a tactic that has since been copied by every team in the game. These were innovations that caused an outcry at the time but now this sort of professionalism is an integral part of football. I also began to develop some of my own methods of intimidation, one of which was to claim the ball with my foot up around chest height, not only to protect myself but to distract the opposing forward and make them hesitant, giving me the advantage in a challenge for a fifty-fifty ball. Many years later in his column in The Sun *newspaper, Jimmy Greaves argued that I was the first goalkeeper to adopt, or invent, this tactic, although many others have copied it since, including that infamous challenge by the West German 'keeper Harold Schumacher in the World Cup against France. The boss has been very unfairly treated by the press as he never once told us directly to do this sort of thing. The decision was always made on the pitch; we had a team full of leaders and some really hard players who would sometimes take the law into their own hands.*

The Welsh wing wizard Leighton James recalls what it was like to face Leeds United, especially at Elland Road.

I remember going there as a youngster in the dressing room before the matches; the next thing there was an almighty rumpus outside. The Leeds team, to a man, were banging with their fists and kicking the door. They were screaming obscenities and saying they couldn't wait to get us on the pitch, where they would do all sorts of things to us. This may have intimidated most teams, but that Burnley side had some real hard men as well; people like Colin Waldron and Jim Thompson could mix it with anyone. As a flair player I had licence to go forward knowing that I had a minder, the England full-back Keith Newton. If anybody kicked me the others would exact revenge. Leeds had some real hard men as well; they didn't come much harder than Billy Bremner, who would dish it out but also take it. Apart from Allan Clarke their team was full of hard players. Clarke was more of a sly player, someone who would throw a punch as the opponent was facing the other way. He did this once with Colin, who turned around to confront him and I've never seen the colour drain from someone as quickly as it did from Clarke that day.

This high level of professionalism was also anathema to the match officials, who had a particularly hard time controlling their matches, a view endorsed by one of the top referees of the time, Swansea-based John Gow, who recalls:

> Whenever I refereed Leeds I knew I was in for a tough time from the very first minute right to the final whistle. After a few games I became exasperated and decided to stamp my authority from the off. In one game, I think it was against Arsenal, the Gunners won a throw-in within seconds. The next thing, Billy Bremner was in my face contesting the decision. I blew the whistle, called him over and ordered him to take off his shirt and I gave him the whistle and told him I was going to play for Leeds United and he was to be the referee. He and the rest of the players burst into hysterics and I never had a decision questioned again. Once the game was over though, you couldn't have met a more sociable group, especially Gary Sprake. I refereed the controversial game against Wolves when Leeds were going for the double in 1972. Gary had been dropped for the cup final a couple of days before and I would imagine was feeling low and going through all sorts of emotions. Before the game I asked him if he would get a signed football for me to raise money for a school in Swansea. After the game, even though Leeds lost and Gary's chance of another championship was gone, there he was with the signed ball as promised. A true gentleman as well as a top goalkeeper.

Revie was so meticulous in his planning that he built up a profile of each player he wanted to attract to Elland Road.

The boss wanted us to play to win on the field but off it we were to behave like champions in a manner befitting our status. As young, fit and professional sportsmen there were lots of temptations around in the 1960s and 1970s, but the boss instilled in us the values that we were not only representing a football club, but ambassadors for the whole city. The media wanted to get their stories and the boss was mindful of press intrusion, especially those based in London. From the time any youngster or seasoned professional arrived at Elland Road, they were given a code of conduct to follow. Obviously he wanted skilful players with a strong will to win and he sometimes overlooked a ruthless streak, but off the pitch everyone had to have humility, be courteous and behave impeccably. Over the years I sometimes broke the code of conduct and the boss had to come to my rescue on more than one occasion. He never turned a blind eye, but I did get away with far more than any other player.

England international Mike O'Grady, who won a championship medal with Leeds in 1968, recalls some of the incidents that drove Revie to distraction:

> I was Leeds born and bred, so when I signed for the club I knew of some out-of-the-way places where the lads could enjoy a few beers. Unfortunately, with Sprakey around there was no such thing as a quiet pint, even if we were in mixed company. I remember the time Gary, Norman, Lash and I went to the Bingley Arms with our partners on a Saturday night after a game. We were in the bar having a good time when some guys started to stare at us, which you come to expect as we were top players. Sprakey was having none of it and asked them what they were looking at and if they wanted trouble. The landlord ushered us into a back room, but not before Gary had punched one of them. When we got in for training on the Monday I was summoned to Revie's office where he told me to send flowers to the landlady and the partners of the guys who Sprakey got into a rumpus with. I told Revie to fuck off as it was nothing to do with me. I was only trying to calm things down but I don't think Revie expected my reaction, whether or not that speeded up my move to another club, I don't know. Sprakey was even worse if we went on a lads' night out as he was a big hit with the ladies. On one occasion we were in a club in the city centre and these girls were showing an interest in him, but there were Leeds rugby league players in as well and they weren't getting a look in as Sprakey was getting all the attention. So one of them punched Sprakey. Not one to back down he grabbed this sixteen-stone rugby player, picked him off his feet and hung him over the balcony. Wherever we went he always attracted attention of one kind or another. I just wish it was like it is today where the players are separated from the fans in VIP areas – it would have stopped Sprakey getting into so much trouble.

This view is supported by Mick Bates, who remembers:

> Whenever we went out the other guys in the clubs were jealous of Gary. He was a ladies' man, always smartly dressed and good looking. He also had a temper and was sometimes paranoid, a potentially lethal combination on a night out for footballers.

Ex-Leeds colleague and former Manchester United star Jimmy Greenhoff also recalls:

Gary was a big hit with the ladies, but he never chased them. They chased him and their boyfriends hated him. On the park, Gary was a great goalie and all the team were a happy family and I am very surprised to hear that some of our ex-colleagues have criticised his goalkeeping since.

The biggest test of Revie's loyalty to Gary came on the day that Leeds lost out on the championship to Arsenal in 1971, as Gary recalls:

We had finished our fixtures on the Saturday by beating Nottingham Forest 2-0, so on the Monday we all gathered in the Mecca for a night out. Arsenal were away to Spurs looking for the point that would deny us the title. Most of the lads were there to either celebrate or drown their sorrows, but unfortunately the Gunners won the title so we had a few beers too many to take away the pain. In the early hours of the morning someone decided we should have a party at Pete Madeley's flat. Pete was a disc jockey in the Mecca and also the half-time entertainer at Elland Road. There were a lot of girls in the club so we invited everyone and jumped into our cars. Pete was with me in the front and there were two girls who I'd not even spoken to on the night who jumped in the back. As we were driving to the party I lost control of my car, an Austin 1300 GT, on a bend and as I crashed off the road one of the girls flew from the back seat through the windscreen. She was very badly injured, later needing over two dozen stitches in her face. As we were wandering around in the dark one of my teammates pulled up and in a panic I jumped into his car and he took me home. Within minutes the police arrived and asked where I had been that night. Foolishly I told them I had been at home. They said my car had been involved in an accident so could they look in the garage. Obviously the car was not there so I told them it must have been stolen. Just as they were about to take me in for questioning the boss arrived. He took the officers to one side and had a word with them. The next thing was they said they would report my car being stolen. I was fined for careless driving, but once again the boss had saved me, this time possibly from serious charges. Looking back I am not proud of some of the things I did and I have always regretted the injuries that girl suffered. Unfortunately that was the way it was back then, as we got into trouble probably because we had a closeted lifestyle and were quite immature. We relied on the boss to get us out of trouble and he always did.

Despite his innovations and far-sighted management style Don Revie's reputation was always dogged in this period with allegations surrounding certain match-fixing scandals. Such evidence became a vital part of the case against Revie made by the investigative journalist Richard

Stott in 1977 while Revie was still England manager. The *Daily Mirror* submitted a 315-page dossier to the Football Association, most of which Stott repeated in his book *Dogs and Lampposts*. In this book he outlined Revie's involvement in attempting to fix games when he was Leeds manager. Before these accusations were published Revie quit as national team manager and fled to the United Arab Emirates, citing the reason that he had taken too much unwarranted and unfounded flak from the media. Was Revie 'dishonest' and 'corrupt' and the paymaster in attempts to change the outcome of games, or was there a conspiracy theory to remove him from the England stewardship?

Richard Stott, Frank Palmer and their team were in no doubt that Revie had attempted to fix games, but proving it was going to be a mountainous task. The footballing fraternity are loyal to the point of blindness and a closed-shop mentality has always existed. Bonds that have been formed, however tenuous, are hard to break by outsiders. There is an adage in football from the grass roots to the very top of the game: 'What goes on in the dressing room stays in the dressing room.' It was this mentality that Stott had to overcome if he was to get to the truth. The first player to be contacted by Stott was the Nottingham Forest goalkeeper Jim Barron, who recalled being approached by a Revie 'agent' to throw a vital end-of-season game when Leeds were vying for yet another championship. The match in question was an end-of-season affair at Elland Road where Leeds had to score at least four unanswered goals to give them any chance of a second championship title. They were one point in front of Arsenal, whose game in hand was the north London derby against Spurs two days after the final Saturday fixtures, so Revie was hoping that Forest could do Leeds a favour. When Stott contacted Barron he was a hugely relieved man who had been guarding his secret for six years. For his part, Barron had declined the offer and went on to produce one of his best performances, prompting the Yorkshire Television commentator Keith Macklin to remark, 'but for Barron it may well have been five or six'. What had worried Barron was the thought of making a genuine mistake and thereafter being branded as a bribe taker. Gary Sprake also remembers the match vividly.

On one occasion during the game Ronnie Rees, my Welsh international col-league, broke clear and bent the ball around me aiming for the far corner of the net. Luckily for us the ball rebounded off the post back into my arms. Ronnie was holding his head in his hands, looked up and I'm pretty sure I heard him say, 'thank fuck for that, I thought I'd ruined it!' Ronnie may not have been in on it himself, but he knew what went on before the game. Billy Bremner had gone into the Forest dressing room at Revie's behest to try and get the right result. I don't know how many Leeds players Revie used to approach the opposition, but he asked me on only one occasion if I would use my Welsh international connections to smooth the path to victory. I was asked to tap up Colin Green and Terry Hennessey when we played against Birmingham City in the last game of our first season back in the top flight. Revie wanted me to go in at half-time and have a word. We drew the game 3-3 and lost out on goal average to Manchester United in the chase for the title. I wasn't interested and told Revie it was something I would never contemplate. I may have lost out on a championship medal, but my conscience was clear and Revie never asked me again. I know how Colin and Terry would have reacted – they were both dedicated professionals and they would have lynched me off my crossbar.

Andrew Mourant picks up on this theme in his biography of Revie, *Portrait of a Footballing Enigma*, when he quotes Peter Lorimer, who had stated:

> There used to be the odd joke if we were playing a team last game of the season and needed the points and they were in mid table. If you had some of your Scottish pals playing, you'd say 'Hope you're not going to have a real go today.' But if you're talking about us going up to one of them with a couple of hundred quid to say 'You're not going to have a go today' then I've never seen that.

As well as offering inducements to fix results Revie also used some underhand methods, according to the *Mirror*, when trying to strengthen the team. The World Cup-winning midfielder Alan Ball recalls in his autobiography *Playing Extra Time* how packages containing £100 in notes would be delivered to his home and handed to his wife Lesley by a mystery man, on the understanding that Leeds had first refusal on his signature if ever he left Blackpool. In his book, Ball states that this happened nearly every Friday night as the mystery man would say, 'No names, no pack drill, here is an investment.' Thirty years previously, during the *Mirror* investigation, however, Ball recalled how he got involved in dialogue with Revie about forming a midfield partnership with Bremner and Giles. After the initial conversations Ball recounted how he drove to the moors above Huddersfield to meet Revie face to face. 'He was keeping in touch with me so that if anyone else approached me he had his finger on the button,' recalled Ball. Revie's plan went awry for, after winning the World Cup, Ball signed for Everton, with Revie citing the reason that his board would not better the Everton offer to Blackpool. The real reason, Ball claims in his memoirs, is much different. Both Leeds and Everton offered £110,000 but when Ball's father found out about Revie's inducements he strongly advised his son against signing for the Yorkshire club and Revie's plan had backfired. In fact, in 1979 Ball was fined £3,000 by the FA for bringing the game into disrepute. The case against Revie himself was never pursued as at the time they were awaiting the outcome of his libel case with the *Mirror*. Could the mystery man who visited Ball possibly have been Harold Warner, who played a far more important role than that of a simply a court jester to the team? He was allegedly known as the 'Bag Man' and was also, supposedly, the intermediary between Revie and any opposing players who might be willing to make a clumsy challenge in the penalty area, take a wayward shot at goal or a make a few misplaced passes. Whatever the mistake, Warner, it is claimed, would be there at the end of the game with the money in a black bag ready for distribution.

While Ball's evidence suggests that Revie's behaviour could be deemed as bringing the game into disrepute, the former Sunderland manager Bob Stokoe was more rigorous in his criticism of Revie, recalling the time when, as Bury player-manager, Revie offered him £500 to 'take it easy' during a vital relegation game in 1962 in the old Second Division. This was a secret that Stokoe kept for fifteen years, apart from telling his chairman immediately after the game. Revie, according to Stokoe, approached him an hour before the game with his offer and, despite being rebuffed, still brazenly asked the astounded Stokoe if he could have a word with the Bury players. Stokoe informed his players who, according to the Bury manager, responded by play- ing above themselves in a 1-1 draw, which was ironically just enough for Leeds to avoid relegation. It was Stokoe who memorably led his Sunderland team out at Wembley before perhaps the greatest ever cup final shock in 1973, when his Second Division team humbled the mighty Leeds, the cup holders. This was a match where a long-stand- ing score was settled for the Sunderland manager, as Stokoe stated, 'I don't think that you could ever put into words how I felt seeing him [Revie] trudge off at Wembley.'

The *Mirror* investigation also claimed that Revie tried to influence results as Leeds were pushing for promotion to the First Division in 1964. According to the reporters, Revie offered a bribe to the Newcastle United captain Stan Anderson, whose team lay ten points adrift of table-topping Leeds. During the investigation Anderson would neither confirm nor deny this approach by Revie, adding that if it ever came to court he would deny any impropriety having occurred. When pressed by the investigating journalists, Anderson concluded:

> I am still in the game… Why are you doing it, why just go for Revie? The game is full of cheats; he was more successful at it, that's all.

While not proving conclusive, the whispers throughout the 1960s, culminating in the imprisonment of some players, would seem to corroborate Anderson's theory that match fixing was endemic at this time. This is a view endorsed by Peter Lorimer, commenting in his autobiography *Leeds and Scotland Hero*:

> The facts of what really happened are a matter of conjecture, but what is indisputable is that many, too many, suspect things happened in the game itself, and particularly involving Leeds… but I remain utterly convinced that football in general was awash with illegal incentive monies.

The *Mirror* investigation also alleged that Newcastle were at the centre of attempted match fixing as Leeds tried to consolidate their runners-up spot in the 1965/66 season. This time they would not reveal the identity of the mystery man who offered the inducement to Newcastle's acting manager Jimmy Greenhalgh, but insisted it was not Don Revie. Greenhalgh informed his experienced captain Jim Iley of the approach, who in turn informed the rest of the team. A member of the team that day, legendary goalscorer Bryan 'Pop' Robson, told the investigation:

> I know there was talk of money flying about… the boys were not interested; we went out and beat them.

Robson scored one of the goals in Leeds' 2-0 defeat. It was Newcastle, in the 1972 season when Leeds were chasing the double, who were once again the alleged focus for Revie's inducements when the Leeds manager tried to use a former Leeds player, the late Terry Hibbitt, as the go-between. Hibbitt had been transferred to the Geordies but was still allowed to train occasionally at Elland Road where, according to the Newcastle player, Revie propositioned him. Hibbitt told the *Mirror*:

> I feel very sad about the whole thing, but I can't deny what you put to me. The *Mirror* has carried out a very thorough investigation. I don't want to shout the details of my experience all over the newspapers. That would make me feel as if I was publicly crucifying Don Revie. I feel sad because despite everything he was a good manager who really cared for his players, whether first team stars or young apprentices and he took a close interest in their wives and families.

One of the few people Hibbitt confided in at the time was another goal-scoring legend, Malcolm Macdonald, who went on to score the only goal of the game.

> I remember Terry telling me and my first reaction was one of laughter. It is the only time that I've known that sort of thing to happen, an approach aimed indirectly at me. My only reaction to it was one of grim determination, that there was no way we were going to lose that match. It was a real spur to go out and do well.

That incident may have been Macdonald's first experience of alleged bribery, but it would not be his last encounter with controversy, as Revie was to become his national team manager. Macdonald recalled in his memoirs *Supermac: My Autobiography* how, after equalling the England scoring record with five goals against Cyprus, he was asked to do a television interview. Before the interview Revie informed the waiting journalists that McDonald wanted £200 before he would talk to them. They all had a whip-round; the cash was raised and handed to Revie and the interview was carried out. According to McDonald that was the last anyone saw of the cash and he didn't find out about it until several months later.

Three weeks after the 1972 Newcastle game Leeds travelled to Molineux in search of a League and cup double after beating Arsenal at Wembley two days previously. Leeds had tried to get the game moved to allow the players to get over the exertions of the weekend. Once again their pleas fell on deaf ears at the unforgiving FA, who decreed the match should go ahead as England had European Nations' Cup fixtures and Wolves were still to play in the UEFA Cup final. This was to be Leeds and Revie's most important game; victory would ensure the double, a rarity in English football at that time. The day before the match, which Leeds lost 2-1, the *Sunday People* revealed that an attempt had been made to fix the game, with offers made to Wolves' players to throw the match. An inquiry was held but was to prove inconclusive as no evidence was found after a shroud of secrecy descended and no-one could identify Revie's agent or middleman. Five years later, during Richard Stott's investigation, the identity of the middleman was revealed. It was Mike O'Grady, the former Leeds winger, who was on Wolves' books at the time of the game even though he was on loan to Birmingham City. The investigating team confronted O'Grady, who admitted to being the go-between. When questioned about the incident he replied:

> It was me. No-one else was involved, just Revie and me. It was a one-to-one situation and I just did as I was asked and made an approach. I never received any money so I am not implicated, I never received a penny. It was suggested I go and see what the reaction would be, which I did but the Wolves player I spoke to said it was a no go.

According to the *Mirror* the player approached was Bernard Shaw, who promptly informed his manager Bill McGarry. He in turn gathered the players together to warn them of the money that was perceived to be flying around and to be careful. The *Mirror* further alleges that during the match many appeals were made by Leeds' players to their opposite numbers to take it easy and to give away penalties. The winger Dave Wagstaffe was having an inspired game and cries from the touchline urged him to 'take it easy, we'll see you right.' At the heart of the Wolves' defence centre half Frank Munro was urged to concede a deliberate penalty. Four months after the game both Wagstaffe and Munro admitted to the *Sunday People* that attempts had been made to fix the game, although they both declined. Munro confirmed that he had two offers of large sums of money, one before and one during the game if he would give away a penalty.

> I am not saying how much was offered but it was a lot.

This is an accusation Munro repeats in more forthcoming terms in the more recent book *Running With Wolves*, alleging that Billy Bremner, acting upon Revie's behalf, had twice offered him

£5,000 to give away a penalty. He claims it was not just a spur of the moment decision on the pitch but a pre-meditated act before the game as well.

> I got a call on the Sunday from the Mount Hotel [Leeds' team base]. That was when he [Bremner] first made the offer. He said I am to give away a penalty and I get five grand. I was tempted, five grand in 1972 would just about buy you a house. From what I understand I believe it had gone on for years. Don Readies they used to call him. I'm sure that's why he finished up so unpopular in the game.

This theme is supported by the legendary Arsenal captain Frank McLintock who recalls, in his recent autobiography *True Grit*, how he was also offered an incentive to take it easy in an end-of-season game. Leeds were away to Arsenal in the penultimate game of the season, a season that saw them finish five points behind champions Manchester City. So the outcome of the match was inconsequential, as they were once again assured of a top-four finish but had an unrealistic chance of overhauling the leaders. McLintock revealed how Revie came up to him and said:

> You and Barbara should have a nice holiday this summer. In fact, you could go anywhere in the world you wanted as a guest of Leeds United. Just take it easy out there tonight.

McLintock described his reaction, how he lost his rag:

> 'You come up to me and ask me to take it easy, are you fucking crazy?' There was no ambiguity about what Don had said, he was a flawed man in flawed times.

Another attempt by Revie to change the outcome of a game had once again gone awry as McLintock scored in Arsenal's 4–3 victory. However, McLintock also offered a balanced and objective assessment of Revie, endorsing Gary's own perception of the manager he regarded as the best in the game. McLintock argues:

> For one bad thing, there were ninety-nine good things about Don. He was the sort who would drive hundreds of miles, sit outside a player's house until 7 a.m., knock on the door and charm the life out of his parents.

Gary states:

Revie's alleged attempts at fixing matches were doomed to fail. Nearly every team that was approached was in mid-table security and had nothing to play for. Once the approaches were made and the teams became aware they raised their game and had a burning desire to put one over us. The boss should have believed more in our ability, we could have won most games we played without any outside influence. Even though we beat Forest it wasn't the result we wanted. Two-nil was of no use, we had to win by at least four goals. I know it's hypothetical and hindsight is a wonderful thing, but would Jim Barron have played as well as he did in what was for him a meaningless, end-of-season game if he wasn't so incensed by what went on?

This is a view endorsed by Terry Yorath in his autobiography, who states:

> The day after our win at Wembley, a Sunday newspaper published allegations that Wolves had been offered bribes by Leeds to lose the match and there was also a rumour that Derby were going to pay the Wolves players a lot of money to win the game. I was there that night so I know what happened and I remember the Wolves fans telling anybody who wanted to listen that their team hadn't played like that all season. You can't be bribed to win, only to lose, but you can be offered an incentive to win.

As Gary states:

Perhaps somebody at Derby, with or without Clough's knowledge, offered more than Revie, or perhaps the Wolves players were motivated to disprove the rumours they had been tapped up? What is certain is that the controversy did Leeds no favours as Wolves were really up for the game and especially Munro, who scored one of the crucial goals for Wolves.

Many of those who had knowledge of what went on were players still involved in the game, who were loath to sacrifice their careers by admitting the truth to the investigators. For Stott and his team the star witness was going to be Gary Sprake, who had first-hand experience of what went on behind the Elland Road scenes. Having gotten wind of the impending revelations Revie summoned his most trusted lieutenant, the Leeds captain Billy Bremner, to contact Gary. He was somewhat taken aback by Bremner's offer of a testimonial, which was conditional on him not co-operating with the tabloid press. Gary was particularly surprised to hear from Bremner as he had had little contact with any of his former teammates since he left for Birmingham City two years earlier. As Gary says:

What really surprised me was the fact that, with the exception of Paul Reaney, not one of my ex-teammates visited me when I was recovering from life-threatening surgery after my back operation.

Despite several further telephone calls made in an attempt to buy Gary's silence he rejected their advances. Revie himself made one last attempt to gag him, arranging to meet Gary in what was then the stereotypical cloak-and-dagger meeting place synonymous with football, the motorway hotel. If a manager was summoned to be sacked, his successor courted or an under-the-table offer made to a player, it was always in such an environment. It is totally unlike today, where brazen would-be suitors court players, managers and directors of football in five-star hotels and restaurants in the full gaze of the paparazzi's prying lenses.

Despite Revie's desperate final efforts, it was too late. He was met by Gary's solicitor Bob Evans, who informed him that Gary had already signed for the *Daily Mirror*. The *Mirror*, with information gleaned from Gary and others within the game, alleged that Revie had agreed to fix important games on five separate occasions during his managerial reign at Leeds. It was alleged that the games involved were earlier in his Leeds reign while trying to avoid relegation and later when Leeds were pursuing championship success. The revelations were earth-shattering in the world of football and the fallout was felt most severely in Leeds. Most of the undeniably highly talented side took the side of their former manager, repaying, perhaps blindly, the faith and loyalty he had shown them over many years. Many of the players were infuriated by what they read, and some to this day have never again read the *Daily Mirror*, believing the revelations to be no more than a character assassination.

Even though Gary was deemed to be a star witness he actually played a very small role in the investigation, claiming he saw Revie and his agent trying to influence the one game against Forest and also revealing that Revie had paid him not to play for Wales. He did not, as Peter Lorimer claims in his memoirs, write an article for the paper or comment on any allegations surrounding the controversial Wolves game in 1972. For Gary Sprake, however, these admissions cost him thirty years of hostility from some former teammates and some supporters who have been inculcated with stories of betrayal. At the time of the revelations Gary's late wife Kathy gave a prophetic interview to the *Mirror* suggesting that both she and Gary were going to lose a lot of friends and possibly make a few enemies.

> I know we will be criticised for staying silent for so long. I know that some people will be so upset that they will label Gary a traitor, a Judas. I hope when the fuss has died down they will be able to understand why Gary had to speak out and we will all be friends again. I am so happy that at last Gary had the guts to help put the record straight, though he had little option in the end. By the time the *Mirror* approached us they were armed with so many facts we knew it was time to come into the open and tell the truth. Don Revie has been discredited, but neither of us will forget how well he treated us when Gary was one of his boys. He always looked after his players and their families like they were his own children. Any problems, he wanted to hear about them. Although I knew the things he was doing were wrong, I pushed it to the back of my mind because I couldn't believe he would do anything to harm the team. Revie was such a dominant influence in our lives, almost like a father, that I never dreamed of questioning anything he did.

Don Revie had indeed played a major part in Gary's life for thirteen years, standing loyally beside him when he got into some off-the-field scrapes; paying him above-average wages and being more of a father figure to him than to any other player on the Leeds United staff. Why then, did Gary Sprake choose to co-operate with the *Mirror* investigation? Gary explains:

Revie was always great with me and looked after myself and the other players extremely well. When I asked for a transfer in 1973, however, our relationship changed and we were never very close after that. What annoyed me at the time was that it was never a money issue, it was all about me playing first-team football. The boss expected loyalty from us, but there were many times when I was at Leeds that Revie would use other clubs' interest in him to get the board to raise his money or get a longer contract. When we played AC Milan in the Cup-Winners' Cup final in Greece he called all the squad together the evening before the game and we were stunned by what he had to say. He told us that the final would be his last game in charge as he had accepted an offer from another English club. This demonstrates that loyalty works both ways and that Revie was prepared to use it as a tool when it suited him; for example, to improve his contract with Leeds. Although we were well paid, when players moved from Leeds they inevitably increased their salaries, as Norman Hunter points out in his book about his move to Bristol City, and it was the same when I joined Birmingham.

After Revie got wind of my part in the Mirror *investigation he and Billy phoned on numerous occasions to offer me both a testimonial and a job with the Admiral Sports Company. They automatically assumed that I was doing it for the money. If that had been the case I would have taken them up on their offer. At the time of the investigation ridiculous claims were made about how much I had been paid. Someone said that I had received £30,000; others said it was £15,000. They were all a pack of lies. I actually received £7,500 for it before tax. I remember at the time the Leeds president Lord Harewood saying those involved did it for financial gain and we were tainted. I found those comments to be particularly offensive. Everything I got from the game was through talent and hard work. I never had the privileged background that hereditary titles bring, I had earned all that I had and after I finished with football through serious injury I never sought financial help from anyone, not even the PFA.*

Some of my ex-teammates and some Leeds fans think that I betrayed Don Revie and Leeds United for the money or because I held a grudge after he dropped me for David Harvey. I know that Peter Lorimer made a similar accusation in his memoirs, saying that I had the knives out because I had been dropped by Revie for the 1972 cup final. But this was never the case as, after thirteen years of loyal service that may have cost me my health from the cortisone injections and playing through the pain barrier on numerous occasions, the only betrayal was on Revie's part. After I left for Birmingham in 1973, he promised me a testimonial in 1975 and we shook hands on it, although there was nothing in writing. I phoned Revie on many occasions after I left but he never once returned my calls. He would leave it to others to tell me that it would happen soon. After the service I had given Leeds I was hurt and thought it terrible that he went back on his word. If I had taken Revie up on his belated offer of a testimonial when the Mirror *controversy broke out, I would have got well over £20,000, far more than I received from the* Mirror, *so I can state categorically that money was never the issue. I don't think I betrayed the fans because they had a right to know the facts and my old teammates also knew what went on. If what I said was untrue it would have left me open to litigation, but no-one sued me or even threatened to. I have no regrets about the article, I simply told the truth. The most disappointing thing for me was that the football authorities didn't make use of the evidence. They had a golden opportunity to clean the game up once and for all. Throughout my career there was always one bribery scandal or other. Since then other allegations have emerged over the years, most notably the claims against Bruce Grobbelaar that he was paid to throw games.*

When the paper later repeated the allegations against Revie and Billy Bremner, Billy sued the People *for what they and Danny Hegan said about the Wolves game, and I was called to the Old Bailey as a witness. I think the* People *had claimed Billy had asked the Wolves player Danny Hegan to give away a penalty and Billy would 'see him right'. When I turned up at the court at nine in the morning Danny was already there, but he was unfit to give evidence. When Billy's lawyer asked if I was aware of the offer I just said I couldn't remember, so Billy won his case and received about £100,000. Billy was a wonderful player, one of the best in the world in his position and a Leeds legend. After he won the court case he should have forgotten about the whole thing. However, I am aware that after that he would criticise me a lot during after-dinner speeches and also in front of Leeds' fans, sullying me both as a player and a person. Both Billy and I knew what went on, the real truth. The fact that he continued to say these negative things and tried to influence others' opinions of me reflects worse on him than it does me. At the end of the day I played a very small part in the Mirror investigation and if I had not given evidence they would have run with it anyway. They had more than enough to go on with all the other witnesses. The pressure on my family was intense, I received many threatening phone calls before the story came out because there were wild rumours circulating that the whole dossier was based on a 'kiss and tell' book that I was writing. Certain ex-teammates have not co-operated with this book because they believe it is going to be of the same ilk. When people read this book I hope they will have a better understanding of my motives. I just hope this sets the record straight and after thirty years we can all move on.*

Comments made in January 2006 by managers Mike Newell and Ian Holloway generated enormous debate on the back pages of both the tabloids and broadsheets. Their comments, alleging corruption in football, seem to suggest that that the issue of illegality within the beautiful game has not gone away. Sven Goran Eriksson's controversial allegation regarding the possibility of some Premiership managers being open to corruption has only fuelled these rumours. It is evident that Don Revie's reputation is not the first and will not be the last to be tainted by rumours of such underhand behaviour. It is only to be hoped that the closing of ranks in certain circles and the criticism of both Newell and Holloway by some in the game do not lead to the two men being ostracised by their peers – the fate suffered by Gary Sprake for his part in similar revelations all those years ago.

RETROSPECTIVE:
A REPUTATION RECLAIMED

Gary has never been invited back to Elland Road to any official function, even to the twenty-fifth anniversary dinner to celebrate the FA Cup win. In February 2005 Gary's enquiry into why he had not received an invite to another Revie reunion went unanswered by the club. Peter Lorimer recalls in his autobiography that despite his own willingness to forget the past some of his ex-colleagues didn't feel the same way. Indeed, at the Premiership game at St Andrews between Birmingham and Leeds in 2004 both Norman Hunter and Eddie Gray ignored him completely. This was very different to the positive comments on his departure from Leeds, when Don Revie had paid a glowing tribute to one of his favourite sons, recalling two memorable saves in a career of outstanding saves; one of which was in the Fairs Cup final in 1968 and the other against Liverpool in the FA Cup in 1972. Keith M. Edwards recalls that:

> Gary could have nothing to do for most of a game and then in the last minutes he would pull off an amazing save that would help win Leeds the game. I remember that Don Revie stated in both public and private on many occasions that only two 'keepers in the country were capable of this standard of goalkeeping: Gordon Banks and Gary.

This is a view echoed recently by England's most capped goalkeeper, Peter Shilton, who told the authors that:

> Gary Sprake was one of the best all-time Welsh goalkeepers and a real character. Like all goalkeepers he is remembered for one or two high-profile mistakes but he contributed much to the success of the great Leeds United team of the 1970s.

Revie lamented at the time that not only had Leeds lost a brilliant goalkeeper but also one of the family, somebody he regarded as a son. Two years later Revie would disown his favourite son and until his death refused to even acknowledge Gary's existence. Yet at the time Revie stated that Birmingham had got themselves 'one of the greatest goalies that has ever lived'. Concluding his eulogy Revie said:

> We hope he and his family will be happy in the Midlands and they must remember that the door at Elland Road is always open to them.

How unfortunate that the door has been firmly shut for the last thirty years. Teammates that were likened to brothers have labelled Gary a pariah. Former colleagues Paul Reaney, Eddie Gray, Mick Jones, Allan Clarke and David Harvey won't even mention his name or talk about someone whose reputation has remained untarnished in the eyes of the most important people, the Leeds fans. It is very interesting to note, however, that despite their negative attitudes in conversation while researching this book Gary still uses the collective terms 'we' and 'us' to describe any conversations about his former Revie teammates. Despite thirty years of negative publicity and no official acknowledgement of his achievements Gary was recently voted thirty-eighth in the all-time Leeds top 100 players poll by readers of the official club magazine *Leeds! Leeds! Leeds!* Not a bad epitaph for a player chastised as nothing more than a liability by some commentators. Many ex-colleagues in their biographies have argued that David Harvey was a safer 'keeper and strengthened the Leeds team. Yet Mick Bates' comment on the comparison in 2003 recalls differently:

> David Harvey was not in the same league as Gary and I should know, as I sat on the bench for many seasons watching both of them.

Keith M. Edwards reinforces this viewpoint:

> David Harvey was a very good 'keeper and always looked solid but Gary was in a different class. Gary would regularly make spectacular world-class saves and he was capable of winning matches on his own. When he was fit David would never get a look in.

While the mistakes Gary made could be counted on one hand, there is no denying their monumental significance at the time, and especially for his reputation since. However, the gravity-defying saves, the faultless positioning, the taking of crosses and often foolhardy bravery are all assets that deserve greater recognition. That famous night in Budapest has been acclaimed by some to be Gary's finest hour, with those spectators present witnessing a save in the final minutes that was of true world-class standard. It is one that the Hungarians still talk of in awe, when Gary took off to stop a magnificent free-kick that was bent around the wall and was dipping into the far corner at speed. Between 1964 and 1972 there were many more outstanding performances that suggest that Gary was one of the best, if not the best goalkeeper in Britain, better than Banks, Bonetti, Jennings, Stepney, West et al. Banks had a sound temperament and vast experience, with the save from Pelé in the 1970 World Cup acclaimed as the greatest ever. However, after that tournament he failed to dominate his area with the same supreme confidence. Bonetti had agility and anticipation and was adept at starting attacks with quick throw-outs. West was temperamental and easily rattled. Gary was all of these things: agile, brave, temperamental and prone to the odd mistake. Yet he was also strong at cutting out crosses (Revie once remarked he was 'like a guy taking bullets out of the air'). For every 100 crosses that dropped into the twelve-yard area round the goal, Gary would claim 99 cleanly. Revie argued that Gary was one of the game's bravest 'keepers, throwing himself at forwards' feet with reckless abandon. This is reinforced by Manchester United hero George Best, who in his 1968 book *Best of Worlds* picked Gary and Leeds colleague Billy Bremner in his Great Britain All Star XI.

Dai Davies, who followed Gary as Wales' custodian believed him to be the 'most naturally gifted' goalkeeper ever. Gary could also distribute the ball quickly and accurately. Another vital point is made by Mike O'Grady, the England winger and Leeds teammate who found him a joy to play with, arguing that his swift distribution allowed immediate counterattacks that added extra yard of space for him to operate in. From the time Gary made his dramatic debut in 1962 to the premature end of his career in 1975, the highlights and record-setting moments far outweigh the high-profile blunders. He was the youngest goalkeeper ever to play for Leeds and also the youngest goalkeeper to have played for any of the Home Nations. During the 1968 championship-winning season he conceded a then-record lowest amount of goals and was ever-present in the Leeds team that suffered the fewest defeats. At the time he was also the most expensive goalkeeper in the history of the British game when he transferred to Birmingham City in 1973.

In his first 300 games for Leeds Gary conceded only 284 goals, a proud record of less than a goal a game. On 113 occasions, more than one game in three, he kept a clean sheet. Statistics can of course be juggled to suit any argument but as Gary's reputation rose so too did

Leeds' rise to prominence. This is evidence, therefore, that Gary was an integral part of one of the finest club sides ever seen. In his autobiography *Marching on Together* Eddie Gray argues that Leeds were successful in spite of, not because of, Gary Sprake. His view is perhaps partly motivated by Gary's later involvement in the controversial allegations surrounding Revie. Indeed, in comments made before the scandal and reproduced in the *Official History of Leeds United 1919-97* by Andrew Mourant, he states that:

> I was always a great fan of Gary Sprake. I think he suffered through exposure on television and found that hard to handle. On form, he was marvellous – a natural with great hands, great at stopping shots and crosses with great distribution. But he did one or two unfortunate things. When Gary was younger I've not seen a better 'keeper.

The statistics mentioned above offer compelling evidence that Gary was, in fact, one of the most important links in the well-oiled Leeds United machine. Support for this argument came from many neutral observers, such as the legendary Liverpool manager Bill Shankly, who was not averse to plucking players from relative obscurity and turning them into superstars. In a game at Anfield late in the 1969/70 season, when Leeds were vying for the championship with Everton and Chelsea, Shankly recalls a wonder save by Sprake from Ian Callaghan that ultimately changed the game.

> For a while now Gary Sprake has been a goalkeeper of international standing. He has emerged as a truly great 'keeper. He has often turned games for Leeds by producing wonder saves. Sprake has emerged as one of Europe's if not the world's greatest.

In his fascinating book on the art of goalkeeping, Francis Hodgson states that Gary's acquired reputation is very hard on him. He argues that for many years he was the first-choice goalkeeper in one of the most famous defences there has ever been. His analysis of Don Revie's persistence with the 'keeper is in complete contrast to the arguments prevalent among some of Gary's former colleagues.

> It was not, it could never have been, a con, he clearly was a very fine goalkeeper. It was inconceivable that Don Revie would have kept him in the side if he thought he was not good enough.

Hodgson views the situation in a totally different light, arguing that the reputation derives more from the negativity surrounding the image of the Leeds team itself.

> The Leeds team of Sprake's era was hated as very few teams have ever been. They were a very hard side founded on a hard defence. Leeds were a great side but conveyed an aura of lack of sportsmanship and sleazy toughness that was resented around the country much more than I think they realised at the time.

If you wanted to get at Leeds then Gary Sprake became the obvious scapegoat as, in such a successful team, any mistakes would make him an obvious target. What better way to undermine a team's reputation than introduce an element of comic satire, within which the goalkeeper became the focal point? It is unfortunate that thirty years later this well-trodden path is still travelled down by far too many commentators who do not display the dispassionate objectivity of Hodgson.

It is evident that many who never saw him play (and whose only knowledge of him would have been the negative demonised view portrayed by the media over the last thirty years) have been able to realise that, despite the brickbats, the controversy and the mistakes, Gary Sprake deserves to have his reputation reclaimed among the Leeds United greats. It is with some hope, therefore, that this biography, which has had Gary Sprake's wholehearted co-operation, will go some way to justifiably reclaiming his reputation. He is not asking for forgiveness nor favour, but a chance to put the record straight in response to those who have too frequently used his name as a convenient scapegoat for their own ends. Even more importantly, it is a chance for a Leeds United legend to thank the people who count most, the fans, for their support and to offer a fascinating memory of what was truly a remarkable career. He was no angel and neither was he flawless, as the handful of key mistakes testifies too. Gary also had a fierce temper and could and would mix it with the opposition as much as any of his teammates. Yet he was certainly not the unreliable error prone 'keeper that has so often been reported upon since. In fact he was, as the evidence from the contemporary match reports proves, a wonderful 'keeper in one of the greatest British sides of all time. Although the mistakes are an ever-present reminder of the past it can be suggested that 'Careless Hands' as an epitaph for Gary Sprake is a myth created by the media and a long way from the real truth.

Gary's own words are an appropriate conclusion to what has been hopefully a truer reflection of the past than has appeared in many of the biographies and histories of the Revie period thus far, with notable exceptions such as Bagchi and Rogerson's *The Unforgiven*.

My main hope is that the readers of this biography will have had a chance to judge me on my real record and not that mythical image unfortunately created by some of my former colleagues, aided willingly by some critics in the media. What is most important for me personally is that I would like to be remembered for my excellent and consistent service to Leeds United from 1961 to 1973. I have no problems with commentators stating that I made high-profile mistakes because I did make some, but to suggest that this was part of some inherent flaw that was characteristic of my goalkeeping skills is simply untrue. I can laugh now at the 'Careless Hands' moniker. Although it wasn't funny at the time, the Anfield incident has become one of the great sporting mistakes and I can appreciate the humour in it like anybody else. However, I don't think this has had any real bearing on the actual Leeds fans' view of me as a player. The overwhelming majority of Leeds fans who I meet or send me photos to be autographed are appreciative of how much I loved playing both for them and for the club. Some may have had their views of me tainted by the allegations about Revie but I think most, even if they don't agree with what I did, realise by now that I was nothing if not honest. I wanted the fans to hear my side of the story and to judge me for my actual performances on the field rather than a handful of mistakes and one controversial newspaper article. After all, I played for Leeds United over 500 times and I can live with myself that I always gave everything I could for Leeds and Wales. I only regret that Birmingham fans were never able to see me at my best and that my appearances for the Midlands club were so few. I have now had a chance to tell the real truth about Gary Sprake, goalkeeper for Leeds United, Birmingham City and Wales. My own personal recollections of the period are nothing but positive, the great games at home and in Europe, the trophies I won and all the near misses and even the heartbreaking failures. But most of all, the memories I will treasure till I die are the support of the Leeds crowd and the comradeship of the team that Revie built. Even today, despite the soured relationship with many of my former colleagues, I will always be happy to have been associated with a team whose spirit and collective identity I believe has never been matched by any team before or since. I was proud to have been an integral part of that Leeds team and to have played with so many wonderful players. These are abiding memories that nobody can take away from me, however much some people may have tried.

CAREER STATISTICS

LEEDS UNITED

1961/62
(Nineteenth in Second Division)

League:	1 game	4 goals conceded	0 clean sheets
Total:	1 game	4 goals conceded	0 clean sheets

1962/63
(Fifth in Second Division)

League:	33 games	34 goals conceded	13 clean sheets
FA Cup:	3 games	4 goals conceded	1 clean sheet
League Cup:	2 games	5 goals conceded	0 clean sheets
Total:	38 games	43 conceded	14 clean sheets

1963/64
(Champions of Second Division)

League:	41 games	31 goals conceded	17 clean sheets
FA Cup:	3 games	3 goals conceded	1 clean sheet
League Cup:	3 games played	4 goals conceded	1 clean sheet
Total:	47 games	38 conceded	19 clean sheets.

1964/65
(Runners-up in First Division)

League:	41 games	48 goals conceded	12 clean sheets
FA Cup:	8 games	4 goals conceded	5 clean sheets
Total:	49 games	52 conceded	17 clean sheets

1965/66
(Runners-up in First Division)

League:	40 games	33 goals conceded	17 clean sheets
FA Cup:	1 game	1 goal conceded	0 clean sheets
League Cup:	1 game	2 goals conceded	0 clean sheets
Fairs Cup:	11 games	10 goals conceded	4 clean sheets
Total:	53 games	46 conceded	21 clean sheets.

1966/67
(Fourth in First Division)

League:	39 games	32 goals conceded	15 clean sheets
FA Cup:	7 games	4 goals conceded	2 clean sheets
League Cup:	2 games	1 goal conceded	1 clean sheet
Fairs Cup:	10 games	8 goals conceded	4 clean sheets
Total:	58 games	45 conceded	22 clean sheets

1967/68
(Fourth in First Division)

League:	36 games	25 goals conceded	17 clean sheets
FA Cup:	5 games	2 goals conceded	3 clean sheets
League Cup:	7 games	3 goals conceded	5 clean sheets
Fairs Cup:	8 games	2 goals conceded	6 clean sheets
Total:	56 games	32 conceded	31 clean sheets

1968/69
(Champions of First Division)

League:	42 games	26 goals conceded	24 clean sheets
FA Cup:	2 games	4 goals conceded	0 clean sheets
League Cup:	3 games	3 goals conceded	1 clean sheet
Fairs Cup:	8 games	9 goals conceded	2 clean sheets
Total:	55 games	42 conceded	27 clean sheets

1969/70
(Runners–up in First Division)

League:	37 games	33 goals conceded	9 clean sheets
FA Cup:	7 games	3 goals conceded	6 clean sheets
League Cup:	1 game	0 goals conceded	1 clean sheet
European Cup	8 games	2 goals conceded	6 clean sheets
Charity Shield:	1 game	1 goal conceded	0 clean sheets
Total:	54 games	39 conceded	22 clean sheets

1970/71
(Runners–up in First Division)

League:	35 games	19 goals conceded	24 clean sheets
FA Cup:	4 games	5 goals conceded	2 clean sheets
League Cup:	1 game	1 goal conceded	0 clean sheets
Fairs Cup:	9 games		
	(+1 sub)	5 goals conceded	6 clean sheets
Total:	49 games		
	(+1 sub)	30 conceded	32 clean sheets

1971/72
(Runners–up in First Division)

League:	35 games	18 goals conceded	21 clean sheets
FA Cup:	5 games	2 goals conceded	3 clean sheets
League Cup:	2 games	0 goals conceded	2 clean sheets
UEFA Cup:	2 games		
	(+1 sub)	0 goals conceded	1 clean sheet
Fairs Cup			
Play Off:	1 game	2 goals conceded	0 clean sheets
Total:	45 games		
	(+ 1 sub)	22 conceded	27 clean sheets

1972/73

European Cup:	1 game	0 goals conceded	1 clean sheet
Total:	1 game	0 goals conceded	1 clean sheet

1973/74

UEFA Cup:	1 game	1 goal conceded	0 clean sheets
Total:	1 game	1 goal conceded	0 clean sheets

Grand Total:	**507 games (+2 sub)**	**394 goals conceded**	**236 clean sheets**

BIRMINGHAM CITY

1973/74
(Nineteenth in First Division)

League:	15 games	21 goals conceded	3 clean sheets
FA Cup:	2 games	4 goals conceded	0 clean sheets
League Cup:	3 games	4 goals conceded	1 clean sheet
Total:	20 games	29 conceded	4 clean sheets

1974/75
(Seventeenth in First Division)

League:	2 games	2 goals conceded	0 clean sheets
Total:	2 games	2 goals conceded	0 clean sheets

Grand Total:	**22 games**	**31 goals conceded**	**4 clean sheets**

WALES

Under-23s:	5 games	10 goals conceded	0 clean sheets
Full Caps:	37 games	51 goals conceded	8 clean sheets

BIBLIOGRAPHY

Ball, A., *Playing Extra Time*, Sidgwick & Jackson, London, 2004

Bagchi, R. & Rogerson, P., *The Unforgiven*, Aurum, London, 2003

Bremner, B., *You Get Nowt for Being Second*, Souvenir Press, Slough, 1969

Carsley, R., *Running with Wolves*, Thoms, Newport: Shropshire, 2004

Charlton, J., *Charlton*, Partridge Press, 1996

Edwards *Paint It White*, Mainstream, Edinburgh, 2003

Gray, E., *Marching On Together: My Life with Leeds United*, Hodder & Stoughton, London, 2001

George, C., *My Story*, Century, London, 2005

Hodgson, F., *Only the Goalkeeper to Beat*, Picador, London, 1999

Hunter, N. *Biting Talk*, Hodder & Stoughton, London, 2004

Kurlansky, M., *1968: The Year That Rocked The World*, Vintage, London, 2004

Lorimer, P., *Leeds and Scotland Hero*, Mainstream, Edinburgh, 2002

McDonald, M., *Supermac: My Autobiography*, Highdown, London, 2003

McLintock, F., *True Grit*, Headline, London, 2005

Mourant, A., *Don Revie: Portrait of a Footballing Enigma*, Mainstream, Edinburgh, 1990

Saffer, D., *The Life and Times of Mick Jones*, Tempus, Stroud, 2002

Saffer, D., *Leeds United's Rolls Royce: The Paul Madeley Story*, Tempus, Stroud, 2004

James, S., *Third Man to Fatty's Leg*, First Stone, Lydney, 2004

Jarred, M. & MacDonald, *Leeds United: The Complete European Record*, Breedon Books, Derby, 2003

Toshack, J., *Tosh*, Butler & Tanner, London, 1982

Yorath, T., *Hard Men, Hard Knocks*, Celluloid, Cardiff, 2004

If you are interested in purchasing other books published by Tempus,
or in case you have difficulty finding any Tempus books in your local bookshop,
you can also place orders directly through our website

www.tempus-publishing.com